P9-DVH-961

DATE DUE

PE 27 '99			
MR 1 8 '99			
AP 8 '99			
FE 10 '05			

DEMCO 38-296

THE COST OF
DICTATORSHIP

THE COST
OF
DICTATORSHIP

The Somali Experience

JAMA MOHAMED GHALIB

LILIAN BARBER PRESS, INC.
New York, 1995

JAN .96

Riverside Community College
Library
4800 Magnolia Avenue
Riverside, California 92506

DT 407.3 .G4 A3 1995

Ghalib, Jama Mohamed.

The cost of dictatorship

First published in the United States of America in 1995 by

LILIAN BARBER PRESS, INC.
P.O. Box 232
New York, NY 10163

© Jama Mohamed Ghalib 1995

All rights reserved. No part of this publication may be
reproduced, stored in a retrieval system, or transmitted, in
any form or by any means, electronic, mechanical, photocopying,
recording or otherwise, without the prior permission
of the publishers.

Library of Congress Cataloging-in-Publication Data

Ghalib, Jama Mohamed.
    The cost of dictatorship : the Somali experience / Jama Mohamed
Ghalib.
        p.   cm.
    Includes appendices and index.
    ISBN 0-936508-30-2. — ISBN 0-936508-32-9 (pbk.)
    1. Ghalib, Jama Mohamed.   2. Police — Somalia — Biography.
3. Politicans — Somalia — Biography.   4. Somalia — Politics and
government — 1960–   I. Title.
DT407.3.G4A3   1995
967.7305′092 — dc20   93-36919
[B]   CIP

Designed and typeset by Smith, Inc., New York,
and printed in the United States of America

TABLE OF CONTENTS

MAPS &
DIAGRAMS

FOREWORD

THE OGADEN WAR of 1977–78 apart, Somali affairs made little impact on world consciousness until the unprecedented suffering that accompanied the famine of the early 1990s was featured on TV screens throughout the world. Response was neither immediate nor much considered, though few will deny that Operation "Restore Hope," 1992–93, was a noble and necessary gesture. True, despite its undoubted achievements, history may well reveal that the dominant pressures leading to a new and unaccustomed "humanitarian" intervention role for the US military had much to do with the internal politics of the US presidency and the frustrations of captains of the aid industry and charities. But of the good intentions of the general public there can be no doubt. The operation was simplistic and too late to save many Somalis. Yet for those who did survive, it halted a terrible cycle of hunger, disease and suffering. Then everything went sadly wrong. The US and UN military soon found themselves in over their heads in Somalia. That is not to blame them. When confronted by unanticipated opposition, they responded as they were trained. However, African crisis situations are invariably complex and not for the dilettante.

Tragedy in Rwanda followed hard on that in Somalia and wider instability is clearly evident in other parts of Africa. With the Cold War no longer a factor, a fresh Africa-centered approach to such problems, examining and explaining their root causes is clearly more essential than ever. Somali writers and scholars have begun to take over Somali studies and interpretation — not to mention creative writing — and academia's neocolonial days of unequal "collaborators" and "informants" are clearly passing. This can only be good. But much more Somali writing is needed, and this work is one timely contribution. The author is not a scholarly graduate, but a largely self-educated man of affairs, and none the worse for that. The unique panoply of change in north-eastern Africa, as recounted by the author, has many a close parallel in the so-called Third World. He has written an important, perceptive and original book.

A remarkable facet of Mohamed Jama's story — for he recounts his country's woes against the background of his own full and fascinating life — is that he never gives up hope. This interpretive account of events in the Horn of Africa, rests on an underlying constant — the author's courage and integrity. He never loses his Islamic faith, his democratic convictions, his personal standards or his sense of duty. I am fortunate in having had sight of a letter he wrote in 1990 to worried members of his family some years after his personal standards had led to his falling conspicuously out of favor. It read

> [with regard to your expressed] worries regarding our security, I would have thought that you have had guidance on such matters. During a school vacation, on one summer evening back in 1981, I took four of you — the eldest — out and highlighted what you might expect in this world of ours. My council to you all was that your primary obligation was the pursuit and completion of your studies and that growing up would soon enough place responsibility on your shoulders. The same is true of my position today. I always do my best to avoid open risks but the prevailing situation dictates an obligation to contribute to the search for a solution to our national crisis.

Discarded by a dying but still powerful and vicious regime, as a former insider and an acute observer, Mohamed Jama set out to chronicle the events that underlay and led up to the tragic situation in which Somalis find themselves in the mid-1990s. In so doing, he throws much new light on the recent history of the Horn of Africa, for example, on why Somalis in the north have demanded their own independent state.

It is a recognized — if not uniquely Somali — virtue to say what one thinks without fear or favor: a virtue the writer shares. In that general context it has been recorded that, toward the end of World War II, Hitler once instructed a court hearing charges of conspiracy, "Don't let them talk too much." The former Somali ruler, Siad Barre—although he himself talked interminably and published volume after volume of speeches—likewise sought to repress the natural outspokenness of the Somalis. That has already proved a vain hope. This book sets out the root causes of the Somali tragedy, and allocates the blame for the destruction of national institutions and the corruption of many leading officials, largely on the deposed dictator. But it also asks that justice be done and moreover be seen to be done.

Born a camel-herder in colonial Africa, Mohamed Jama Ghalib has seen it all, as he struggled to improve himself, become a police officer, then a commissioner and finally a cabinet minister. He witnessed the independence of his country and others; corruption in the first generation of civilian politicians; the ambitions of a modern major-general; and the euphoria, albeit misguided, that largely greeted a "bloodless" coup d'etat. He beheld the introduction of a form of African (garrison) "socialism," only to see it collapse into oppression, still greater corruption, social and economic chaos and even attempted genocide. He survived the dark days of intimidation and terror, popular uprisings, famine, civil war and—in reaction—rampant tribalism (clanism): all the cost, he declares, of the dictatorship of Major-General Mohamed Siad Barre—a cost as yet unaccounted for.

The author was a professional policeman of what may be called "the old school." His pride in the former Somali Police Force, which is being rebuilt, permeates his writing, as does his firm belief in democratic processes and his distaste for the abuse of power. The natural repugnance he experienced as improper powers were seized by the dictator's own security services led to his taking up the pen in defense of his ideals.

Again it was Hitler who once said, "If we cannot win, we will drag half the world [down] with us." Toward the end of his rule, Siad Barre uttered almost the same words on Somalia. In 1990 he rejected an appeal for peaceful change made by a group of Hawiye clan elders in the Somali capital, with the threat, "When I came to Mogadishu there was one [paved] road built by the Italians. If you force me to stand down, I will leave the city as I found it. I came to power with a gun: only the gun can make me go." The elders turned sadly away. It was a matter for the soldiers, who were already in the field.

At times of crisis in the history of any peoples or nation, natural divisions widen. A difference between statesmen and mere politicians, is that the former play a healing role but the latter often only an exploitative one. Somalia, whose regions have historically eschewed central authority, is no exception. An emphasis on regional government and development is inevitable in the future. The lessons of this book, showing as they do how realization of this fact has been grasped but not yet successfully implemented by the new Somali generation of would-be leaders, are of continental and wider relevance.

After she had edited an early draft of the manuscript, Dr. Bettina Wolff, who teaches courses on Somalia, remarked to the publishers, "A major strength is that this is the record of a Somali who spent his professional career in the impartial pursuit of law and order, in an environment that is widely seen by the general public as lawless, chaotic and without structure or rule. Surely this aspect must be of great interest to Americans, just as his inside knowledge will be of fascination to Somalis and others. It is surely an important book."

The Cost of Dictatorship is indeed a major contribution to the little known story of how — humanitarian issues apart — Somalis endeavoring to overthrow dictatorship, have to date scarcely been understood, let alone assisted, by the often frantic and ill-considered activities of the international community. Mohamed Jama Ghalib can also serve as an inspirational role model not only for young people from economically depressed backgrounds but members of minority communities worldwide. His book can also hearten, even at this late hour, the wise who recognize that ultimately only Somalis can rebuild and restore Somalia — with enlightened help, of course, but on their own terms and under their own chosen leaders. For sure a daunting task but we must wish them well.

Richard Greenfield
Office of the Chairman of Council
The Africa Centre, London

PREFACE

I AM A SOMALI. MY NATION inhabits a beautiful land of cool mountains, rich tropical river valleys, wide savanna plains and semi deserts beyond one of Africa's longest and most spectacular coastlines. Cliffs, reefs of coral and sandy beaches define what is today called the horn of Africa: the northeastern limit of the continent. Known since the days of ancient Egypt and the civilizations of south western and south eastern Asia, it was not colonized until the last quarter of the last century. After no great time however — nowhere as much as ninety years and often much less — the portions of our lands then ruled, latterly as a United Nations Trust by Italy and as a protectorate, by the United Kingdom, regained their independence and in 1960 united to form the Somali Republic.

As an experiment in democracy, it failed, being overthrown by a military coup led by Major General Mohamed Siad Barre in 1969. Experiments with scientific socialism — which also failed — followed, but worse the seeds were set for the development of a harsh, oppressive and corrupt dictatorship, supported in turn by the Soviet Union and the United States. Our young nation's institutions were destroyed.

A long and courageous but little known struggle came to be waged by my fellow countrymen and women and at last, after much suffering, the dictator fled from the capital early in 1991 and from the country in mid 1992. Sadly, disorders and horrific famine followed in many areas in the wake of popular uprisings. The United Nations and the United States government, and others eventually felt constrained to intervene with military force and welcome humanitarian assistance, but perhaps with little real knowledge of how the Somali tragedy — the sad legacy of dictatorship — had come about.

I have lived through it all, thanks be to God, as a Somali, as a police officer, as commissioner and as a minister and I have long cherished a desire to write from my experiences of the background and particularly of Siad Barre's specific role because I felt that he was only able to develop and maintain a totalitarian regime for as long as he did, because he was allowed to impose an almost total news blackout over so long a period of time. This was especially true in the north of our country during the most critical years—between 1981 and 1988, before the escalation of civil war—when the forces of the Somali National Movement (SNM) attacked targets in the main cities of Burao and Hargeisa. Siad Barre retaliated by the total destruction of those towns and the news blackout was broken. It was not, however, ended, for with the evacuation of foreign nationals and their complete withdrawal from the whole north for the remaining period of the rule of Siad Barre, world interest again waned.

Siad Barre thus retained room to maneuver and he and the stalwarts of his regime continued to propagate a great deal of disinformation for both internal and external consumption. Although most Somalis took what he said with more than a pinch of salt, at the same time abroad much of his disinformation remained unchallenged. The outside world had few alternative sources of information until the hundreds of thousands of refugees fleeing from the destroyed cities and elsewhere were interviewed by various human rights organisations, journalists and other parties and individuals. Group complaints and case histories of individuals describing the nature and malpractices of the Siad Barre regime belatedly came to play an important role in enabling the outside world to begin to appreciate the dreadful reality of the totalitarian regime under which we Somalis lived; its dimensions and how these greatly contributed to its ultimate demise.

Even so, case histories alone lacked descriptive details of the personal traits of Siad Barre himself, his demented behavior and intrigues and his interactions with the other actors who operated his rubber stamp institutions: that is to say they did not fully reveal the collective notoriety of his regime. A volume such as this cannot include all the many shocking reports and accounts of solitary confinement, torture and murder.

Likewise, there is insufficient space for much ordinary information about the Somali people, our culture and customs, or population estimates, and details of the geography, topography, climate, and natural resources, of the region. Since a number of books have been written and published during the last three decades or so (though until recently by and large by non-Somali writers and researchers), I have only attempted to fill whatever gaps appear to have been left uncovered by the various reports and have concentrated on the Siad Barre era. By the nature of his employment in the police, Siad had access to additional information on cases of murder, torture, corruption, the instigation of civil strife and state-sponsored banditry. Thus could he foster inter-clan feuds and mistrust, to a degree previously unknown to the majority of the Somalis. In order to provide a framework, and help the reader identify more directly with the tragedy which has befallen the Somali people, I have deliberately set out to recount my own life and personal experiences prior to and during the Siad Barre era, but there are few areas of this book which have no bearing on its main theme — the terrible cost of dictatorship.

When the United Somali Congress (USC) forced Siad Barre to flee Mogadishu, I had still to start actually setting out this book and even felt I should perhaps drop the idea altogether and concentrate on the future — but I was trapped in the capital for a period from November 1991 onward, due to the outbreak of factional fighting within the United Somali Congress (USC). This reactivated my interest in the sad legacy of the Siad years and presented the opportunity, because I recognized senseless internecine strife as the direct consequence of the misdeeds and misrule of Siad Barre. I still do.

My writing, along with my small transistor radio which kept me up with news of the outside world, helped much to minimize the frustration of my stay and the risks to which — among others — I was constantly exposed. Eventually I managed to leave Mogadishu, the city where I had lived for the best part of my life, for nearly thirty years — once among the safest and most peaceful places in the whole world . . . and I carried with me the first draft of this manuscript.

Jama Mohamed Ghalib
Hargeisa 1994

ACKNOWLEDGMENTS

I AM GRATEFUL TO ALL who have encouraged me to write and to many Somali friends who have provided me with so much material. Of course, I alone accept full responsibility for any shortcomings and for the whole text and content of this book, but their help was invaluable.

I would particularly like to thank Dr. Bettina H. Wolff of Lake Lure, NC, USA, for having kindly edited an early draft of my manuscript under the severe handicap of having to work without my being there as I was not at the time able to travel to North Carolina because of personal constraints. Bettina taught my daughter Faiza when she earned her Master's degree in Management from the California State University (Fresno/SIDAM project, Mogadishu 1983–85) and thus became, together with her husband, Jack Donovan, my long time golf mate, very good friends of our family.

I would also like to thank Dr. Terry Walz, of Lilian Barber Press for his encouragement and Professor Richard Greenfield, Chairman of the Council of Management of the Africa Centre, London, and a long term friend of the Somali people, to whom I am indebted not only for having kindly written the Foreword, but also for having provided a great deal of invaluable advice and help during my research work in England in 1992.

I am indebted to my daughter Faiza who typed and repeatedly retyped my original manuscript each time I revised it and to Sara Nicoll who similarly labored over the revised text: also to my sons Saeed — who sold his own car to finance some of my research travels — and Khadar, who helped in locating vital research data in the United States.

The cover was designed by Nancy Carey; the historical chart by Russell Bianca and the illustrations, apart from one courtesy of *Africa Report* and my personal documents, are all from the Greenfield Collection.

And lastly, but not least, to some Somali friends who prefer not to be named but who gave me generous financial contributions without which I would not have been able to conclude the task of writing this book, to the staff of the British Public Records Office in Kew and to Ambassador Abdullahi Said Osman, Assistant Secretary General of the Organization of African Unity (OAU) and his staff, for having afforded me access to materials in the O.A.U. library in Addis Ababa.

I would like, however, to dedicate this book to all those Somalis, within and without the government, who, in defying the dictator, gave up years of their freedom, endured unspeakable hardships and in so many cases sacrificed even life itself, in defence of the dignity and civil liberties which they held to be the God-given birthright of every Somali, regardless of gender, class, or — and especially — clan affiliation. By their courage they offered proof that as a nation, we still possess that nobility of spirit, which, if God wills, even now will enable us, with the informed and sympathetic help of our friends, to rebuild our shattered society and country and avoid the pitfalls of the past.

CHAPTER ONE

A NOMAD JOINS THE POLICE FORCE

I WAS BORN A NOMAD in the vicinity of Buur–Armo (*Buur* is a hill) in the countryside to the east of the northern town of Erigavo. I was the youngest of my parents' six children: three boys and three girls. My eldest brother died as an infant so I never saw him. Perhaps I would still be a nomad today had my mother lived beyond the tender years of my early life. My mother came from the Warsengeli of the Darod clan who inhabit the eastern corner of the former British Somaliland Protectorate westward up to and including my birthplace. My father however, came from one of the Isaaq sub-clans of Hargeisa. With the non-existence of modern communication and motor transport in those days, inter-marriage between distant clans was very uncommon.

In her youth my mother, a nomad herself, lived with one of her older sisters, also living in the Erigavo district, married to a man of the Dolbahante sub-clan section, the Bah Abdalla. It was their leader, the late Abdi Nur 'Hiddig' (*Hiddig* is a star) who is alleged to have attempted the assassination of Seyyid Mohamed Abdille Hassan (whom the colonial authorities whom he fought all his life called the Mad Mullah) inside the latter's own fortress at Taleh. When the attempt failed, Abdi escaped on horse back. Under such circumstances it was the common practice for the 'Mullah's' followers, the *Darawishta* (Dervishes) to kill and massacre all the relatives of an escapee or a deserter, including even children and pregnant women, in order to deter future assassination attempts and desertions. Related nomadic population would also be attacked.

Many settlements of the Bah Abdalla thus abandoned the Erigavo district area, as we know it today, fleeing as far as the ancient Somali port of Berbera to seek the protection of the British authorities. My mother accompanied them. Somalis are Muslims but a few such families were given refuge by the Roman Catholic Church established in Berbera to which they became converted. My parents had met in Berbera and were married there. They later moved south of Hargeisa the northern capital, to the *Haud,* a grazing area which stretched into what is today eastern Ethiopia. Well after the defeat of Mohamed Abdille Hassan in the 1920s, my mother again visited Berbera, perhaps to shop for food and some cloth. Berbera at that time was an important shopping centre. There she met some camel caravans of her own people from beyond Erigavo. Carrying my youngest sister on her back, she decided to accompany them on their return to see her own mother again. A return journey to the Hargeisa area would not be easy. It required a long period of preparation and waiting to find suitable and safe caravans. A year or so passed and then my father joined her, having taken the same route himself in search of her. In the event they both remained together in the Erigavo area for the rest of their lives. Both my elder brother and myself were born there and my two older sisters also later rejoined the family.

My father died there when I was about six years of age. I remember that it was during the *Gu* or rainy season, the best part of the year for nomads. The camels had just rejoined our *Rers* or settlements. Sometimes when the camels are taken to distant places for grazing or watering purposes and are separated from the *rers,* many camel *kadins* or herds are grouped together for security reasons. When the camels return to the settlements they are normally separated again into their respective *rers.* At the time when my father died they had not been separated; perhaps the elders had yet to decide whether the camels would stay with the *rers* or not. So the *kadins,* still grouped together, were camped at one *rer* and all the small boys from the various *rers* would rush to the camels' encampment to enjoy the almost forgotten taste of camel milk.

Association with camels is considered more honorable for boys and young men than association with sheep and goats and it signifies the attainment of at least the age of adolescence. I was one of those who had gone to stay with and care for the camels. Early one morning I overheard the older men saying among themselves "Mohamed Ghalib died." They were preparing themselves to go for the burial. I think I knew quite literally what death meant, but did not really understand its effect nor what difference my father's death would make. Later that same evening I went to our *rer* and saw my mother and sisters mourning and recognized their grief. Only then did I begin to realize that we had lost a loved one. I did not cry.

My mother also died some 8 or 9 years later and her death meant a great deal of unhappiness to me. I was quite a grown up boy by then, but I still wept and cried loudly. In our country, grown men are expected to face the realities of their life and their problems and thus be able to control their emotions. So my brother, five years older than myself, did not cry in public, but as we slept side by side the night following our mother's funeral I could hear him sobbing throughout the night. Although my brother and sisters did their very best to care for me, they could not fill the vacuum. I became restless and wanted to leave, without knowing why. Whereas both my brother and I had refused to leave after our father's death, when his cousin had come to us and had wanted to move us to the Hargeisa area, I just hated staying any longer in the place where my mother had died. It was as if I blamed the environment for her loss. Perhaps I was spoiled by excessive maternal care, being her youngest child. Anyway, I left to plunge myself into life in the town.

I do not know even today my exact date of birth, but that is not unusual in any nomadic society. Subsequent reconstruction and calculations, after I became acquainted with dates and the modern calendar, suggest that I was probably born between 1931 and 1933. I discovered later I first came to Hargeisa in 1947. The Second World War had ended two years earlier, but its effects stayed with us. This period marked the beginning of modern political awakening in all the Somali inhabited territories; an awakening which was contemporaneous with that of other colonial peoples all over the world, particularly in Africa. For the first (and last) time all the Somali inhabited territories except Djibouti were then temporarily under

British jurisdiction following the defeat of Italian forces. Later I learned that the British Foreign Secretary, Ernest Bevin, proposed that all the Somali territories be lumped together and mandated to Britain in a Trusteeship. That might well have encouraged the already simmering Somali nationalism.

Indeed, there was a great deal of economic and social exchange between the inhabitants of the Somali territories in those days. All talk in the teashops and the streets of Hargeisa centred upon experiences during the world war, the way of life of various other Somali groups and the ongoing activities of the Somali National Society (SNS), which, dating from the nineteen-thirties, was one of the forerunners, if not the very first, of all modern Somali political organizations. My reaction to these surroundings, as I would come to realize later, was like someone watching a film or a play, without understanding the language of the actors. The whole scene was in total contrast to my earlier placid — though in other ways hard to cope with — nomadic environment.

As a nomadic child or even an adolescent it had been hard and demanding to accompany and care for animals all the way to distant locations, always seeking grazing or water. Sometimes I went all day without water or food before returning home in the evening. In the *Gu* season, however, when there was plenty of everything, young adults of both sexes would be involved in folk dancing almost every night and we would envy them their adulthood. We youngsters would play a game called *Loof,* either in the daytime or under the moonlight, involving our throwing stones into a hole from a distance of about 10 yards. Whoever got nearest would win the round. It was similar in principle to the ancient game of golf, I was to learn when later I started to play, for children in Scotland had also played in the same way. Of course different rules followed modernisation which I have always thought resulted from subsequent commercialisation: the use of manufactured balls, clubs, bags, etc. As children, we too could play singles, but when playing doubles we would call one's partner *jaalle,* a Somali word that I never heard again after my nomadic life until twenty-five years later, Siad Barre, searching the Somali vocabulary for a semblance of socialist flavor, which was hardly apparent, coined it to correspond to comrade.

In Hargeisa I stayed at the tailors shop of a cousin of mine, Mohamed Haji Hirad, the first son of my mother's youngest sister, but I made very little progress in learning his trade. I was always afraid to cut someone's new cloth into pieces for fear of spoiling the material and upsetting my cousin's clients. I found another interest. Within a year or so of my coming to town, a branch was opened of the Somali Youth League (SYL), a political grouping founded in Mogadishu in 1943, which was active and strongest in the former Italian Somaliland, then under British military administration (BMA) but which had also spread throughout all the other Somali inhabited territories. It's social activities in Hargeisa included the teaching of English language through evening classes. I joined the lowest class; that for beginners. In those days electricity in Hargeisa was limited to the european residences and government offices. A kerosine *Tilley* or pressure lamp was used during our class, but it was turned off soon after the lesson was over. I had to wait for daylight the next morning to read my exercises and to review the lesson taught the previous evening.

After some time I gained employment as an office boy in the Department of Public Works. I was in fact recruited on April 16, 1948 by a Mr C. J. Martin, later to become Somaliland's Chief Accountant and then the Government Information Officer. After leaving Somaliland he was Head of the East African Service of the BBC for many years. However, back in 1948 on secondment from the Treasury he was Public Works Finance Officer, a post which included responsibility for personnel matters. (I would meet him on many subsequent occasions, even after his retirement, and would always regard him as my benefactor.)

Office hours started at 8 A.M. and I had to wake up very early every morning except Sunday and walk more than two miles from the area of the town where I lived to the Public Works offices located at the other side of the *tug,* a dry riverbed that divides Hargeisa which only floods after heavy rainfall. I went first to the Indian quarters every morning to collect the office keys from the head clerk to open the offices so that the cleaners could make things ready before the starting time. But although they were only intermittently available those days, I continued attending evening classes.

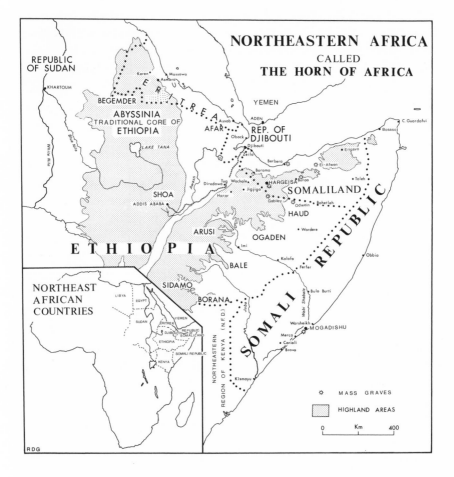

NORTHEASTERN AFRICA
CALLED
THE HORN OF AFRICA

REPUBLIC
OF SUDAN

KHARTOUM

Keren Asmara

BEGEMDER

ABYSSINIA
TRADITIONAL CORE OF
ETHIOPIA

LAKE TANA

SHOA

ADDIS ABABA

ETHIOPIA

ARUSI

SIDAMO

BORANA

NORTHEAST
AFRICAN
COUNTRIES

Massawa

ERITREA

YEMEN

ADEN

Assab

AFAR

Obock

REP. OF
DJIBOUTI

Djibouti

Zeila

Borama

Berbera

Diredawa Tug Wachale

Harar Jigjiga

Gabiley

Odwein Boherleh

HAUD

OGADEN

BALE

Imi

Kalafo

Ferfer

Wardere

Obbia

C.Guardafui

Bosaso

Erigavo

El-Afwen Taleh

Burao

HARGEISA

SOMALILAND

SOMALI REPUBLIC

Webi Shabale

Bula Burti

Warsheikh

Merca MOGADISHU

Coriali

Brava

White Nile

Blue Nile

Awash

Juba

NORTHEASTERN REGION OF KENYA (N.F.D.)

LIBYA EGYPT

SUDAN

YEMEN

ERITREA

DJIBOUTI REPUBLIC SOMALILAND

ETHIOPIA

SOMALI REPUBLIC

KENYA

Kismayu

✿   MASS GRAVES

       HIGHLAND AREAS

0   Km   400

RDG

I was financially hard put to live on my very small salary. In order to earn a bit extra I caddied on the golf course for one of the European officers under whom I worked, who played two or three days a week. Office hours in the afternoon ended at 4 P.M. and we would walk a mile to his house to collect his golf clubs. While he changed, he would give me a cup of tea and one or two biscuits. When the game was over he would pay me half an East African Shilling (fifty cents). That would buy me a modest dinner in the evening. It would have been wonderful had he played every day but as it was for three to four nights a week I would go without dinner.

As I worked during the day and had to use my lunch break to walk the long distance home and back, I had little or no time to learn during the day. I therefore had to study in the evenings. When scheduled, evening classes were held every other day. In 1950, one of the best evening classes was taught during September to December by the late Yusuf Ismail Samatar, then the headmaster of the only government school in Hargeisa. That class was organised for a mixed group of Somalis with different levels of literacy, and it was taught in the Somali Officials' Union Club under electric lighting. But whether or not I was attending evening classes, every night I studied with some colleagues, all of us underprivileged.

Invariably we had difficulty with lighting. We could not afford a *Tilly* lamp, nor even a hurricane lamp which was much cheaper. Even if we had one, we could not have afforded to buy fuel for it. Instead we borrowed candles from the offices, sometimes without permission, and so ran the risk of being dismissed. However, the head clerk, Mr Nambiar, was a kindly man who would often allow me to take some. One colleague worked in the Post Office where more candles were used than in ordinary offices and he often brought us them, though not without risk. Perhaps the lack of adequate light explains why I had to have reading glasses at an early stage.

In 1952, after passing the necessary test, I was admitted into the clerical establishment. In Hargeisa government clerks were a pool service under the governor's secretariat and I was posted to the police headquarters. I was all too aware of my lack of education and continued self-directed studies. I devoted a great deal of my spare time to learning to type which in those days was a real achievement for a clerk. This skill was to benefit me immensely in my various subsequent activities and even in my personal life. I was regularly assigned by the chief clerk to do typing work and I was always happy to be given such opportunities. I typed a lot for the deputy commissioner of police with whom I established a good working relationship. Also, I was always assisted and encouraged to improve my career by Abdullahi Abby Farah, who was the only Somali with officer status in the police department. He was my immediate boss as the police pay and quartermaster.

At Police headquarters there were two civilian fingerprint classifiers employed at the fingerprint bureau, both of them having been recruited from Mogadishu during the British Military Administration of Somalia, though one of them was originally from the Somaliland Protectorate. They worked under a European who was also the Immigration officer. The southerner, Ahmed Muddei, who later became the first Somali Mayor of Mogadishu, took his annual vacation leave in 1953 back to Somalia, which by then was a UN Trusteeship under Italian Administration. Once in Mogadishu, he resigned his position. Fearing that the only other trained fingerprint classifier might also leave, he was offered opportunity to enlist into the force with the rank of Inspector. This did not involve any pay rise but he accepted the offer. Then the vacant post had to be filled.

Early one cold February morning in 1954, I was sent for by Deputy Commissioner John Temple. My first reaction was that he would give me something to type which I would have been happy to do, but he told me that he would give me a test. There and then I had to write a letter asking for a transfer to Burao because I was a married man and the rents in Hargeisa were very high (in fact I was not then married). I followed his instructions and guidelines, perhaps not as well as I should have; I do not think that I even made the lines straight. I could hardly hold the pen both because the weather was cold, and I was not sufficiently clothed, and because of the pressure of the test itself. However, my examiner appeared quite satisfied with my scribbles. Because of my being in the clerical service the secretariat had to approve any change in my status but I was soon afterwards offered opportunity to join the police force with the rank of sub-inspector, which carried a pay rise above my clerical grade.

The arrangement was in fact cleared before I was asked for my consent, but I discovered later that Temple had discussed it with Abdullahi Abby Farah and might have assumed that I was aware of what was going on. The terms were that for six months I would be trained in the identification of fingerprints in the bureau and then be required to undergo basic police training at the Police Training School, Mandera, for at least a further six months. My final acceptance into the police force would therefore depend upon satisfactory completion of those two types of training. I accepted the offer, fulfilled both pre-conditions and formally became an enlisted policeman on April 1, 1955, with the already agreed rank of sub-inspector. While at the Police Training School I had worn a police uniform with the badges of rank of a sergeant, in an acting capacity, but had still drawn my clerical salary. In truth the real incentive had been the pay rise, but the training I had undergone ultimately greatly influenced my personal outlook and interest in a career in the police force.

There was a great deal of resentment amongst long serving policemen of various ranks to the two of us joining the force with such comparatively high ranks. It was unprecedented in the history of the Somaliland Police Force; previously every Somali had been required to join as an ordinary policeman at the very bottom with no preferment whatsoever. Both the commissioner and his deputy therefore gave firm undertakings that we would be permanently employed in the fingerprint bureau, as a closed department, and that our appointments would in no way prejudice the careers of other members of the force.

However, when at the end of February 1955, I reported back to police headquarters at Hargeisa upon the completion of my training at Mandera, both the commissioner and his deputy who would have finalised my formal transfer into the police force from the clerical service were away on leave. Acting in their two respective posts were two other senior police officers seconded from the districts, who shared the sentiments of those long service policemen who had resented our new ranks. I was compulsorily granted all my clerical accumulated leave. It was three months before I could join the force. It was the heart of *Jilaal* or the dry season and not a good time to take a vacation and I pondered how to make the best use of the time.

Every year the police force sent some policemen for vocational in-service training under the auspices of the Department of Education. A basic requirement for such training was an intermediate school (the second highest educational institution in the country) certificate or its equivalent. I considered myself to be equivalent in English but that could only be proved by taking a test. I decided that I should go to Sheikh, a town in the mountains, in order to study and look for a chance to take the Intermediate Leaving Examinations there. I left almost the next day. The first batch of police officers sent for vocational training were there and they introduced me to some of the Somali teachers. I found accommodation with the bachelor teachers and ate with them. The bachelors lived in the block of quarters where the Teachers' Club was located and there was a small library.

At that time Sheikh was the centre of education for the whole of Somaliland. The Somali people — especially in the north — had long resisted the establishment of schools (other than traditional Quranic schools) upon the suspicion of proselytizing. This was not without justification, as the first western schools in the country dating from 1891 had been Catholic missionary schools. That at Dhaymole, about thirty-five miles inland from Berbera, had in fact converted some children. It was the existence of such schools and the availability of alcohol which had so angered Seyyid Mohamed Abdille Hassan as to afford him pretext for his twenty-year-long rebellion against the colonialists' until his final defeat in 1920. One strict precondition for the eventual establishment of government schools was the acceptance only of those boys who knew the Quran well.

Apart from the schools in Sheikh, there was only one elementary school in each of the six districts of the Protectorate until the early nineteen fifties when district elementary schools doubled or tripled in number and intermediate schools were opened in every district and in some other appropriate centres. But there was only one two-class secondary school for the whole country, at Sheikh, up until the time of independence and the first girls primary school was only opened in Burao, in the early nineteen fifties. I had heard about

Sheikh but only as a legend. Now I was to live there for the next three months.

Situated fifty miles from Berbera to the north and forty miles from Burao to the south, Sheikh stood at the head of a tortuous nine mile long pass, on the summit plateau of the Gollis range of mountains, at a height of over five thousand feet above sea level. Its wonderfully moderate climate could be rather cold, at least for the tropically born, especially during the winter months. I soon got to know everybody and was introduced to Yusuf Haji Adan, the second most senior Somali education officer. We discussed my needs and interests. I said that I wanted to study with classes in the intermediate schools. He told me to come to the headquarter offices of the Department of Education — the only government department with headquarters outside the capital, Hargeisa, the next morning so that he could take me to Mr Badham, the deputy director.

I went there the following morning and as I reached the office verandah, Yusuf came out of Badham's office. On catching sight of me he immediately turned back, asking me to enter the office and informed the deputy director about my case. Badham asked me what my police rank was. "Acting Sergeant," I said. He gave me a note to Mr Lloyd, the principal of the Intermediate School with instructions that I be allowed to join the classes and I presented that note the same morning. I was then referred to one of the Somali Assistants, Hashi Abdulla, who sat in the next office.

Hashi asked me which class I wanted to join. "Seven," I replied, it being the highest intermediate class. Hashi then asked me, "Do you want something of your choice or do you want to do what is good for you?" "Whatever is good for me," I said. My preference was to sit with the Sevens because I wanted to take the leaving examinations with them, but I had not previously said that to Yusuf, Badham or Lloyd. Hashi then remarked that the Sevens were only doing revision for their leaving examinations and it was therefore better that I join the Sixes who were taking serious lessons. He added that the syllabuses of the two were quite similar.

I went into class six, but could find no vacant seat. One of the pupils from Hargeisa, Dair Abdullahi, a nephew of Yusuf Haji Adan, recognised me and asked me to share his seat with him. That particular class was taught by Hassan Adan Gudal who had returned from the Sudan where he had taken his secondary education. He was then waiting to go to a university abroad. Since 1919, small grants had been given for students to study in the Sudan. While Hassan awaited acceptance, he was seconded to the education department in order to teach. I benefitted a great deal from class six and have never regretted Hashi's advice, despite my original desire just to study for exams.

Three weeks later, the timetables of the Intermediate Leaving Examinations were posted on the bulletin notice boards. I went to Hashi and said that I wanted to sit for the English of those examinations. Hashi referred the matter to Lloyd and he to Badham. Schools did not officially work in the afternoons in those days, but as the summer term was about to end, there were many sports competitions between the boarding houses of the schools, which were personally organised by Badham himself and almost everybody went to the sports field in the afternoon to cheer on those activities. At the end of the games on the day of my request, Lloyd called me and told me that Badham had approved my taking the examination and that I should prepare myself.

I made intensive preparations, answering hundreds of old examination questions and asking almost every Somali teacher to correct them for me. I also read the text books of the Sevens. The day came and English was the first subject to be taken, at 7 A.M. The invigilator was the most senior Somali education officer, the late Mohamoud Ahmed Ali, who had already met me at the Teachers' Club. He was pleased at my attempting the exam, especially since I was essentially self-taught. It was a very long paper lasting until 11 A.M. In the afternoon I took the second part which was an oral conducted by Mr Lloyd. Thereafter, I resumed my lessons with the Sixes until the summer vacation.

Hassan Adan Gudal was transferred to the Information Department, Hargeisa, pending his university acceptance and as I helped him load his luggage on the truck, Badham revealed that he was going also to Amud in Borama to collect the examination papers after their correction by Mr Darlington, another well known education officer. He would let me know how I had done. I thanked him as they left. The schools all closed down and the teachers took their vacations. Only Nur Haji Jama who was taking a promotion examination, and myself were left at the bachelors' quarters. I continued my private studies while I awaited the result of my examination.

Early one morning Mr. Badham sent for me and as I entered his office he congratulated me, adding that out of seventy-two boys only seven had better results than mine. I had worked hard for this but successes seemed often aided by mere chance. Mr Badham asked me if I would like him to write to the commissioner and suggest that I was a suitable candidate for a vocational training course. I could hardly breathe for joy. I thanked him again and left Sheikh that same morning for Hargeisa, stopping at Burao for a few days. It was the end of May and my three months leave was about to expire. I would report to police headquarters, and Deputy Commissioner Temple would again be in charge. The process of my transfer to the police force was completed the same day that I reported for duty. I resumed work at the fingerprint bureau where I remained working and waiting for a further year.

CHAPTER TWO

STRUGGLE TO BECOME A PROFESSIONAL

It was 1956 when I was sent to the Vocational Training Centre
(VTC) at Sheikh for a one year course, having already established
the equivalence of eligibility. I was to study law. We were also taught
English and I used the opportunity to the maximum as it was my
longest period of being taught English in a formal context and for the
first time by an Englishman. I had to correct much of what I had
already taught myself. It was however success in my law examinations
which proved to be the turning point for my future career. I passed
individual law subjects with high marks: Criminal Procedure Code:
the Penal Code: the Law of Evidence and the Local Laws (Ordinances,
Rules and Regulations enacted by the Governor of the Somaliland
Protectorate). The next stage was an official examination in Hargeisa
set by a judge of the High Court and the Attorney-General.

A question often appeared in the Protectorate's Law Examinations
Local Laws paper on the use of the Sheikh Pass. Motor vehicular traffic
using the pass was regulated by two Police control posts, one at each
end of the pass with hourly intervals between downward and upward
journeys, during the hours of six in the morning and five in the afternoon. The pass was closed to traffic during the whole night since
livestock crossing took place between sunset and sunrise. This route
has since been rebuilt, as part of the Burao to Berbera asphalt road, and
restrictions on its usage no longer apply.

Just before the completing of the course both the commissioner
and his deputy proceeded on leave pending retirement, the latter

perhaps partly because of the appointment of a much younger police officer as the new commisioner of police. When I was reposted to the police headquarters after independence, I came across a telegram addressed to the Governor of Kenya, copied to the Governor of Somaliland Protectorate. It read as follows:

> The post of the Commissioner of Police in the Somaliland Protectorate will be vacant shortly. Since that territory is undergoing some constitutional changes, it is desirable to secure the services of a first class police officer. We have in mind Assistant Commissioner of Police, D D P Cracknell who has had relevant experiences in Somalia and hope you can release him for this appointment.

David Cracknell's selection proved a positive contribution not only to the Somaliland Police Force, but the entire administrative system of the Somaliland Protectorate. He was progressive and anticipated early constitutional changes in the country. Unlike many other expatriate officers, he had seen changes involving the folding up of the Union Jack before: in Somalia, at the end of the British Military Administration in 1950 and in Eritrea in 1952. In both cases he had been commissioner of police.

One of Cracknell's early decisions was the Somalization of all officers at the police station level and at the district level a year later. His early Somalisation policy was a success. By the time of independence the Police Force was considered to be not only a fine British legacy but one of the best institutions in the country. Most other heads of department had followed suit as far as Somalization was concerned and those which had not done so early enough were caught off guard, as independence was to come much earlier than anticipated.

It surprised no one that the new commissioner set aside my return to the fingerprint bureau; I must have filled a small square in his 'Somalization' puzzle, for I was posted to Berbera as the station officer. That was April 1957: an important time, for me, for I met my wife there and we were married on 19 December that same year.

This was the first time that I was assigned to normal police work and I was very conscious of my shortcomings in practical police performance. Even so, I was enthusiastically looking forward to learning a great deal from my juniors in rank but seniors in experience and service. The responsibilities of the officer–in–charge of a police station included all manner of station work, but the priorities were the prevention of crimes, the proper functioning of the criminal investigation branch, the presentation of cases to the courts and their prosecution, and the care and custody of prisoners. I endeavored to involve myself in every aspect of police work. At night, I always inspected police foot patrols on their beats and would often accompany plain clothes detectives on foot on their assignments. Those functions were gaps in my police experience which I knew I had to fill.

Berbera, then the country's only port city, was very prosperous in those days. But during the *Kharrif* period, the hot season, May–September, the majority of the wealthy merchants would close down their goods stores with little or no regard for security arrangements. They left to do business elsewhere, often also taking vacations in cooler parts of the country. As criminals knew this very well, the *Kharrif* time was also the peak crime period. Many thieves and shop breakers would come to Berbera from other towns during this season. Many of our plain clothes detectives who had known those criminals in other towns would recognize them and immediately report their presence. That was the benefit of long police experience.

In the Somaliland Police, men had been transferred to a new district almost every two years. There were six districts in the country and most policemen with twelve years of service had served in every district and therefore knew many habitual criminals. We had to fight these criminals as best we could. While the experienced policemen were doing a good job of keeping the habitual criminals under very close watch, it was my responsibility as the station's law expert (my only credential so far) to devise ways and means of confronting such criminals with the law. The Criminal Procedure Code contained a provision for the arrest of habitual criminals and vagrants without any common place of abode. They could then be required to execute bonds to keep the peace for at least a year.

Despite our vigilance, there were several shop break–ins, so I had all known habitual criminals rounded up as suspects and applied for their remand in custody for the maximum period of 14 days allowed by the law, pending investigation. This was granted by the court. In the meantime, I arranged for fingerprints to be taken in order to prove that those detained were habitual criminals. Certificates of their previous convictions from the fingerprint bureau in Hargeisa coupled with the fact that none of them had any common place of abode, established the two necessary ingredients which could be presented to the court upon the completion of their remand period. The court considered them all liable to be required to execute bonds to keep the peace. The execution of such bonds required sureties from property owners which they could not provide because no one would stand guarantor for the behavior of habitual criminals.

The magistrate, who was also the District Commissioner (DC) Mr N.L.P. Thomas, again remanded them in custody and wrote to the High Court for a ruling because the law did not specify what further steps the court should take when such bonds could not be executed. The High Court ruling was a setback. The Chief Justice ruled that the application of that provision in the Criminal Procedure Code was inapplicable to Somaliland where the majority of the people were nomads without any common or permanent place of abode and he ordered the immediate release of the habitual criminals. I was disappointed but learning fast.

Apart from the local laws, all the other laws in force in Somaliland were Indian laws, based on English law as the legal source. Somaliland had originally come under the Government of India. The Chief Justice must have considered that those particular provisions were originally intended solely for Indian society and a different culture and environment from that of the Somalis. The habitual criminals in question were never nomads themselves having always lived in the towns, but being habitual criminals they remained without permanent places of abode because society would not accept them. No one would even rent a house to known criminals. Anyway, they got away with it and that was the end of that legal battle. Perhaps I had been over zealous, but I set out to try and find some other legal framework within which to work.

The possibility of getting a common ruling applicable to all of them was slight. They were again on the loose; and they knew our weakness and the vulnerability of the merchants' property, locked up as it was in unguarded stores. I busied myself for a day or two searching the law books for an alternative legal avenue. There was a provision in the Criminal Procedure Code that permitted the arrest of any suspects in the commission of a crime and their detention for twenty-four hours, but thereafter they had either to be taken to court or released. Since they were habitual criminals could they not always be considered suspects for offences against property of which there were daily occurrences? That would not, however, be enough because we could only reasonably suspect a few of them for each such case and arrests of only short duration would not solve our problems. I wanted to neutralise all habitual criminals for the entire *Kharrif* period.

So, I continued digging into the law books. There was another provision in the Township Rules for the prevention of nuisance in public places in order to safeguard public health. I considered a plan to round up all habitual criminals one evening, upon the first opportunity of their becoming suspects. They would then be placed in cells, awakened early the following morning and temporarily released when they would urinate in public, thus committing a nuisance in contravention of the Township Rules. However, needless to say my conscience bothered me. Was I not twisting the law and provoking the commission of an offence? I felt very strongly that I was not only acting in good faith, but was also duty bound to protect the property of innocent people. I went back and read again my first police training notes. The first lesson in theory at the Police Training School read: *The first duty of the Police is the preservation of people's lives and the protection of their properties.* It was certain that if those habitual criminals were left alone, the loss of people's property was inevitable. Surely I had to act with my mind and not with my heart. Right or wrong, I went ahead with my plan.

About twenty habitual criminals were taken on the same day to the Subordinate Court where they were convicted and sentenced each one of them to 14 days' imprisonment against which there was no appeal. That was still only a short period of relief, but surprisingly — and in retrospect perhaps fortunately — the criminals themselves resolved the problem. Unable to stand the pressure we had brought to bear on them, they left Berbera immediately upon their release. No doubt they would commit some crimes in other towns, but to me that seemed a lesser evil since Berbera was the priority as there were more goods at risk in Berbera than in all other five districts combined. It was the supply base for all the other towns and the hinterland as far away as the Haud and the Reserved Areas, across the border with Ethiopia, where British Commonwealth forces retained administrative control for wartime strategic reasons. Meantime, we went on record as having reduced criminality in Berbera to an unprecedented low level for the *Kharrif* period of 1957.

My early efforts to increase Police efficiency were sometimes compromised by weak public relations. The Criminal Procedure Code contained schedules showing which offences were allowed bail and which were not. I would discover later, in the old days illiterate Somali police officers who did not know the law, often allowed bail even for people accused of very serious crimes, like murder for example. Lacking proper skills of investigation, police officers were also inclined to turn problems over to tribal elders for disposal. Subsequently this practice came to be tolerated by many police officers even when they were educated and knew the law. Whenever elders came to me to stand surety for people in the lock-up, I would always simply look at the book and deny bail for non-bailable cases, which in the circumstances stunned most local leaders. One very powerful clan chief vowed not to set foot in Berbera while I was there and confined himself to his local village after the DC had supported my stand. That clan chief later became a good friend of mine, but only towards the end of my term.

A pro-independence demonstration intended as a peaceful event when two British members of Parliament visited Berbera, turned into a riot during March 1958. The disturbance was provoked by the District Commissioner's failure to stop his car in which the two MPs were riding so that they could read the written slogans which the demonstrators had on display. The demonstrations were sealed off by a riot police cordon and both the senior District Police Officer, Mr Roach, and I were present. When the DC's car passed by a second time the demonstrators threw stones, some of which hit the DC's car, but without causing any harm to the VIPs. We then used tear gas and dispersed the crowd with no injuries either to the police personnel or to the rioters, although we later arrested about a dozen, including the ring leader, Mohamoud Jama Urdoh who was jailed for two years. Upon his release, Mohamoud and I also became good friends. He had been arrested many times before on similar charges and he would always say that that was the first time that he had been dealt with fairly, without any police excesses.

David Cracknell initiated a total transformation of the Police Training Programme, recruiting a very experienced police officer, Superintendent Leslie Tompkins, who had not only worked in a number of colonial police forces: in Italian Somaliland, during the British Military Administration, Eritrea, Nigeria and Aden, but had also served in the British police in Bedford. After he took over the Police Training School in 1957, Tompkins drastically revised the training syllabuses which had previously focused on semi-military subjects such as drill, arms training and musketry. The new syllabuses largely comprised advanced legal studies and practical police techniques. At the Vocational Training Centre in Sheikh, only the English in which the laws were written had been explained and even that depended upon the kind personality of the principal of the centre, Mr Tanner, for there were no law instructors. After the new training was introduced the Somaliland Police discontinued sending candidates to Sheikh. I think my group was the last. Superintendent Tompkins also introduced and edited a police journal, "The Bush Telegraph" for the exchange of news among the members of the police force. There were no newspapers in the country at that time. I had the privilege of serving under Superintendent Leslie Tompkins as a law instructor at the Police Training School, Mandera and gained a great deal from his experience.

In late June 1957, I was summoned from Berbera to Hargeisa to sit for the official Somaliland Law Examination. Previously I had taken one subject at a time; I now had to take all four subjects on two successive days, becoming possibly the first candidate and certainly the first Somali to obtain a credit pass in the history of the examination. I was very proud when the Law Examination results were published in the Government Instructions and were gazetted. This gazetting later entitled me to membership of the 'Special Roll,' of the Somali Bar

Council and also to my later becoming a Notary Public and an advocate. At the time it was also a qualifying factor in selection for further training in the United Kingdom and eventual promotion to gazetted officer rank. I was the fifth Somali to be sent to the Metropolitan Police Training School at Hendon, north-west of London. I arrived there in late August 1958. My first child, a daughter, was born while I was at Hendon.

Many types of police courses were offered at Hendon: for recruits, promotion courses, advanced training, etc., but we mainly concentrated on the Metropolitan Police Criminal Investigation Department (CID) courses. I was excited to be even vaguely associated with the famous Scotland Yard. As a Colonial Course later renamed an Overseas Course we were administered separately by a supervisor, a retired former senior colonial police officer, assisted by an active police officer seconded from one of the colonial police forces and we also took some of our studies separately. During our first orientation, the assistant supervisor boasted that his boss and he would know within three weeks who would be the winner of the Baton of Honour. This kept us on our toes. There were short tests almost every day, for several weeks. These were mainly memory tests known as 'Quick Think Tests', but they counted towards the overall examination results. I achieved very low or even zero points in most of those tests, having come from Somaliland where life was slower even in its capital, Hargeisa. We had very few asphalt roads with fewer traffic signs and no advertising or similar publicity pictures on street walls. London bewildered me. Before leaving Hargeisa, I had called on my commissioner to take courtesy leave and remember him telling me that as soon as I got to London I should buy a notebook to write down anything I did not comprehend. I really did not understand what he meant at the time, but those 'Quick Think Tests' made me recall his advice. For some time I grew somewhat demoralised, not only because several weeks had already passed and for the first time since I had started to learn I was doing badly.

At long last, law studies commenced with more familiar subject matters. When the examination came I surprised the assistant supervisor, who was invigilating us and who must have by then already written me off, by asking for more paper at a time when almost half the class had already handed in their answer papers and had left the room. After answering all the questions, I had always made it a practice to use whatever time was left for review and corrections. I think I was the last person to leave. When the assistant supervisor gave me extra paper he took the first pages of my answers and read them whilst standing beside my table. Then, taking them with him, he went out of the room. I was thrilled, knowing that he was going to show my answers to the supervisor who was in his office just opposite the classroom. He came back after a few minutes, put the papers back on my table and resumed his invigilation. That same afternoon the supervisor himself was the invigilator and as he was distributing the examination papers he said to me, "I believe you did very well this morning." "Thank you Sir" I answered him. I found that remark very reassuring and it did much to close a long period of frustration.

I scored high marks in both law examination papers, coming first and second and did averagely well in the practical tests: case investigations, examination of mock scenes of crimes and the overall preparation of police case files, etc. All in all, I was lucky to finally secure a comfortable pass and the thirteenth or middle position out of 25 foreign students. The average police experience of our whole class was just over ten years; I had the least number of years, barely four, and was thus quite content with the final outcome.

My return from Hendon and my posting to Hargeisa coincided with the visit in February 1959 of the British Colonial Secretary, the Right Hon. Alan Lennox-Boyd. His was the first visit of its kind in Somaliland's history since Winston Churchill's some forty years earlier. He made a policy statement regarding our country's future, saying that if after general elections in one year's time the people of Somaliland wished to have a closer association with the people of Somalia (meaning Italian Somaliland) Her Majesty's Government would facilitate any necessary arrangements. Britain had already agreed, in 1956, not to oppose such a development. Mr. Lennox-Boyd then appealed for respect for law and order, but at the same time warned that it would be unfortunate if the resources needed for election arrangements had to be diverted for keeping the peace and for security.

The police had made a good impression. The Colonial Secretary wrote to Commissioner Cracknell on 9 February 1959 about the "long hours" of duty put in by the "fine force" which had looked after him. He went on to make a statement about the police and political development still relevant in Africa, in the Somali Republic not least

> I fully realise how important my statement on future constitutional progress is to the Somaliland Police. It enables you to approach your duties with greater determination of purpose and confidence in the future.
>
> The smooth carrying out of the programme upon which we must now concentrate together will depend greatly upon the efficiency, impartiality and strength of the police. I know you all understand this clearly and I wish you the greatest success in carrying out your important task.

February was mid *Jilaal,* the dry season extending from November to March, and in Hargeisa unlike Berbera the peak period for crime was during the *Jilaal.* It was my second posting as a station officer, but for me Hargeisa was quite different from Berbera. I had previously lived here for many years and knew many more people than I had in Berbera. More people would confide in me to help them solve problems and many more would voluntarily co-operate and offer information. My public relations improved tremendously.

In my capacity as police station officer, I was also in charge of driving tests. I was very proper and strict with young learners. But one day, a very elderly and popular clan chief came to me and said he wanted to have a driving licence. He did not know me, but I remembered seeing him drive a short wheel base Land-Rover three years earlier when I was at the Vocational Training Centre at Sheikh. My first reaction was that he might have lost his old licence, but was surprised when he quite frankly admitted that he had never had one. I directed him to the Traffic Licensing Office and asked him to pay the testing fees and bring me the testing authority from that office. I gave him the benefit of my having seen him drive in the past and certified him as having passed without putting him to the test. He could not have passed.

The whole following year was a very challenging one for the police. It was marked by continuous political campaigns involving rallies and other electioneering activities. Although a Legislative Council had been convened in 1957, the forthcoming election would, for the first time, decide on the full composition of the Protectorate government. Attention focussed on two main parties: the Somali National League (SNL), a resurgence of the former Somali National Society (SNS) led by Mohamed Haji Ibrahim Egal, and the National United Front (NUF) formed in the wake of the handing over to Ethiopia by Britain in 1954-5 of the Somali inhabited Haud and Reserved Areas, and led by Michael Mariano. Within the Protectorate, both parties drew their support mainly from the Isaaq clan who were the majority. A third party, the United Somali Party (USP) which drew its support from the non-Isaaq groups also came into being, to protect minority interests. It later entered into coalition with the SNL.

As I have explained, the Commissioner of Police's Somalization policy had a positive impact on the local situation. Our politicians had direct access and contact to senior Somali officers with no need for interpreters as used to be the case. Most European police officers had been reassigned to police headquarters and to specialised units where they had little or no face to face contact with members of the general public. The result was that during a whole year of heated election campaigning there was no single disturbance in the entire country, the governor, Sir Douglas Hall's secret report to London a week before the election "I shall be surprised if there is no trouble anywhere — ," notwithstanding.

Both main parties committed themselves to early independence and union with Somalia to the South. While the NUF generally followed a moderate policy line — that of cautious negotiations for union and bargaining with the southern leaders for power sharing, the SNL capitalised on its rival's moderation and adopted a radical platform without any pre-conditions on the unity issue. This step would be long regretted, not for the union aspect itself, because that had been the long-standing wish of the overwhelming majority of the Somali people, but for neglecting to bargain and safeguard the North's rights.

The Somaliland Constitution (Order-In-Council) of 1960 provided for the appointment of four elected ministers including a chief minister (The Leader of Government Business). Although the SNL won an overall majority at the election on 17 February 1960, i.e. 20 out of 33 seats, they nevertheless lived up to their coalition contract with the USP, who won only 12 seats, and then allocated two portfolios to the latter party. Significantly, the SNL, whose radicalism naturally appealed to the mass of the voters, won twenty seats of the twenty-one Isaaq constituencies. For the NUF, only Michael Mariano, the party leader, won his seat. Michael had been a favorite of the Protectorate authorities. Some former NUF sources maintain that after the SNL election victory Michael handed over his file containing notes on Somaliland's negotiations with the Southern leaders to Mohamed Haji Ibrahim Egal who became leader of government business. I regret not having ascertained the truth from Michael himself before his death, despite many opportunities. I later asked Mohamed Haji Ibrahim Egal, but he denied it. Some Southern politicians who were then key ministers assert, however, even today that when the Somaliland ministers went to Mogadishu for unity talks and they were asked for their conditions for union, they said that they had none. If true, with the hindsight of history, this clearly demonstrated a most naive, even tragic, idealism on the part of the then leaders of the north.

CHAPTER THREE

INDEPENDENCE
AND UNION

AFTER HER DEFEAT IN THE Second World War, Italy renounced all rights and title to her former African colonies. The Four Powers, who were victors in that war (Britain, France, USA and the USSR), could neither reach an agreement on the destiny of those former Italian colonies nor support an earlier Bevin Plan which proposed the lumping together of all Somali inhabited territories in the form of a British administered trusteeship. Such a trusteeship is believed by Somalis to have been strongly opposed by both the USA and the USSR, who, for different reasons, favored returning Somalia to Italian Colonialism. The USA is thought to have believed that Western style democracy would be more likely to redevelop in a post-war, post-Fascist, impoverished Italy if she were strengthened by the return of her former colonies.

Stalin, however, took the view that with the return of those colonies to Italy, communist forces would gain the upper hand in Rome and he could then use Somalia as a stepping stone into black Africa where communism was barely known at that time. Moreover, according to former Yugoslav deputy leader Milovan Djilas, Stalin had said that he would not support the British proposal for a Greater Somalia Trusteeship because the British were already too powerful in the region. The Four Powers then referred the matter to the United Nations where, in 1949, the General Assembly adopted an historic resolution (by a single vote, that of a latecomer, Haiti) placing Somalia under an Italian administered United Nations Trusteeship for a period of ten years with the specific instruction that it be prepared for independence.

Despite early attempts to reintroduce her former colonial policies, Italy lived up to the UN trust requirements, taking the first step in 1950 by establishing a Territorial Advisory Council appointed by the Italian Administrator. Municipal elections were held in 1954 and the first elected Legislative Assembly consisting of 60 Somali deputies was established in May 1956. Ten seats reserved for foreign residents, Arabs, Indians, Italians and Pakistanis were never filled. Somali ministers with some executive powers were installed under the first Somali Prime Minister, Abdullahi Issa Mohamoud, who served until independence in 1960. Local administration at the regional and district levels was also Somalized. For the second Legislative Assembly, all Somali elections were held for 90 Deputies in March 1959.

Much less thought had been given in this regard in the Protectorate. When it came, the path to independence was thus fairly precipitate. There were three partly external pressures influencing the British authorities. The first was developments in Egypt, where General Mohamed Naguib and Colonel Gamal Abdel-Nasser had overthrown the monarchy on 23 July 1952 and inspired a new generation throughout the middle east. From 1953 onwards, Egyptian educational institutions accepted many Somali students — and this at a time when places in Somali schools were very limited. On their return young Nasserites soon radicalised the local political scene, to the consternation of some more conservative Somali leaders. A second pressure was the perceived need of sections of the British Government to minimize friction with the Imperial Ethiopian government, led by the astute emperor Haile Sellassie, even at Somali expense. The handing over of the Haud to Ethiopian administration in 1954 had deeply divided British officials. There had even been resignations. But to the Somalis it seemed not only an unmitigated disaster, but a betrayal. As a people we overwhelmingly lost faith in the protection treaties with the British. During the six years after this transfer and prior to independence, the very word *Protectorate* became anathema to most Somalis. Many quite rightly believed that had it not been for the handing over of those territories, so vital for the transhumantic life pattern of herdsmen and herds alike, there would hardly have been the emotional desire for an immediate union with the South, nor even the demand for immediate independence, rather than customary and careful due process leading to eventual decolonization, as had happened or was underway elsewhere in Africa.

Thirdly, as British internal memos now released also demonstrate, there was a desire to keep in step with Italy. A note on 'Somali Union' used at an April 1960 Cabinet meeting in London comments

> The Foreign Office [is] only interested in Union to the extent that to oppose it might give Nasser or [the] Russians [a] chance to fish in troubled waters. We would prefer [the] Protectorate to develop on parallel lines to Somalia towards independence, working under our guidance for "close association" with Somalia and normal relations with Ethiopia. [JG10/11/1G-F.O. 371 14699-96]

The Somalis in the Protectorate — and elsewhere — knew what they wanted. Somali Unity aspirations were of long standing having been pledged as early as the 1940s by leaders of various Somali clans living in the five different, but adjoining, territories. These were the British Somaliland Protectorate, the Italian administered U.N. Trusteeship of Somalia, French Somaliland (later Djibouti), the Ethiopian administered Ogaden and the Northern Frontier District (later Province), of Kenya. Somalis aspired towards reunification into a Greater Somali Union. As a first step, the first session of the first elected parliament of the Somaliland Protectorate meeting in April 1960, unanimously voted for immediate independence and union with Somalia. Independence was approved by Britain to take effect on 26 June, 1960, four days earlier than the pre-planned independence of the South, which itself had been brought forward from 2 December to 1 July 1960, with the approval of a General Assembly of the United Nations.

With regard to the projected union of the Trust Territory and the British Protectorate, on 27 May 1960 the Italian Government advised the Trusteeship Council of the United Nations

> . . . the people of the two Territories have already democratically shown the desire of uniting in a single independent state. This of course will be

a development following the independence of the Trust Territory and as such is not within the terms of the Trusteeship Agreement. To these developments, which transcend its responsibility as an Administering Power, the Italian Government in the circumstances could be but a witness. In fact those results will and must be solely the result of the converging aspirations and wishes of the peoples of the two Somali territories. The only part that is becoming to Italy is to formulate its wishes that this important event take place — as indeed seems to be the case — in accordance to democratic principles and be in the interest of the prosperity and welfare of both peoples and of the maintenance of peace and tranquility in the area.

The South as we have seen, had undergone a longer and more thorough political process preparative to Independence. The southerners' greater involvement in governmental processes and their consequent political maturity was soon reflected in the discussions which took place. At a meeting of Somaliland and Somalia leaders held in Mogadishu during mid-April 1960, the two parties agreed to unite as one Republic with a parliamentary system of government. It was also agreed to set up various committees to unify the different administrative, judicial and financial systems. It was further contemplated that upon the Independence of both territories, representatives of the two sides would sign an Act of Union setting out the terms of the Union and thus making it legally binding on both sides.

The Constituent Assembly of Somaliland passed resolutions and a proposed *Act of Union* during the April to June period, 1960 and submitted drafts to the Constituent Assembly of Somalia. The latter debated a different version of an Act of Union (Atto di Unione) and also approved it, but only the day prior to Independence. Where the two texts differed, they were referred to the two governments of Somalia and Somaliland to finalize and submit a single text to the National Assembly. That was not done for neither government met again, probably due to the pressure of work on their respective Independence celebrations. However, at a meeting held just prior to the Independence of Somalia, its Constituent Assembly had added a new clause to the constitution for the election of a provisional president by the new National Assembly (comprising the Legislative Assemblies of the two respective territories) Clearly, such a vote should have taken place only after the signing of the Act of Union of the two Somali territories, Somalia and Somaliland. Somaliland members of parliament however, participated with their southern colleagues and voted in the election of the provisional president without the prior signing of any Act of Union. Such participation might well not have been constitutionally proper.

On July 1, 1960, the provisional president signed a decree, with much less substance than the stipulated Act of Union would contain, and which was not subsequently submitted to the National Assembly for conversion into law in accordance with Article 63 of the constitution. It could be argued that it did not therefore have any legal binding force, thus finally becoming a dead letter. It was not until seven months later, on January 31, 1961, that a new Act of Union was finally adopted by the National Assembly which had been formed on July 1, 1960 by the merger of the two respective Legislative Assemblies.

In view of the above and other legal anomalies, it is evident that it could be argued that the Union of Somalia and Somaliland, despite its practical implementation at every level of government and in every sphere of society for more than thirty years, might not after all have been legally validated. Predominant legal opinion, however, owns that such a long period of total integration together with the absence of any claim of invalidity, would override any other arguments.

When Somaliland and Somalia merged as the Somali Republic, notwithstanding the legal anomalies stated above, the first National Assembly was formed by bringing together the members of the two former Constituent Assemblies, numbering 33 and 90 respectively. However, it must be pointed out that the resultant representation did not reflect the actual population ratios of the two former States. According to the population counts accepted by the two European former administering powers, the two states had the following population estimates:

		Source:
Somaliland (North)	640,000	(1951 General Survey of Somaliland Protectorate by John A Hunt).
Somalia (South)	1,275,584	(1955 census by the administering power as reported by Prof. Bruno Cherubini).
Total	1,915,584	

Although the southern census was made four years after the estimate in the North, it is evident that about 1/3 of the population lived in the North and 2/3 in the South. Furthermore, election for the Somaliland Assembly was based on the single constituency system while that of Somalia was based on proportional representation. This latter system was to be adopted throughout the Republic for both the 1964 and 1969 general elections. Disproportionate representation and the change of the constituency system were among the many underlying factors which contributed to the rapid development of disenchantment among northerners with the union. They were aggrieved that they could not influence any decision making process because of their unbalanced minority representation in the National Assembly.

	Southern Somalia	Northern Somalia
Population	1,275,000	740,000
Census date	1955	1951
Population ratios	66.6% (2/3)	33.4% (1/3)
No. of Parliamentary seats	73.2%	26.8%
Seat/population ratio	1:14,167	1:19,394

In hindsight, in order to make National Assembly seats conform more closely to population ratios, one of the following two alternatives should have been adopted:

ALTERNATIVE I: (Seats changed)

South:	66.6% of 123 =	82 seats	instead of 90
North:	33.4% of 123 =	41 seats	instead of 33
	Total	123 seats	123

ALTERNATIVE II: (Southern seats unchanged but seats adjusted for the Northerners)

South =	90 seats
North =	45 seats
Total	135 seats

Leaders of the South had in fact made a last minute suggestion that the Union be delayed a few months whilst such anomalies were resolved, but that view had received no northern support. At the time, I noted with alarm that the people of Somaliland had forced the union upon the South so precipitously, that they alone had to pay the price by accepting a southern constitution, southern flag, southern capital and a southern Head of State — who also appointed a southern Prime Minister. When the first National Government was formed, southerners assigned to themselves all the key portfolios including Foreign Affairs, Interior, Finance and Commerce. The President of the National Bank was a southerner as were the commandants of the armed forces. The single important post it seemed to me, that was allocated to the north was the presidency of the newly constituted National Assembly — but I did not then know how important for me analysis of Somali politics was soon to become.

THE CLAN-FAMILIES AND CLANS
OF THE SOMALI NATION

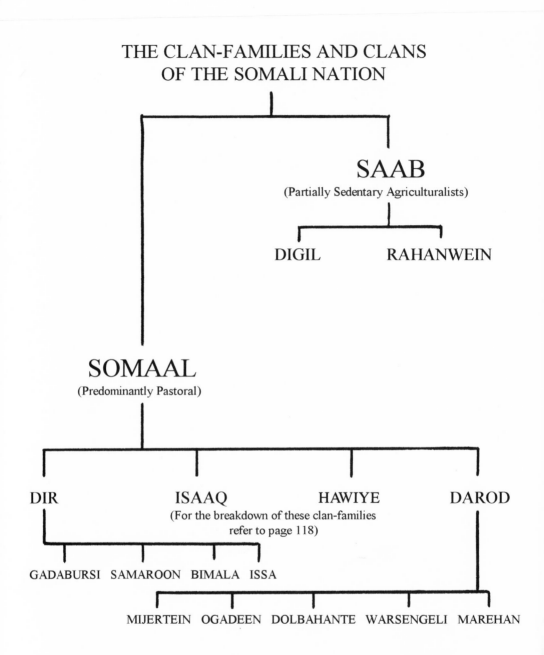

SAAB

(Partially Sedentary Agriculturalists)

DIGIL   RAHANWEIN

SOMAAL

(Predominantly Pastoral)

DIR   ISAAQ   HAWIYE   DAROD

(For the breakdown of these clan-families
refer to page 118)

GADABURSI SAMAROON BIMALA ISSA

MIJERTEIN OGADEEN DOLBAHANTE WARSENGELI MAREHAN

(The above list is of main groupings, especially those mentioned in the text, and is not intended to
be comprehensive.)

CHAPTER FOUR

COMMAND OF THE
SPECIAL BRANCH

I N J U N E 1 9 6 2 , I W A S again sent back to the United Kingdom on
a British Council sponsored course of study at Bramshill House Police
College described as "near Basingstoke" in Hampshire. Bramshill
House was in fact quite isolated from any populated or built up area,
standing in the centre of a large estate of more than ten square miles.
From a bus stop at its main entrance one had to walk a good four miles
to reach the college premises. Also, during our few short vacations,
which really were 'long week-ends' from Friday morning to Monday
evening, most of us had to walk that four miles distance to and from
a bus to the nearest railway station at Reading or Basingstoke. The
estate was originally owned by a member of the nobility before it was
bought by the British Home Office during the 1950s to become the
permanent site of the Police College, at the time the only one of its kind
in England and Wales.

Many smaller buildings had been constructed to accommodate
and service those enrolled at the college but the mansion itself remained
largely unaltered. Upstairs, at one end of the 'first floor' — or second
as it would be counted in America — was a large library, with, it seemed
to me then, a copy of every book that had ever been printed. At the
other end of the floor were the offices of the commandant of the college
and his staff, some conference rooms, and a chapel. The commandant
had an apartment flat on one of the floors still higher up. The whole
ground floor, apart from the reception at the main entrance to the
building was devoted to recreation and other amenities: bars, lobby

facilities, etc. There were pianos and many indoor games: billiards, ping-pong, badminton, chess, dominoes, etc. I played most of these games but not the piano. Out-door sporting activities included golf and tennis and I was an amateur player in both.

Outside the mansion were the newly built facilities. Nearest was the sick bay where I was at one time a lone in-patient, and the catering block or 'mess.' Beyond that was a second block consisting of an auditorium, lecture halls, classrooms, and a gymnasium. Furthest were the living quarters for both the teaching staff and the students, interspersed with the academic directors' offices. The courses were taught by three departments: Law; Police Procedure; and Liberal Studies. Each programme was of two months' duration, and each department was further subdivided into a number of 'syndicates.' I belonged to syndicate eleven of the Law Department. Unlike Hendon, there were no examinations but after the morning lecture one had to spend a great deal of time in the library, preparing discussion papers against stern deadlines.

Since the main objective of the Police College was the development of leadership, the Commandant of the College was a retired British Army General of the Sandhurst type. Liberal Studies were taught by academics seconded from nearby universities. On the assumption that the average policeman would not, at that time, have the desired academic background, the aim of this aspect of the curriculum was to broaden our general outlook. I had been a stranger not only to the English language but was largely self-taught without regular schooling even by my own country's meager standards. I must have been the greatest beneficiary of those liberal studies. Despite the shortness of the course, I have ever since considered it the most important educational experience of my life. I was brought up to date with the past and guided toward understanding the future.

To this day I continue my self-education: hardly a day passes without my having recourse to an English dictionary for new vocabulary. I have later tried to learn Arabic, but although I have broken the first barriers, I have not gone as far as I wished (the same can be said of my Italian language efforts). However, I can now understand Islamic principles better and can read some of the Holy Quran. I was orally taught only the minimum requirements of Islam as is the sad case for many non-Arabic speaking people. While at Bramshill College, I met many British police officers who like myself had also been to Hendon and I was often amused by their recollection and criticism of the 'Quick Think Tests', I had so much dreaded. There was good news from home. My second son, Khidar, the fourth of my nine children, was born in Hargeisa.

At the request of the Somali government after leaving Police College, I attended early the following year a course on Intelligence and Security under the auspices of the relevant British Services. The reason for this was that I had been selected to become the head of our Police Special Branch. In 1965, I went for similar training in the United States, a Public Safety course followed by an Intelligence course. Apart from many similarities in the field of intelligence and its trade craft, I recall they both had one very special focus in common: how to fight communism. I was not convinced by either course that that was a Somali security priority but one of my British instructors sagely remarked, "Whatever we teach you to use against communism you can always use against your other enemies." That was so. However, my American Chief Instructor told me that he regretted not having been able to convince me that communism was a threat to my country. At that time, in the judgment of every Somali, the main threat was perceived to be the imperialist ambitions of neighboring Ethiopia.

Upon my return home from the United Kingdom, I took up my new assignment as Head of the Special Branch in the Somali capital, Mogadishu, in March 1963, and was immediately faced with a great deal of both internal and external political tension. Feelings were running high in the North. Former Prime Minister Mohamed Ibrahim Egal and Sheikh Ali Ismail, then ministers of education and defence respectively — the only two Isaaq ministers in Prime Minister Abdurashid Ali Shermarke's government — had resigned the previous year. In the very month of my new assignment, Somalia broke off diplomatic relations with Britain over the latter's handling of the issue of the future of the Somalis who lived in the Northern Frontier District of Kenya (NFD). Bowing to pressure from Kenya's emerging politicians, The United Kingdom Government disregarded a report indicating that an overwhelming majority expressed a desire to become part of the Somali Republic. Those relations remained severed for the next five years.

The Somalis in the Ethiopian ruled Ogaden also revolted that same month which led to Ethiopian subversion and military reprisals against Somalia. Those, in turn, were to lead Prime Minister Abdurashid Ali Shermarke to seek and obtain arms from the Soviet Union since he had failed to get a favorable deal from the West who were distracted by their good relations with Haile Sellassie. In his arms deal with the Soviets, Abdurashid went over the head of President Aden Abdulla Osman, which further compounded internal political tensions, although at that time he received great popular credit for obtaining the arms because of a nationwide defense consciousness. In the general elections held in March 1964 his SYL party won an overwhelming majority while Abdurashid himself was elected unopposed but even so, President Aden Abdulla Osman did not reappoint him as prime minister, preferring Abdurazaq Haji Hussein.

The pressure of work on my office was thus formidable. The Police Special Branch, although coming under the commandant of police, was the sole intelligence and security service in the whole country. The National Army had a small untrained novice intelligence unit and the Chief of Staff, General Daud Abdullah Hersi relied heavily on my office. I served him faithfully with the Commandant of Police, General Mohamed Abshir Musa's blessing. The relationship between those two very different officers was amicable and characterised by mutual understanding and personal trust. Daud had been Abshir's deputy in the police force before he became the first commandant of the newly created National Army on the eve of independence in 1960. Unlike Abshir, Daud did not involve himself much in the capital's social life and generally he would be available at his home. I frequently reported to him there, mostly in the evenings when he was quite relaxed and thus able to absorb the differing aspects of my briefings without our being interrupted. In contrast, I always had to see Abshir during office hours.

I also worked very closely with each minister of the interior, of whom there were two during my tenure: the late Mohamoud Abdi

Nur in Prime Minister Abdurishid's government and Abdulqadir Mohamed Aden in his successor Abdurazaq Haji Hussein's government. I would occasionally call on several others including the foreign and finance ministers to brief them on matters affecting their respective responsibilities. Throughout I also enjoyed cooperation and a good working relationship with the Chief of Cabinet in the Prime Minister's office, Dr. Ahmed Shire Lawaha, a man with a very good sense of urgency and sensitivity to confidentiality — two important qualities in which I found most other senior southern civil servants lacking in those days. Fortunately, he held onto that office during my whole tenure as the Head of Intelligence and Security.

I would very seldom report in writing about personalities, whether government officials or ordinary civilians, but would maintain dossiers on any sifted and reasonable allegations against personalities, which would be filed and preserved in the intelligence archives. I would usually write only to the minister of the interior and the chief of cabinet in the prime minister's office. Nor did I ever write about cabinet ministers, unless specially requested by the prime minister, which only happened once during my tenure. I would, however, verbally consult General Abshir who might in turn brief the prime minister. I would not myself normally have any direct contact with the prime minister for my only line of communication was through the chief of cabinet. I was delegated to act freely by General Abshir whose complete trust I enjoyed but I was very proud of both my decorum and loyalty to my superiors. If we ever had to report direct to the prime minister, and that was very seldom, I would have Abshir sign the communications.

Prior to independence the Police Special Branch had been headed by General Mohamed Siad Barre. Before the latter became second-in-command of the National Army, his police career had been associated with general mishandling and had earned him some public mistrust. In order to restore public confidence in the police, after independence General Abshir had forbidden special branch personnel from making arrests. If arrests were necessary, they had to use uniformed police units to make them. The two men were very different and this came to the fore when, sadly, General Daud died in 1965. Mohamed Siad Barre assumed acting command of the Somali National Army. His appointment to that post was confirmed a very few months later.

Mohamed Siad's appointment marked the end of the cordial relationship which had developed between Police Commandant Abshir and the new army commandant's predecessor. It also adversely affected our sharing of intelligence, which had been primarily for the benefit of the army. While Abshir never suggested any variation of the working relationships, Mohamed Siad's representative abruptly absented himself from attending weekly intelligence meetings chaired by the chief of cabinet in the prime minister's office. Siad must have felt confident that his past experience and the army's novice intelligence unit which he soon sought to expand were sufficient to serve his needs. Nor did I come to know him on a personal level since informal meetings, such as I had held with General Daud, were discontinued.

The commandants of the army and police were permanent participants in National Security Committee meetings held under the chairmanship of the prime minister, with the defence, foreign affairs and the interior ministers also present. Such meetings primarily concerned matters of national defense which directly touched upon the responsibilities of the army commandant, but they also covered other general aspects of national security. As I have indicated, Ethiopia was at that time considered the main threat to our defense and national security. Police intelligence near to and across our border could provide better analysis of movements and intentions than could the army. Abshir was, therefore, far more knowledgeable than his counterpart, as Mohamed Siad must have recognised. Perhaps because of this, when he met me one evening at a reception given by Abshir, he asked to come with me after the reception was over. I agreed, waited for him and took him for a drive around the town. He acknowledged his department's weakness in intelligence collection and evaluation and asked me many questions. Finally he came to the point: he wanted me to train his men. I agreed, but suggested that he should first contact Abshir. I later informed Abshir who was in agreement too but Mohamed Siad took his time to write to Abshir. Although it was decided I should soon transfer to Hargeisa due to tensions there; that move had to be delayed for several weeks so that

I could complete the requested training for the military intelligence.

I came to recognise the depth of the ill-feelings Mohamed Siad harbored towards Abshir stemming I supposed mainly from jealousy over the latter's popularity. Both, together with Daud and several other police officers, had been trained by the Italian Carabinieri in Rome during the Italian administration in the mid fifties. In the Italian system examination results from such training always counted towards seniority. In 1958 Abshir, who was from the Mijertein clan, had been appointed the first Somali Commandant of Police, with Daud, an Hawiye, as his Deputy. Mohamed Siad had then invented a petty story which he sold to his own Marehan clansmen and many other non-Mijertein Darod people, that in those examinations he had stood second and therefore should have had Daud's position. That story was revived during the 1970s after Mohamed Siad's coup d'etat, specially by his cousin, Abdurahman Jama Barre. When I asked Abdurahman about it, he replied that it was a collusion between the Hawiye and Mijertein politicians for Darod/Hawiye power sharing.

Years later, in 1981, as the minister responsible for refugees in Somalia, I paid a visit to Sweden where the late Abdullahi Issa was then ambassador. Abdullahi was a very decent man from whom I always learned a great deal of Somalia's political history, may God rest his soul. He had been prime minister and was also acting as his own minister of the interior, after dismissing Musa Boqor, when the appointments of Abshir and Daud had been made. I specifically asked him about Mohamed Siad's claim of being superseded. Abdullahi Issa's father had died when he was a child and his mother, a Marehan, had brought him up with the help of her own clan. He felt that he owed that clan a debt of gratitude. Nevertheless he told me that according to the report he had received from the Italian Carabinieri, the examination result was: Abshir, Daud, Mohamed Siad, etc. in that order. He remembered the exact position of each officer even to the very last one. He also said he received protests from members of the Marehan on behalf of Mohamed Siad and he had then handed the file over to Adan Shire Jama (Adan Low), a Marehan, who was his Under-Secretary of the Interior, requesting him to show it to the Marehan elders so that they should know the truth. However, that Mohamed

Siad bore a grudge seems to have affected subsequent events.

During the period of military cooperation with the Russians, the police, in contrast received substantial technical advice, assistance and equipment, from western countries, particularly Germany, Italy and the United States. The military, or more properly Mohamed Siad Barre, took maximum advantage of the weakness of a government that had subordinated its authority to popular emotion and enthusiasm for the newly formed National Army. Siad's army personnel would always harass and mishandle western diplomats, especially the military attachés, during arms deliveries, under the pretext of preserving national military secrets. The real motive for their abuses must have been either to erode western assistance to the police force because of resentment against Abshir, or Siad sought to please his benefactors, the Russians. Initial, but as yet unconfirmed reports from the KGB archives, appear to suggest the latter.

CHAPTER FIVE

INTELLIGENCE AND COUNTER-INTELLIGENCE

T HE ONLY FOREIGN AMBASSADOR WHO knew me personally was the Sudanese ambassador, Ahmad Salah Boukhari, a very high calibre diplomat, who played an important role in the mediation effort undertaken by his government in the Ethio-Somali war of 1964 which led to the Khartoum agreement. That instrument was perhaps the best instrument of its kind worked out in the whole horn of Africa. It not only worked well for the twenty-six years it was designed for, but its provisions remained a solid basis for solving disputes right up until the collapse of the Somali state and the fundamental changes initiated in Ethiopia after the departure of the two dictators in the nineteen-nineties.

The Sudanese have always understood the nature of the Ethiopian empire-state, as we had to — for Ethiopia was the number one enemy of both our countries in those days. That is not to say that some Ethiopians were not very good people, but I learned that other Ethiopian officials could be unnecessarily difficult. During a Public Safety Course in the USA I was one of a group of police officers attending from many parts of the world: Africa, Asia and South America. Three African countries, Egypt, Ethiopia and Somalia were represented. There were four of us from Somalia, while all the other national groups numbered one, two or three. At the end of the course I was selected as the leader of an exercise and workshop to deal with an assumed insurgency. An Indian Officer was selected as my deputy. Each one of the rest was given a specific assignment. One of three Ethiopians, a certain Colonel

Barakat, behaved obstinately and was quite uncooperative, although the other two officers were excellent men. Probably he wanted to sabotage the workshop just because I was a Somali. I decided not to quarrel and delegated my deputy to deal with him for the rest of the time and the operation was a success.

The main counter-intelligence target for the Police Special Branch was the Ethiopian Embassy. Ato Ahadu Sabure, the incumbent ambassador, was a capable and honest diplomat. Ahadu never knew me personally though he might well have known about my existence. He spoke both Arabic and Somali fluently and had good working relationships with all our key ministers. I remember him on one occasion, even at a time of hostilities and tension between the two countries, appearing at the airport VIP lounge where some ministers were waiting to welcome Oscar Kambona and a team of Tanzanian ministers on a mediation mission between Ethiopia and Somalia. He was the only foreign diplomat invited to that welcoming reception because of his obvious interest. He was teasing about the Ogaden and said in Arabic, "You are devils," to which Abdurazaq, then Minister of Communication and Transport, quipped, "But in our own home," (indirectly accusing Ethiopia of aggression). Ahadu took the joke in good part. He stood for good neighborliness between our two countries and although most Ethiopian diplomats in those times were often overshadowed by their intelligence officers, Ahadu appeared an exception. I was sorry, later, to learn that Ambassador Ahadu Sabure had spent years in detention under the Mengistu regime.

We soon identified a certain Tawelde, whose diplomatic cover was that of First Secretary in the Ethiopian Embassy, as the assigned Intelligence Officer. He was active but without any undue excesses. We recognised that he had to be active because at the time the underlying revolt amongst the Ogaden Somalis and sections of the Oromo, was beginning in earnest: it led to open war between the two countries before many months had passed. The population of the Somali Republic was very sympathetic towards all Somalis still under foreign rule.

There had been friction between the Christian highland kingdoms of Abyssinia (Ethiopia) and the largely Muslim people to the southeast and east at several times throughout history. But during the scramble for Africa Ethiopia greatly expanded and the then Ethiopian emperor Menelik II laid detailed claim in letters to the heads of European states to areas long populated by Somalis, Oromo and others which he intended to colonize. Ethiopian troops occupied the city of Harar in January 1887. Soon afterwards, military expeditions began years of raiding and burning Somali settlements and looting herds to the south and east. On the other hand, effective Ethiopian administration of the Somali inhabited Haud and Ogaden regions can only really be dated from the late 1950's after Britain had withdrawn from the Reserved Areas she had occupied during the Second World War. The people of the area had never accepted alien rule, be it from the European colonialists or the Amharic speaking Abyssinians. Small wonder, in the 1960's when the British and Italians departed, that Somali populations in Djibouti, Kenya and the Ogaden grew more than restive. The degree of sympathy and support extended to them by our government became a priority target for Ethiopian intelligence officers, including Tawelde.

Tawelde, we noted, was a bachelor or at least had no family staying with him. He had a Somali mistress called *Hilla'a* or lightening, perhaps because of her beauty. On one occasion he was alleged to have bitten her, perhaps after they had quarrelled, and she complained to the police. Thereupon, it later transpired, the head of our counter-espionage, Major Farah Sugulle, maneuvered the handling of the case to create a sensational scandal; this without my knowledge. Early one morning a local Italian language daily, *L'Unione*, carried on its front page the woman's photograph, lying on a hospital bed, half naked to show wounds on her thighs. A passport size photograph of Tawelde, which could only have been supplied by our office, was printed and the rest of the page was filled with the story of her complaint. Farah Sugulle was euphoric when he brought that paper to me, but he soon read disapproval on my face. I have a natural weakness whereby people can easily detect my negative reactions. He quickly denied that he had organised the scandal or arranged the press report, but admitted he had supplied a photograph of Tawelde. It was not only a negative act from the intelligence viewpoint, but could have been counter-productive because the Ethiopians could have but did not do something similar to our diplomats.

The Ethiopian Ambassador, as might be expected, delivered a formal protest, personally calling upon the Foreign Minister, the former prime minister, Abdullahi Issa. Abdullahi was equally annoyed, protesting furiously and in person to the Minister of the Interior, Mohamoud Abdi Nur. Most ministers including our minister were unhappy over the scandal. Many senior officials including ministers kept commenting on the issue and sought my assurances that 'the Siad Barre era of intelligence misuse,' of which they had become reminded by the Tawelde affair, was not about to be repeated. I undertook that henceforth the counter-intelligence unit would be under my close personal control and I constantly lectured the counter-intelligence personnel against excesses and on the need for credibility.

Tawelde was immediately withdrawn, only to be replaced by a much tougher and more aggressive intelligence officer—a certain Petru. He was more senior than Tawelde and became the second man in the Ethiopian Embassy, acting as chargé d'affaires in the absence of the ambassador. It was a time of great military activity: movement of our army personnel to and from the Soviet Union for training purposes, arrival and departure of Soviet military advisers, the delivery of large quantities of armaments—not to mention the presence of Ogaden rebel leaders. The Ethiopian intelligence network was thus very effectively strengthened and their activities evidently reflected a large budget increase. Whilst our intelligence organization was still in its embryonic stage, the skills of our adversary had been built up over centuries, even if only recently upgraded into modern form of organization and capability.

To combat increased foreign espionage, the need arose to tap some of the Ethiopian embassy telephones—the first operation of its kind in independent Somali history. I wanted it done discretely in the safest possible way to avoid leakage. That called for the cooperation of the ministry of communication. I personally approached the chief technician at the main telephone exchange complex and sought his advice. He said that it was perfectly feasible and he was quite prepared to cooperate from a national security point of view, but that I should first obtain permission from his superiors. He was a good civil servant and I could not agree with him more. I thanked him saying I very well understood the need for that, but at the same time it was vital that as few people as possible should be involved. He suggested that in that case, I had better approach the minister directly since only he could put a limit on the number of people involved.

Fortunately the incumbent minister was my former minister of interior, Mohamoud Abdi Nur, with whom I had a good working relationship. He was a nationalist who trusted me completely but he did not much like the idea. I convinced him that it was a vital national interest but, I promised that the ambassador's telephones would not be tapped. Technically, I later discovered, that undertaking would not be wholly fulfilled. The minister approved my request, but he had one more condition: the practice of tapping would not be extended for use against Somali politicians. I gave him my assurance, and he instructed the chief telephone technician to cooperate with us and promised that he would be the only other person in his ministry involved.

We found that the Ethiopian embassy had five lines connecting with the main exchange, of which two were direct lines to the ambassador's office and residence, another was only for the intelligence officer and the remaining two were for the embassy exchange. We tapped the last three telephones, but found that both the ambassador's office and residence were also connected through the embassy exchange and there was no way of insulating the ambassador from the tapping. His two direct lines were left free to the best of my knowledge, at least during my tenure of office.

The tapping was a successful operation. Within two days we had arrested seven of our armed forces personnel, both army and police, including two from special branch staff itself! Although there was not sufficient evidence forthcoming to secure their conviction by a court, they were nevertheless disciplined and dismissed after a period of detention. There were only two civilians arrested, a man and a woman. Both were later released on the grounds of insufficient evidence. The most important part of the operation, however, was the disruption of the Ethiopian espionage network which it would take them quite a long time to restore.

At the invitation of the Somali prime minister, Mr. Chou En-Lai,

Prime Minister of the People's Republic of China, paid a four day visit to Mogadishu in February 1964 during the latter's famous extended tour of Africa. I was put in charge of his security which was well coordinated with the protocol arrangements. Any security operation that conflicts with protocol only serves to defeat the object of such important visits. I attended all the preparatory meetings invariably chaired by my friend Dr. Lawaha, the Chief of Cabinet in the Prime Minister's office.

The first item on the agenda for the second day of the visit was the official meeting of the two governments scheduled for 8 am at the Council of Ministers Hall. I told the head of the security escort to await instructions before escorting the VIPs and went to check if the prime minister was ready to receive his guest. I found Abdurashid in an unhappy mood. None of his ministers, with the exception of the foreign minister, Abdullahi Issa, had yet shown up and the prime minister's secretary was busy telephoning ministers' residences. Abdurashid asked me to delay the VIP's departure from his residence. Without asking him how long, because I felt that the prime minister would not know, I delayed Chou En-Lai's departure for one hour. Our guest had to be informed through his own chief of security, before he dressed, so that he could relax.

A large banquet in honor of Mr. Chou En-Lai was held on the last night of the visit. The only western ambassador present was that of France as other western countries had no relations with China at that time. I was included in the list of participants, but I did not feel that I was entitled to be and so took my seat at a far corner. During the toast time, Chou En-Lai walked around and surprised me by approaching, glass in hand, and saying *shiffo*. This was the exact literal Somali expression for a toast, but I could not have produced it myself. Like *jaalle* it was another Somali word that I had not heard since my nomadic adolescence. When babies choked at breast-feeding and coughed, mothers often said *Shiffo*, calling for "good health." I admired the skill of his adviser/translator whoever he was. After Chou En-Lai's departure, but before he left the airport, Abdurashid personally shook me by the hand and congratulated me on a job well done.

From the privileged vantage point of the Special Branch directorate as well as foreign dignitaries, I was in a position to form my own evaluations of most Somali leaders and would-be leaders. The southerner, Abdullahi Issa's premiership was during the Trusteeship's self-government period preceding the union of the North and South and I therefore had not known him in that capacity. Undoubtedly, he was a unique personality who lived before his time. Very unlike most other Somali politicians of that era, he believed genuinely in supporting whoever became the head of either party — the Somali Youth League (SYL) — or the government, both of which he had led for a long time. He would never try to undermine those who succeeded him. He willingly served under Abdurashid as foreign minister and under Abdulrazaq as minister of health and minister of commerce and industries. Although he was not gifted with charisma, as foreign minister and later as ambassador, he was renowned for the perfection of his sense of protocol. Despite being a self-taught man he would never hesitate to correct his more educated officials in matters of protocol.

When internally and externally criticised for inviting Israel to the 1960 independence celebrations purely on the basis of its membership in the United Nations from whom Somalia was receiving her independence, he skillfully managed, with the help of the Italians, to convince the Israeli government to withdraw its acceptance of the invitation rather than he having to cancel it. That, he considered, would be a serious breach of the diplomatic courtesies to which, he insisted, the young Somali Republic should always adhere. That he bitterly deplored that this issue had been politicized is clear from the secret notes on the unofficial talks held 2 to 4 June 1960 in Mogadishu.

I have included Abdullahi Issa, for the sake of completeness — and no account of Somali national evolution could ignore such a figure — but to return to my time in the special branch, I have already explained that Abdurashid Ali Shermarke left the prime ministry in March 1964 and it soon became common knowledge that he would stand for president in three year's time. In the meantime, apart from attending parliamentary debates and meetings, he did not much involve himself in politics and led a quiet life. Though still belonging to the ruling party (SYL) he was known to oppose the government of his successor, Abdurazaq Haji Hussein.

Soon after he had handed over, I received information that some of our motor scooters which had outlived their usefulness for intelligence work, being too well known, were surveilling and openly trailing Abdurashid. Those scooters belonged to the counter espionage unit whose responsibilities did not in any case include checking on local dissidents or the activities of Somali nationals unless suspected of foreign espionage connections. To insinuate that Abdurashid might have been involved with such things was tantamount to blasphemy.

I had previously discouraged similar activities against Mohamed Ibrahim Egal and Sheikh Ali Jumale, so early the following morning I summoned the head of counter espionage into my office and rather sternly questioned him whether or not it was true that his scooters were shadowing Abdurashid. He had already read my mood, and after some hesitation he admitted doing so. I then asked, "Who gave the orders?" He vacillated a great deal and kept saying that it had been common practice, implying that whenever any important politician took a stand opposed to the government he would be checked out. I demanded a straight answer, which I was finally given, but Farah Sugulle stuck to his rationale that it was common practice. I ordered him to cease all this unwarranted harassment forthwith adding that if he ever found out that Abdurashid was acting against the law of the land he should report it to me in writing but that he was to do nothing more than that. Abdurashid, after all, was a member of parliament, enjoying parliamentary immunity and there was not much anybody could do to him except cause irritation. I therefore suspected that some higher persons in government might well have ordered that kind of provocative harassment. I expected to be asked about my intervention, but my actions were never questioned.

I had little confidence in Farah Sugulle since the Tawelde affair, although he was my second-in-command, and remained troubled over who could have ordered the shadowing of Abdurashid. Farah Sugulle might have acted of his own accord. Apart from being over-zealous, he came from an area in the Mijertein region where the late Haji Musa Boqor, a close relative and strong supporter of Abdurashid, dominated the electoral constituency causing disturbances at every election time.

Out of office, Abdurashid had a daily routine. In the morning he would go to the Lido or beach restaurant, sit in a corner and read a book until about lunch time. In the early evening he would go and watch the first show of a film in one of the cinema houses, come out about 8 pm, and go to the Hotel Shebelli Roof Restaurant for refreshments or dinner and meet parliamentarians and other friends. He would then watch the last show of another film in a different cinema house until midnight. For some time I checked on him at the Shebelli in case the shadowing had continued. I would even sometimes greet him with the due respect of his status. I was known as an officer, though in mufti, and my presence might ward off any undesired followers who might be lurking around. Eventually I had to stop lest Abdurashid himself might suspect me of what I was in fact trying to prevent. I went to these lengths not only because unauthorised surveillance could reflect upon the credibility of my office, but also because it was ridiculous that such treatment be meted out to the man who had been the nation's leader yesterday and might be so again tomorrow. Indeed Abdurashid did win the next presidential election.

He did come to know of my actions, but how is a mystery to me even today. Abdurashid had a plain clothes policeman, a certain *Qulan* or Jack, as his bodyguard who belonged to our office and was in contact with some of our junior staff. At first I suspected that Qulan might have been Abdurashid's source of information, but in that case I would have expected him to boast of it or at least tell me after Abdurashid's election to the Presidency, but he never did. What Abdurashid did not know, however, was the role of Farah Sugulle as the instigator of the surveillance. When he was elected to the Presidency in 1967 I was in Hargeisa and Abdurashid wanted me to be reappointed as Head of the Intelligence Department or Special Branch. When I declined he had Farah Sugulle promoted to the post.

President Aden Abdulla Osman believed that his election defeat was because of his refusal to accept conditions which were later accepted by his opponent. Many years after, we accidentally met at the Mogadishu Airport VIP lounge, and he revealed that prior to that election he had received three northern members of parliament, including Mohamed Haji Dualeh, MP for El-Afweyn (Garadaq), who told him that they represented 21 MPs — by implication all the Isaaq members of parliament—and would vote for him if he would promise to appoint the next prime minister from their group. He had responded at the time that although he could make no such promise that did not mean that one of their group might not be considered for the premiership were he to be re-elected. It was however considered a foregone conclusion that Aden Abdulla's re-election would also involve reinstalling the premiership of Abdurazaq.

Aden Abdulla had been a serious western style President. According to the constitution, the president was not an executive, but a constitutional head of state and Aden Abdulla was just that. Although he had considerable experience of parliamentary work, to avert conflicts he would advise the government and the National Assembly to refrain from any acts of which he might not later approve, but he would not otherwise pressure them in their day to day business, nor would he interfere with the appointment of government officials. Abdurashid was the opposite. He was a typical third world president wanting to okay almost every important government decision, especially appointments of senior government officials. While Aden Abdulla was his own man, Abdurashid had an almost unlimited number of advisers from almost every group of the society. Anyone seeking favors from the government had henceforth to find a kingmaker to recommend his name to Abdurashid or even to present him personally to the president.

Unlike many third world leaders, however, Abdurashid displayed a remarkable lack of personal greed. When he left office after being prime minister, that for a good four years he had little money, was evidenced by his subsequent lifestyle. He continued to live modestly with his family in the same old government bungalow relying solely on the rent of the only house he owned and the ungenerous stipend of a parliamentarian. He had neither business investments nor other sources of income. After handing over the official cars, he drove his own decrepid old small 1100 Fiat car. However, he failed to curb the corruption of some of his ministers. His political cronies and their greedy businessmen friends were heavily engaged in tax fraud and smuggling.

On one occasion I briefed General Qorshel who was acting for

General Abshir as the commandant of police during the latter's absence on a study tour in the USA, about the corruption prevailing in the country. He told me to write him a report which he would show to the prime minister. I prepared a brief of substance without singling out anyone by name. According to Qorshel, Abdurashid took him for a drive out to a number of private development projects in the capital and remarked that any Somali who had money would only spend it to develop the country, implying that the acquisition of wealth, even if by corrupt means, was not necessarily a loss to the nation. That might genuinely have been his altruistic interpretation of economic concepts, for when his successor's government sacked many redundant government employees, Abdurashid criticised that in parliament on the grounds that it reduced the poor people's purchasing power and thus undermined the economy. In any case, although strong with foreigners, Abdurashid was by nature weak in his dealings with our own people.

Although Abdurashid was neither a gifted speaker nor a charismatic personality, he could be very firm. His arms deals with the Russians had leaked out by the end of 1963. The West wanted to pre-empt them before any announcement was made and tried to offer him a counter deal, which would obviously be much less favourable. Three western ambassadors — from Germany, Italy and the USA — asked to see him urgently. He saw all three of them individually in one morning at five minute intervals. He listened and gave the same answer to all three of them in one short sentence, "Somalia no longer seeks arms from the West." When that was later reported by the western media it turned into an internal political triumph for Abdurashid.

Despite the 1964 cease-fire already referred to, being mediated by the Sudanese Government of President Ibrahim Abboud, the 1964 Ethio-Somali war dragged on into the time for Somali political elections. Ethiopia, through violations, sought to prevent the conclusion of those elections hoping to leave the Somalis distracted by endless campaigning. Abdurashid refused to postpone the elections and addressed the nation over the radio to explain Ethiopian intentions. He told the Somali people, "Hold your gun in one hand and vote with the other." The elections were successfully concluded despite Ethiopian air raids on some polling stations. Abdurashid's short sentence inspired a great deal of public confidence and earned Abdurashid an unlimited degree of personal credit and widespread recognition of his leadership. Many believed that played a vital role in his subsequent election victory to the Presidency. Certainly many electorates brought pressure to bear upon their elected deputies for the president was elected by parliament. I did not share that opinion as it was unlikely that the parliamentarians of those days would have much heeded any such pressure. Most of them voted only for whoever best met their self-interested demands. Nor did such pressure dissuade President Aden Abdulla from replacing Abdurashid after those elections with Abdurazaq Haji Hussein of the same SYL ruling party, as the new prime minister.

Abdurazaq was a good administrator. He was much bolder in dealing with domestic issues than his predecessor. He sacked several hundred senior civil servants for various shortcomings as well as many redundant workers. He demanded that all government employees hitherto enjoying slack practices, observe and adhere to official working hours. He restructured the civil service law; abolished the spoils system of appointments and, for the first time in the history of the South, introduced the merit system of fair competition for appointments through reactivated selection interview boards and examiners. He incidentally restored the confidence of the Northern civil servants who had been used to such a system, and assigned more portfolios to the North including the two key ministries of foreign affairs and defence to redress previous imbalances.

Unlike his predecessor, Abdurazaq was never unduly influenced in his decision making. He was the only head of government in Somali history who dismissed ministers for alleged corruption so that they could be prosecuted. His critics, however, accused him of bribing parliamentarians to buy their votes to carry out his programs. But even if that were true, it was a phenomenon which characterized the history of the parliament of those days and which neither his predecessors nor his successors seemed able to do without. Parliament mainly existed, in those days, to safeguard the coalition interests of its members, refusing to sanction the lifting of their immunities. Although Abdurazaq was considered moderate, or even pro-West, he was nevertheless a forthright Somali nationalist. He failed to secure any substantial Western development assistance because of his strong backing for the Somali liberation movements fighting the West's two idols in Africa: Emperor Haile Sellassie and President Jomo Kenyatta in Ethiopia and Kenya.

Abdurazaq's successor, Mohamed Haji Ibrahim Egal, however, reversed the long standing Somali government policy vis-a-vis the Somali liberation movements and restored diplomatic relations with Britain, but that did not earn him any additional western financial assistance either, perhaps because of the failure of his domestic policies, for the west must have foreseen the early demise of his regime. Egal was by far the best orator and the most charismatic of all Somali politicians of that era, but he lacked consistency and determination and was often therefore defeated in his political goals. Egal's prime ministership, ran from 1967 to 1969.

I was re-posted to Hargeisa in April 1966 on the assumption that I might be able to help solve serious intra-clan conflicts because of my knowledge of the area and of the local people. General Abshir's words to me were just that and I believed him. My transfer aroused little interest until a year later at the time of the Presidential election when my successor, Lt. Col. Abdullahi Mohamoud Hassan 'Matukade' (literally one not given to prayer), was accused of involvement in the pre-election campaigns by using his position to back the government supported candidate, the then incumbent President Aden Abdulla. It was only then that some people speculated that my transfer was linked to the protection that I had tried to accord Abdurashid, certain government circles wishing that I could be replaced with someone more pliant. Another factor which lent support to such speculation was that the appointment of Abdullahi 'Matukade' superseded two officers senior to him. I paid little regard to such talk. For to me, the complex problems facing the North presented a new and very important challenge.

CHAPTER SIX

INTRA-CLAN STRIFE

A T THE TIME WHEN I was re-transferred to the North, the Ethiopians were carrying out serious acts of terrorism on our side of the *de facto* border, mainly along the margin of the Borama district. A few bombs had even been exploded inside Hargeisa. Our semi-settled agricultural population living near Borama, were continuously being harassed to pay taxes for which they were receiving neither services nor security. They played on clan rivalries and sought to destabilize the whole nation, which certain Ethiopians wished to incorporate within their own empire. Our *Illalo* or interim peace-keeping auxiliary unit, camp at Quolujet, eighteen miles west of Borama was attacked. A bomb exploded, burning and destroying a tent, but causing no human casualties. Then one of the Illalo guard at the district commissioner's house in Borama itself was murdered in a night raid. Such Ethiopian terrorist operations were perhaps in response to rebel activities deep inside the Ogaden. They were being organized and managed from Aw-Barre, by their District Commissioner, a certain Fagadhe, who under the Mengistu regime, later became the senior Security Officer for the Somali populated areas of Ethiopia.

On arrival at Hargeisa on April 21, 1966, I lost little time in studying and appreciating the situation and without delay launched a counter operation. We managed to arrest the ringleader of the Ethiopian collaborators, a certain Ahmed Bahdon, who was convicted and sentenced to a long term of imprisonment. We also retaliated with bomb explosions ourselves. We had an overall advantage over our adversary. Since both sides were using Somali agents, we always had a better chance of turning their agents into double agents than they had. For a period every bomb the Ethiopians intended for explosion on our side would first be brought to us intact and we would assign an empty target. They had to be exploded because the Ethiopians monitored the acts of their own agents.

On one occasion, the Ethiopian target was a tractor owned by the department of agriculture at Dila near Borama. We arranged to move the tractor a few hundred yards and allowed the bomb to be exploded at the exact selected spot. However, the Ethiopians suspected their agent had become our double agent and they executed him. The Ethiopians had one advantage over us. They were less concerned than we were about any damage to human lives resulting from their terrorist acts because the common populace on both sides of the border were our kith and kin, not theirs. I owed much of the success of those operations to the efficiency of our intelligence officers stationed in Borama, Abduraman Ali Nur and Jama Khaireh. They always carried out our operations according to plan. Eventually, one thirty-six pound bomb was placed inside the compound of Fagadhe's own residence at Aw-Barre. The Ethiopians ceased their terrorist operations forthwith and we followed suit.

The police in the North, both sides of the boundary line, were always fed with false or exaggerated reports and we had to be careful not to accept them uncritically. We would sometimes receive instructions from Mogadishu to meet our Ethiopian counterparts, i.e. the governors, army and police officers, and on occasion we ourselves would ask for such meetings. Once, before attending a meeting at the border post of Tug-Wachale, we were receiving confusing reports of nearby Ethiopian troop movements. The Ethiopians regularly made deceptive moves in order to obscure their military strength. They would withdraw some units from certain locations to reinforce others, only to reverse the process the week after. One question arising would be whether troop numbers had actually increased at specific Ethiopian garrisons. Substantial military increases would necessitate structural command changes, i.e. from company to battalion, from battalion to brigade, or even from brigade to division, but we could only know the truth from the Ethiopians themselves, not, of course, by asking them directly for they would probably not tell us the truth, or worse, would feel entitled to ask us similar questions. We had to read between the lines.

One day we were to meet the Ethiopians, led by their military governor of Jigjiga, a certain 'Colonel' Yilma. I had learned that he was a former tank brigade commander, who was also the military commander for the whole Ogaden area, but needed confirmation. Not only did he turn out to be a brigadier, according to his badges of rank, but he spoke consistently as leader of a military brigade. We needed to know that in order to correct false impressions even by some of our own army officers.

Somali army officers tended to overestimate Ethiopian plans — perhaps not always intentionally, in order to seek budget increases from government. I always endeavored to send balanced weekly reports and explain the reason behind any unusual Ethiopian activity. Mogadishu, more often than not, would rely on them. When I did not have accurate information I would only send nil reports. If the army sent any alarming documents I would either be asked to comment, or Mogadishu would wait for my report.

Upon my arrival in Hargeisa after taking over, I also appraised the overall internal situation which I had been following as the head of intelligence. In 1965, a serious clan fight had broken out between two Isaaq sub-clans of Hargeisa (Arap vs Habar Awal Saad Musa). Several government ministers led by the late Abdullahi Issa, former prime minister and foreign minister then the minister of health, visited the area and spent about a month endeavoring tó solve the problem. They took several measures including the replacement of the governor and several other senior officials. Follow-up technical missions were also sent to the North which drew up peace agreements. Both sides were made to sign a bond to keep the peace, but all in vain.

On the spot appreciation of the existing individual problems made a great difference. There seemed three dangerous challenges to the established order of government: civilian inter-clan strife, Ethiopian terrorist operations already described, and widespread contraband. I decided to deal with them all together, but first and foremost I found it necessary to put my own house in order i.e. to clean up the police. I removed anyone whose loyalty and devotion to duty was suspect, whether by being biased or taking sides in the local conflict or over some other matter. I then set up my own agenda: to gather information on individual promoters of the fighting, then without any leniency to seriously deal with all cases until incidents ceased on our side of the border and then to secure that peace.

After compiling a list of those who were promoting the strife, I applied for their detention and internment in Bosaso in the Mijertein region. Within a few weeks we were able to restore peace and tranquility in all the area inhabited by the two fighting groups as far as the boundary with the Haud. Incidents continued to occur intermittently for over a year, but only in Ethiopian administered territory across the boundary line, which at Gumar, the nearest point, was only 38 miles from Hargeisa. We maintained constant mobile police patrols along the entire length of the border south of the Hargeisa district, which is traditionally inhabited by the two fighting groups. All the nomadic settlements were searched for unlicensed firearms and many such arms were seized and those in possession arrested. We worked with the courts to give such cases speedy trial and co-operation was always at hand.

After exhausting every possible means of legal and police action, and having thus attained a reasonable degree of calm, I embarked upon arranging a dialogue between the two sides, upon the premise that permanent peace would only come when the combatants realised that it was in their own interest. Prior to and during this period I had been monitoring the views of various individuals on the possible attainment of peace and had discussed it with many to whom I looked for support. At first I found the majority did not favour resolution of the conflict, especially on the Saad Musa side, so I had to seek out and deal with alternative people. The Arap side was not averse to the attainment of peace, but they were deeply convinced that the other side was, and they were not therefore prepared to take any chances. That meant that they wished to continue their preparedness which was not by its show of force, conducive to fostering an atmosphere of peace. I discovered that the genuine peacemakers on the part of the Saad Musa were, in fact, among those who were least trusted by the opposing Arap side.

From both sides, I selected elders whom I knew had peace in their hearts. They were led by Farah Arrale Guled 'Burgal' on the Arap side and Issa Gabobe on the Habar Awal Saad Musa side. I arranged many secret meetings for them so that troublemakers would not sabotage the peace efforts. The dialogue was many times put at risk by the occurrence of new incidents, but the scale of killings and the number of people participating in the fighting was decreasing all the time. Outbreaks diminished as the people got word of the peace efforts being made. Moreover, missions of elders were continuously sent over the border to further the cause of peace. Later on the peace meetings between the two sides were brought into the open, as peacemakers from both groups gained the upper hand. Finally in September 1967 a peace conference was held, attended by the new minister of interior in Egal's government, Yassin Nur Hassan, at the border town of Beleh Gudadleh, the scene of the original confrontations two years earlier.

The dimension of the contraband trade which engulfed the whole Northern region, the former Somaliland Protectorate, was enormous in every respect. Smuggled goods were not only being displayed in the open by street vendors, but were laid out in front of licensed shops even blocking access and forcing virtual closure of many legitimate shops for whom it was in any case difficult to compete with untaxed goods. The smugglers and their agents, the street vendors, had no need to hire any premises or pay rents, so could afford to sell their goods much more cheaply. Even some families in the police were selling smuggled cigarettes, sugar, etc. from their houses.

It was absolutely necessary that I should first and foremost attack police corruption. I ordered an immediate search of suspected targets in the police quarters. As well as taking disciplinary action against those concerned, I would transfer them out of Hargeisa to other units, not only to cut off their clientele but because, except when totally dispensing with the services of a policeman, it often paid off to remove him from the environment of embarrassment. I had known cases where earlier defaulters, even of a serious nature, were completely reformed by the shock, and made successful career recoveries. I made it mandatory that the occupant of any police quarter found in possession of smuggled goods, apart from legal or disciplinary proceedings, should vacate the house which was free of rent. Those not finding available police married quarters were paid a house allowance, but the cost of rent in the town was twice or three times the allowance. I soon managed to re-establish the prerequisite police loyalty to duty which was so vital for the kinds of odds we were up against. That was achieved at the high cost of dismissing seven policemen and losing several others skilled in anti-contraband operations.

Apart from 'Qat' smuggling which originated in Ethiopia, all other smuggled goods were coming from Aden or Djibouti, both of which were free ports. Most of that illegal trade was heading for Hargeisa which had the largest population and thus offered the best market. I established a special anti-smuggling unit under a very loyal, dedicated and long serving policeman, Chief-Inspector Nur Elmi, known as *Nur-Madobe* or Nur the Black. They had issued to them an efficient motor vehicle, a German one-ton Unimog which would go over all sorts of terrain and could convey any seized contraband goods. They could operate all along the border with the then French Somali-land, now the Republic of Djibouti. Most contraband from that direction was carried by camel caravans and Nur's men proved quite capable of intercepting more than ninety percent of it.

Likewise, another capable and experienced loyal police officer, Jama Warsame, was in charge of anti-qat smuggling. Qat is a mild narcotic, the fresh leaf stalks of which are chewed as a temporary stimulant. We reduced the illicit trade to its lowest ever, both by vigorously combating it and by improving bureaucratic control measures. The hardest part of the contraband problem was to control that coming from the Gulf of Aden along the lengthy unmanned and undeveloped coastal areas. This was compounded by our lack of sea transport even for occasional patrolling. We could only wait until contraband merchandise came inland. As part of the control measures, I also strengthened information gathering. That included the immediate reporting by coastal police outposts of the arrival or even the presence of any dhows, some of which were on our blacklist.

On one occasion, information was personally communicated to me in confidence, of the landing of smuggled goods at Heis on the Makhir coast. There was a possibility of police complicity. I immediately asked Mogadishu for a police plane and flew to Erigavo the following morning, together with my assistant, the North-East police division commander. Arriving there without any prior notice, we found that three trucks had carried the smuggled goods, but only one had been seized by the police patrol assigned to that task. After several days of intense investigation we concluded that the patrol commander, a sergeant, was in fact mislead by his men, although he was to blame for not being sufficiently vigilant. We dismissed five policemen and fined the sergeant.

On another occasion we dismissed two more policemen at the coastal outpost of Elayu including the wireless operator for failing to report the arrival of a blacklisted dhow. On the whole, we were succeeding even in this difficult area of coastal contraband although only by a fifty percent margin. Meantime, licensed shops reopened and legal trade took off again.

On my recommendation the government of Abdurazaq Haji Hussein approved the payment of about thirty percent of the proceeds of the sales of seized and auctioned contraband goods, together with the fines imposed upon smugglers, to policemen responsible for the seizure, arrests and investigations in such cases. The enabling law enacted at that time remained in force up to the disintegration of the Somali state, 1990–92. When I think back, I sometimes think these efforts to bring peace to the North are perhaps the best contribution I have been able to make to the cause of the Somali people.

RULERS OF THE SOMALI NATION

THE LAST COLONIAL DECADE, 1950-60

BRITISH SOMALILAND PROTECTORATE	THE ITALIAN ADMINISTERED UNITED NATIONS TRUST
Governor	*Administrator*
Sir Gerald Reece 1948-54	Giovanni Fornari 1950-53
	Enrico Martino 1953-55
Sir Theodore Pike 1954-59	
	Enrico Anzilotti 1955-58
	general elections 1956
	Aden Abdulla Osman
	President of Legislative
	Council 1956-60
establishment of	
Legislative Council 1958	Mario Di Stefani 1958-60
general elections 1958	
Sir Douglas Hall 1959-60	
general elections 1960	
Mohamed Haji Ibrahim Egal	
Leader of Government Business	
INDEPENDENCE 26 June 1960	
(5 days pass before)	**INDEPENDENCE 1 July 1960**

-----------------------------------union as-----------------------------------

THE SOMALI REPUBLIC on 1 July 1960

President
Aden Abdulla Osman

Primeminister
Abdurashid Ali Shermarke

general elections 1964
Abdurazaq Haji Hussein

period of the 'triumvirate'
general elections 1967

Abdurashid Ali Shermarke   Mohamed Haji Ibrahim Egal

(assassinated, 15 October 1969)

MILITARY COUP D'ETAT BY THE ARMY AND POLICE
Led by Major General Mohamed Siad Barre, 24 October 1969
THE SOMALI DEMOCRATIC REPUBLIC

CHAPTER SEVEN

THE TRIUMVIRATE, COMPROMISE AND CORRUPTION

The Last Civilian Government (1967–1969)

T HE PRESIDENTIAL ELECTION of June 1967 ran to three ballots in the National Assembly, but eventually saw the installation of Abdurashid Ali Shermarke as the second president of the Somali Republic. Mohamed Haji Ibrahim Egal was appointed as the new prime minister, but he did not seem to have the same authority and power as his predecessors. Abdurashid had apparently unilaterally styled himself as an albeit undeclared executive president which Egal had to accept, having just reappeared center stage after being out of office for almost five years. More significant, perhaps, was that the government appeared to be taking the form of a triumvirate of Abdurashid, Egal and Yassin Nur Hassan.

Yassin Nur Hassan was minister of interior, but he appeared to be the third man, if not the second, in the new government thus overshadowing the elderly and respected nationalist Haji Farah Ali Omer, minister of finance, who had also been appointed as a nominal deputy prime minister. Perhaps that arrangement had been agreed to prior to the presidential election campaign that had brought them to power. Egal had resigned from Abdurashid's government in 1962 and the two men had long since remained far apart. To Somalis, their alliance seemed a strange marriage. They were reconciled through the mediation efforts of mutual friends, like Ismail Nahar and the veteran SYL campaigner Musa Boqor, but their new association was dictated by mutual common interest—a political ambition for power. The respect and support of the clan provided a base.

That together with Yassin they might have reached an accord for power sharing became even more apparent during the campaigns for the 1969 general elections. Knowledgeable observers suggest the triumvirate drew up and agreed upon spheres of influence over the electoral constituencies. Under that agreement the North (formerly Somaliland) would be regarded as Egal's domain, though he would consult with the two other partners of the triumvirate before taking final decisions on the choice and fate of candidates contesting in the purely Darod clan areas of Las-Anod and Las-Qoreh and on other Darod candidates contesting the Bohotleh and Erigavo districts. All the purely Isaaq areas and westward into the Issa and Gadabursi clan areas would remain totally under Egal's discretion.

Likewise, the whole South would be under Abdurashid and Yassin; Egal would be consulted before decisions were taken on the Hawiye areas, but all the Darod and Digil/Mirifle areas would be totally beyond the sway of the prime minister. This became evident when Abdulqadir Mohamed Aden 'Zoppo' (the lame), formerly minister of finance in Abdurashid's government and later minister of interior and the second strongest man in Abdurazaq's government, was flatly refused opportunity to register his candidacy in Bur-Aqaba for clan reasons. Egal owed 'Zoppo' a great deal since during the whole period that Egal was out of office, 'Zoppo' had always met the former's requests on behalf of his political cronies. Nevertheless, when 'Zoppo' complained to Egal, the prime minister could only tell him to go to Abdurashid. It may be said that 'Zoppo' was unlawfully denied his right to contest those elections and he was not alone, but it illustrates the importance of the clan factor in Somali politics.

Any agreement as to spheres of influence was threatened, however, when Yassin encouraged and promised support for the up-and-coming Abdurahman Mohamed Ali 'Tur' (hunchback) who was contesting Burao. When Egal learned about that, he threatened to support Ali Hussein Gur'a, Yassin's arch rival. The triumvirate's arbitrators, Hilowle Moallum, Musa Boqor and Yusuf Egal, intervened and Yassin backed off. However, Egal alone appeared to have paid any price, as the other two partners in the triumvirate do not seem to have parted with any of their respective powers. To many it seems that what in fact had been shared out was none other than the prime minister's job.

In the 1964 election Egal had been elected on the Somali National Congress (SNC) ticket. However, it was a common practice and not only in the Somali Republic, for parliamentarians to defect from their original parties of convenience soon after they had been elected and to join the ruling Somali Youth League party in order to seek appointments or other favors. Soon after those elections, several MPs crossed the floor and Egal followed suit one year later. That might have been Egal's first step towards his subsequent rapprochement with Abdurashid.

When I was being re-transferred to the North in 1966, Egal had asked some mutual friends to arrange a meeting before I left for Hargeisa, though the two of us had little in common. Ismail Ahmed Ismail conveyed that message to me and I accepted. Anthony Mariano arranged a farewell dinner in my honour for just the four of us at the Tre Fontana restaurant. Egal maintained, among other things, that he had not left his party but that his party had left him, meaning those other MPs who had left the SNC before he did. But Egal was not only a national figure, but also a founding member of the Congress. Other founding members like Sheikh Ali Jumale, Haji Yusuf Iman and others had stayed on, so I was reluctant to accept comparison between him and the other ordinary MPs who defected. I later came to realise, Egal was subtly sending an indirect message through me to the people of the North, in case I was asked why he joined the SYL.

I recall that he also told us a story during that Tre Fontana dinner, that soon after Abdurazaq's first government lost a parliamentary vote of confidence in 1964, Siad Barre, then still second-in-command of the national army, had met Egal and other parliamentarians at Ming Sing, a Chinese restaurant, and said to them, "If you do not stop (such votes) we will do our duty." Egal and his colleagues read this as a direct threat of a military takeover. Infuriated as he remembered Siad Barre's remarks, Egal prophesied that unless a strong government emerged to retire such a dangerous man, he would surely one day overstep the mark. On the other hand, I do not think Abdurazaq's government was influenced by this absurd display of support when it appointed Siad Barre Army chief of staff to succeed General Daud. He just happened to be the most senior officer. By the time Egal recounted this story, Siad Barre had already been appointed. Nevertheless, the next year Egal became prime minister only to be overthrown by Siad Barre after being in office for barely two years.

Several reasons have been given why Egal failed to prevent an eventuality that he had himself seen long before coming to power. There were differences of opinion within the triumvirate about Siad Barre; while Egal and Abdurashid were in agreement that, since he did not have any military training background, Siad should, upon a pretext, be sent to a staff college in the Soviet Union, and then replaced during his absence, Yassin had disagreed. Siad Barre personally said to me later, that he had used Dahir Haji Osman, the then powerful director-general of the ministry of the interior, to influence his cousin Abdurashid in his own favour, and he believed that had stopped his being sent to Russia. Again the clan factor: Dahir is believed to have been mothered by the Marehan—the small clan to which Siad himself belonged.

After Abdurashid's election to the presidency, several members of his new government who had visited Hargeisa, including Ali Mohamed Ossoble 'Wardhigley,' minister of health, and Salad Elmi Dhorwa, vice-minister in the council of ministers, told me that the president wanted me to be re-posted to Mogadishu as the head of intelligence and security to replace Abdullahi 'Matukade.' I later met my former minister of the interior, Mohamoud Abdi Nur, then the minister of public works, who was visiting the North and he confirmed this. I confided in him the events surrounding the shadowing of Abdurashid which the latter, although he would not have known the role I played, might have heard about. I asked his opinion as to what would be the reaction of the triumvirate if, by the same token, I were not to allow the shadowing of Abdurazaq, then in the opposition and who, unlike Abdurashid, had left the SYL ruling party altogether. His guess, like mine, was that they would not tolerate it. I requested him to inform Abdurashid that I was not interested in returning to that post. The President then had Farah Sugulle promoted and appointed.

Egal's type of government, or rather that of the triumvirate, unfortunately came increasingly to be characterised by an unprecedented degree of injustice and corruption. Many people believe that if Abdurashid had survived his last inspection tour of several regions of the country, he would have replaced Egal in order to insulate his presidency from growing government unpopularity. After Engineer Ali Sheikh Mohamed, the man most feared by Egal as a possible substitute, declined to show any interest, the personalities mentioned for the new premiership included Michael Mariano and Omer Arteh Ghalib.

Michael had been a leader of the National United Front, which had brought groups and individuals together to protest the Anglo-Ethiopian agreement of 1954. He was a government employee and he became a leading member of the Legislative Assembly. At the time he was minister for planning and coordination. Omer, a gifted intellectual, had long been an advocate of Somali re-unification. A strikingly tall and courteous man, and a gifted linguist, Omer once told me that if he were to have come to terms with Abdurashid—meaning, I gathered, if he had been appointed prime minister—then Siad Barre would have been transferred to the defence portfolio. Omer was to be the lone member of the old Parliament included in Siad Barre's first government where he served as foreign minister for six years and was considered for the secretary generalship of both the OAU and the Islamic Organization of the Non-Aligned Conference, but later he was detained and spent many years in solitary confinement.

In what proved to be the last days of civilian rule, within a year after coming to power, in July 1968, the triumvirate, in a bid to prepare for the 1969 general elections, replaced all eight regional governors and the forty-eight district commissioners. Most of the new appointees were hand picked by parliamentarians and other prospective candidates supported by members of the triumvirate. After taking over, all the new regional governors were summoned to a pre-election campaign conference in Mogadishu. Similarly, all police division commanders were called for a meeting at police headquarters, Mogadishu. The northern police command was independently structured; I had two divisions under me with two commanders. Thus, apart from the headquarters staff, I was the only participant senior to the division commanders at that meeting.

Unofficially, the campaign had already started, as far as individual politicians including ministers were concerned. One of the objectives of the meeting was general briefing and appraisal. Most of us reported campaign excesses and anticipated areas of confrontation. Regrettably, some of the participating senior police officers conveyed distorted reports of our discussions to members of the government and the triumvirate. At the end of our meeting the commandant, General Abshir, took us to the president on a courtesy call. We went to Villa Somalia, the presidential residence, and met Abdurashid. He was extremely angry. Somewhat hastily he told us, "Whatever complaints there may be about forthcoming elections will be matters for the courts and will be no concern of yours. Your responsibilities will be solely that of security, law and order." The President would have been quite right in a situation where things were normal, but not when the government and its protégées were allowing all manner of excesses whilst their competitors were denied the minimum degree of fair play. No one knew that better than the president himself. Many of us were totally dismayed by the president's outburst, but General Abshir, who had been present the day before at an address by the prime minister at the governors' conference, did not share our pessimism. He totally accepted Egal's assurance to the governors that he wanted the best kind of free and fair elections which he hoped would be a model for the rest of Africa. Abshir was much encouraged: Egal, after all, was the prime minister and the head of the executive branch. Such optimism was to be short-lived.

The governors' conference was of a much longer duration than ours which lasted only for a few days. Most governors recommended the transfer of their police counterparts before the election campaigns officially started. Abshir received instructions from the minister of the interior demanding the immediate transfer of several senior police officers whom the minister described as undermining the government's election policies. Abshir in turn asked for detail and reasonable proof of those allegations and in the meantime took no action on the minister's instructions.

Meanwhile, a new electoral law was published, giving almost unlimited powers to governors and district commissioners. It was accompanied by an explanatory circular issued by the minister of the interior. Both the Election Law and the minister's circular stressed the prohibition of police entry into any polling booth, unless summoned by the chairman of a polling station. Abshir criticized those instructions, issuing his own circular stressing that, according to the Criminal Procedure Code, which he considered to override the Election Law, the police could enter any place if they suspected the commission of a crime. The rigging of elections was of course a crime. Abshir had touched a hot issue. The triumvirate retaliated swiftly by issuing overnight a presidential decree which transferred most of the functions of the commandant of police to the minister of the interior. The Election Law, the circulars, and all related developments had already become widespread public knowledge. Interest was immense. All non-SYL political parties, about 80 of them, addressed the issue on their parties' platforms and subsequently at their campaign rallies, accusing the government of an intention to rig the elections.

General Abshir resigned the day after the presidential decree and in so doing received unprecedented public acclaim from friend and foe alike. Pressure mounted on the triumvirate and, rather cunningly, they sought some accommodation with Abshir, through arbitrators or power brokers. They were prepared not to implement the decree if Abshir would withdraw his resignation and take his vacation leave during the elections. Afterwards there could be a round table meeting of reconciliation to resolve differences. When Abshir resigned, my colleagues, the two division commanders, Belel and Omar-yare, and I pledged our support for him and offered to resign in solidarity, because we felt that the role of the police was becoming politicized. In the meantime, however, I got word that Abshir was being persuaded to withdraw his resignation. I wrote to him and advised him not to yield to what I considered only a time-gaining ploy. I did so because it had long been common knowledge how much the triumvirate hated Abshir because of his close association with the former president, Aden Abdulla Osman and the former prime minister Abdurazaq Haji Hussein. Abshir's removal from office was surely the triumvirate's deeply desired goal. It was my conviction that it was more honorable for him to leave over that issue rather than wait and give them a chance to dispense with him 'when the tide was out.' Abshir replied that he chose to accept the advice of mediators because he did not want to be considered rigid and inflexible; and furthermore, he could not ignore the advice of important friends like Musa Boqor whose support he would not like to dispense with.

The minister of interior, having been relieved by Abshir's temporary departure from the official scene, did not even issue any subsequent instructions to override Abshir's circular which in fact was the last such instruction to the police force on the elections and the Election Law. The governors, however, were implementing the minister's circular and his interpretation of the election law. I decided to wait until polling day and then uphold the instruction of the police high command; in the meantime I would let sleeping dogs lie and would not argue about trivialities.

Legally speaking, Abshir's interpretation might have been incorrect for two reasons. It was commonly held, at least in the British legal system, that when two laws conflicted, the one of a later date would override the other, based on the premise that when the last law was being enacted the legislature had known about the existence of the first law. Secondly, it was also commonly held, again in the British legal system, that when an ordinary law and a special law conflicted, the special law should prevail. Hence, there was little doubt that the Election Law was both a special law and one of a later date than the Criminal Procedure Code. My interpretation, however, was that I should uphold Abshir's instructions because, though Abshir argued on legal grounds which were not rebutted in any case, his instructions to the police force were primarily of an operational nature. Also, I believed that election rigging would trigger off serious violence and it was my clear duty to do everything possible to prevent such disturbances.

During the campaign I received reliable information that some of the candidates who were contesting in the Northeast Region, and who were not favored by the government, were plotting to kill the governor, Hassan Mohamed 'Waqooyi' (a Darod) and the Burao police station officer, the number two man, Lieutenant Abdullahi Hassan Sultan (an Isaaq). To avert any future retribution under traditional customs, Darod were assigned to kill the governor while Isaaq would kill the police officer.

Soon afterwards, I received one of those candidates, a former senior civil servant whom I had known very well, in my office in Hargeisa and I asked him if such a plot existed. He said it did, but he would not name the plotters. When I warned him and reminded him of the futility of resorting to such a serious crime, he said that they had exhausted all their patience and had given up hope that the elections would be conducted fairly and freely. They felt they had to take drastic action sooner rather than later in the hope that others would follow suit in other parts of the country in order to send clear signals to those in power that the people would not tolerate election rigging forever.

He added that there had already been more than enough excesses in favor of the SYL. Since all polling stations were to be in places of their choice, they would have government provided transport to move their voters. Moreover, they were selecting all chairmen of the polling stations. His group would be prepared, he said, "to tolerate all that, if only there were no fraudulent voting." When I said to him that the police would enter any polling booth upon the suspicion of irregularities which were likely to disturb the peace and tranquility, he seemed relieved, undertaking that if I would only promise that, he and his colleagues would call off their assassination plot. I gave him that undertaking.

The subsequent few months witnessed heated election campaigning. The administrators, both governors and district commissioners, were guilty of the arm twisting of government opponents, in fact of all non-SYL contestants, on countless occasions. There was a provision in the election law that campaign rallies should be held within a certain period and that not more than one party rally would be held each day. All political parties would submit to the relevant district commissioner the dates and number of intended rallies. Finally, the district commissioner would issue an election campaign calendar showing the details of campaign rallies, dates time and place, etc.

The district commissioner was empowered to cancel or vary the conditions for approval of any rally at his own discretion, for reasons of security — real or imagined — or any other reason affecting the public good. However, more often than not, the SYL would demand at short notice that a day allocated to another party be re-allocated to them. They would do that for a variety of reasons. They would claim the day as being of particular interest to them for showing off new members whom they had brought from another party, or to announce some news of importance to their cause. They wished sometimes to score against another party merely by having a rally cancelled and suggesting it was due to lack of support. All such provocative actions invited serious disturbances at any moment. In most cases, however, conflicts were averted by the individual candidates themselves who saw the measures as pretexts to lure them into violence and eventual disqualification.

In Hargeisa, District Commissioner Abdullahi Mohamed 'Degei,' was not altogether devoid of a sense of justice. But he was under severe pressure from a very clever governor, Ahmedaher Hassan, who was himself the originator of many questionable instructions. The governor wanted the police to submit long in advance, the names of policemen to be deployed at polling stations, so that he could compare them with favored lists already supplied to him by the SYL party. We avoided meeting his demands without giving any formal denial. He then went behind the backs of both myself and the division commander, Col. Omer Mohamoud Nimale and contacted the police station commander directly. The latter in turn reported to Omer. Omer and I discussed how the station commander should respond to the governor.

Officially, the station commander usually reported to the district commissioners whilst Omer reported to the governor. I was in overall command of the police in both regions and with all the specialised units, the Field Force, Transport, Communications, CID and Special Branch directly under me. We agreed that Omer should first remind the station commander of the proper chain of command. Secondly, Omer would advise that he as the division commander would himself issue deployment orders when the time came, but in the meantime the station commander could submit his recommendations and forward them to him. We knew that the station commander's recommendations would be influenced by the governor and that the latter would simultaneously receive a blind copy of them. We felt obliged to tolerate this for otherwise he would complain to Mogadishu and there was no longer an Abshir there to protect us.

Both the governor and the station commander were from the South; they often conversed in Italian. In those days, the telephone system in Hargeisa was not automatic. Telephone exchange operators had to connect interlocutors and were in a position to listen to any conversations. Mindful of that, the governor had brought two female telephone operators (both southerners) from Mogadishu. He usually telephoned the police station commander in the evenings when it was quiet and only the girls were on shift duty at the telephone exchange. The station commander would seldom visit the governor to avoid sensitivity, especially after Omer had warned him. We knew that fair deployment of the police in the elections was indispensable but recognised also that we as the senior officers were not trusted by the authorities.

The Somali Youth League, once popular amongst all Somalis, had lost a lot of ground in the North. However it still formed the national government in the capital, Mogadishu, in the South, and from the point of view of its candidates in the North, the 'reliability' or political sympathies of the police, were seen as an issue of some political significance. Discussion thereon, over the telephone, had to be in Italian. In fact, the purpose of transferring the two girl telephonists to Hargeisa was not lost on anybody, neither the police nor the opposition parties, though priorities and objectives differed. We were only interested in ascertaining the loyalty or otherwise of individual policemen and any possible affiliation with political parties. The opposition parties probably wanted to know more, including whatever might be communicated between the governor and the higher authorities in Mogadishu about possible manipulation of the elections.

In the event it transpired that the two female telephonists were won over by some of the opposition parties. With their help, many of the governor's conversations were tape recorded. We learned of those recordings from the political parties concerned, but only insofar as they concerned members of the police. We had already marked some policemen as untrustworthy, but the recordings provided new information.

We planned as follows: three to five policemen were to be allocated to every polling station depending upon their location, population density and the anticipation, or otherwise, of conflict. We had two companies of the Police Field Force stationed at the two regional headquarters Hargeisa and Burao, from which all the other stations could be reinforced. The army allocated to us one platoon to be deployed at every district headquarters so we could requisition for more men for polling stations in Hargeisa and Burao townships.

The uniformed and armed levies, or *Illalos,* serving with the district commissioners, would also be taken into account, but they were under the control of the political authorities. Therefore, all non-police personnel, Army and *Illalos,* were to be assigned to polling stations within the district headquarters township where rigging was unlikely. Then they could safely be mixed with only a handful of policemen. However, only policemen were to be sent to rural areas. The station commander in Hargeisa, under the influence of the governor, endeavored to assign many policemen to locations in Hargeisa which were of specific interest to the SYL party. However, we dispatched them to locations no nearer than Erigavo, about 360 miles away. Since all the deployment forces had to be in position twenty-four hours before voting started and those assigned to far destinations had to be dispatched five days ahead, by the time the governor realised his handpicked men were missing they would be hundreds of miles away. I would not mind by then if he complained to Mogadishu.

The election operations deployment would also affect officers. There had to be additional operations officers. I therefore transferred Abdullahi Hassan Sultan from Burao, where the opposition had lodged complaints about him, and put him in charge of the Ain Area, giving him a short deadline like everybody else. He at once informed the governor. The latter sought to speak to me over the radio, but I avoided him bidding the operator advise he send me a message. He rather incautiously sent me the following text, in English, the official language in the North at that time:

> Col. Belel informed me that you had posted Lt. Abdullahi Hassan Sultan to Ainabo. I want to tell you that Abdullahi Hassan Sultan is helping me on the movement of the Issa Musa tribe from Burao Region to Berbera District as specially requested by the prime minister. So, please cancel his posting."

I did not answer but monitored the departure of the officer concerned for his area of assignment.

The normal movements of nomads could not be prevented but the election law forbade deliberate mass population migrations from one district to another. The use of motor transportation was the distinction. Many weeks before the voting day, we lectured all the deployment forces including army personnel about election procedures. Many of Egal's would–be voters transported from the Burao area, were stopped by the army before reaching Sheikh, the nearest Berbera district and were thus prevented from voting illegally. Egal had no need of such dubious practices. His seat was quite safe and secure but he wanted to be sure to defeat Engineer Ali Sheikh Mohamed (better known as Ali Jirdeh) who was running on another party's ticket. Egal had considered him a possible rival for the premiership because of his assumed friendship with President Abdurashid.

The electoral system at that time was called "The Caution System," whereby the number of valid votes cast would be divided by the number of district seats. Egal perhaps wanted to inflate his party's votes so that Ali would fail to muster the number of votes required for a seat. These actions of Egal's were in contradiction with earlier vaunted pronouncements, offering the election as a "Model for Africa." The governor in Hargeisa, despite his excesses, wanted to prepare the SYL party to win a "caution victory," that is, to win all the seats through the ballot box. We estimated that he would have hated to resort to rigging, but would do so if left no other choice. The governor in Burao was a different phenomenon; right from the first day of his posting he boasted, even in the presence of opposition candidates, that his sole mission was to ensure a safe election result and he would leave the day after to Mogadishu. He was called several times and severely reprimanded, but in vain. At the first opportunity thereafter he would repeat the same story and even boast, "Who says elections cannot be arranged in the North. I will show them."

The SYL candidates of Bohotleh and Las-Anod tried, with government assistance and connivance, to transport voters from each other's district areas. The opposition parties at both ends protested vigorously but were heeded neither by the authorities nor by the SYL. Fierce armed clashes took place at two border crossing points on election day with eleven men killed and many more injured before police reinforcements arrived and restored law and order. These incidents were foreseen and anticipated according to the police reports from Las-Anod. In the deployment of police strength in the election operations, there were ten Field Force men reserved at every district headquarters on polling day to be committed on the first reported incident. Thereafter, recourse would have to be made to the army who would only commit their men upon written orders of the regional governor.

Just two days before the elections I flew with the governor of Burao on our last inspection tour of all the eastern districts, starting with Las-Qoreh, and spending the night at Erigavo. Next day, we stopped over at Garadaq, where the SYL candidate, the late Mohamed Nur Aman, shed crocodile tears when he saw the governor, and complained against the police. Upon investigation, it all boiled down to his unwillingness to accept the impartiality of the police, despite having the rest of the government machine in his favour. It was only during this trip that the governor realised that the police still had control of deployment, despite the directives in the minister's circular. He threatened to cancel the election in that electoral district unless the police relinquished that competence and passed it to the district commissioner. He so instructed the DC in my presence. That was to see if I would yield to his bluff. Most men had already been detailed to their duty polling stations, but in turn I instructed the police operations officer in the presence of both the governor and the DC, that if by 6 pm on the polling day the remaining men were not needed, he should return them to their original bases. And with that we both entered the aircraft.

After the pilot had closed the doors, with the engine already running, the governor ordered him to delay take off. He called the DC and, changing his mind, instructed him to continue the normal election process. We next landed at Las Anod to hear from both the DC and the police station commander alarming reports of the predicted clashes at the border with Bohotleh. All the officials in Las-Anod, myself included, recommended to the governor that he order the deployment of army personnel to seal off routes along the entire border. One platoon would be sufficient since there were only a few trunk roads usable by motor vehicles. He said he would consider that when he got to Burao. We finally stopped over at Bohotleh, the last leg of our tour, and we not only heard similar reports to those of Las-Anod, but two candidates actually fought in our presence as one of them complained about crossings of the district boundary and the SYL candidate arrogantly insisted that they would continue. At this point the governor then promised the deployment of the army. As soon as we took off for Burao, however, he changed his mind. If he ordered the involvement of the army, he explained, the SYL candidates would lose the election in both districts and he would be blamed. They still both lost.

I continued my flight to Hargeisa, landing there well after sunset, in darkness since the airport was not then lit at night. I wished to speak to Mogadishu, and only Hargeisa had efficient radio communication. I called the chief of police operations and informed him of the situation. The necessary manpower was already in place and all that was needed was just an instruction to the army commander in the North or the regional governor of Burao to move an army patrol into the crisis area. He said that he would report to higher authorities and I would be advised in due course. I never was.

In the North, there was only that one incident, serious enough in itself, but with the exception of Mogadishu and a few other electoral districts the whole South was marked by violence. Several newly but fraudulently elected deputies eventually became targets of armed attacks inside Mogadishu after they returned from their constituencies. In the North it was cynically believed that the main reason for rigging elections was to prevent men of any standing or ability being elected. Parliament could then remain what sadly it had become, a refuge for mediocrities who could be manipulated by a small and corrupt elite. It seemed therefore absolutely necessary in the eyes of the triumvirate to exclude independent–minded personalities: Abdulqadir Zoppo's case was a vivid example.

Hitherto, election rigging had been anathema in the North, although the practice was widespread in the South. This was well known and the people were conscious of it. For that reason, direct attempts at rigging were unsuccessful, though the counting of the votes in Burao was falsified. Even that could have been prevented if the opposition candidates had been a bit more vigilant. Both the late Mohamoud Abdi Arraleh, the first Somali Ambassador to the United Kingdom and Hassan Abdi Khaireh, a former prison service officer, knew they could win their seats without falsification. There were more than fifty polling stations. All ballot boxes except one were opened as each arrived at the centre; the votes were counted and the number of ballots per box and station established.

However, the counting of the ballot papers in the remaining box was delayed for more than 12 hours. Arraleh and Hassan Abdi foolishly ignored the outstanding box, believing that even if its whole contents were allotted to the SYL that would not alter the leading positions they had established. Further, they anticipated that that box would only contain the average number of ballots. All the other opposition candidates had already conceded defeat and were no longer interested. Thus it transpired that it was in the absence of any opposition observers, that a number of ballots greater than that of all the other boxes combined were produced newly marked for the SYL. No other party could secure enough votes at the "Caution" level and all five seats were declared for the SYL. The governor made his rhetoric reality and left Burao the very next day after he had declared the election 'results.'

A similar attempt, employing exactly the same method was devised in Hargeisa. There was delay in opening one box and counting its ballot papers. Unlike in Burao, the opposition parties — about 16 of them — became suspicious. All police on duty at the counting center had been changed, in case they had been got at, and to neutralize the possibilities of familiarization and resulting laxity. The political parties were on their guard and in no way could the counting be falsified. Unlike Burao, each seat was won by a different party, the first six including the SYL.

Election rigging would undoubtedly have caused bloodshed in Hargeisa. There were 57 polling stations and after counting the ballot boxes of 56 of them who would be the winners of at least four of the six seats was almost certain. The ballots in just one box could, in fair play, perhaps alter the position of the last two or three but could not upset the overall balance to the extent of switching all the six seats in favor of the SYL. The party with the second greatest number of votes was 'Ubah' (flower) whose leading candidate was Omer Arteh, but his supporters would not protest, because although their preferred candidate would lose, their Isaaq sub–clan Habar Awal Saad Musa stood to gain three others 'elected' on the SYL ticket. Still considering in clan terms, as was customary, the final three seats would all go to the Garhajis (two to the Eidagalla, who actually got none by fair play because they were split into three parties, and one to the Isaaq Habar Yonis group, who in fact won a seat but through a different non-SYL candidate).

The Arap and the Habar Awal Saad Musa, Saeed Ismail, knew they were standing 3rd and 4th after the counting of 56 boxes and they would not accept that that one last box which was clouded with suspicion could change the whole picture. Both groups worked hard, campaigned fairly and, like the rest of the opposition parties, withstood all sorts of pressure meted out to them by the hands of the authorities in favor of the SYL candidates. They had exercised a great deal of restraint, but had reached the limits of their patience. In my judgement, in the absence of rectification of corrupt rigging practices, they would fight against those groups in whose favor the falsification was being made. It would have been a mockery for me to have spent so much energy and effort for so long to bring peace and reconciliation between two groups in Hargeisa and at the same time to condone actions that would have engulfed the whole city and neighboring region in bloodshed. I did not, and direct rigging, though attempted, did not succeed anywhere in the North, apart from Burao.

CHAPTER EIGHT

THE END
OF AN ERA

As anticipated, soon after the elections, Egal was re-appointed prime minister and General Mohamed Abshir was replaced for good as commandant of police by his long time deputy, Jama Ali Qorshel, who by then had come to an accommodation with the triumvirate. Abshir's indispensable friend, Musa Boqor, had deserted him and no reconciliation meeting, such as had been promised before the elections, ever took place. The post of commandant of police was a political appointment and the government had the right to replace Abshir or retire him in a normal manner. Probably they did not trust him because of his connections with former President Aden Abdulla Osman who was married to Abshir's aunt, not to mention his personal friendship with former Prime Minister Abdurazaq Haji Hussein. But they went too far in writing to the police that Abshir was no longer a general.

Abshir engaged the government in a legal battle before the Supreme Court, hiring a famous Italian lawyer named Avvocato Champron. He won with costs, but was never paid because Siad Barre's coup interrupted due process of law. He turned down an offer of the Somali ambassadorship in Paris and instead started his first business as a gas station owner, a sector which Siad Barre promptly nationalised upon seizing power a few months later. Was this the end of an era? The replacement of Abshir contributed to Siad Barre's seizure of power because not only was Abshir a counterweight, he was more popular and influential than Siad Barre even among the army officers, many of whom had served under him as police officers before the formation of the national army.

Meantime, in Hargeisa, an inquiry was initiated on Egal's orders, to be conducted by General Hussein Kulmiye Afreh, then the new vice-commandant of police, as to why the SYL did not win all six seats in Hargeisa. When Kulmiye interviewed me, I said to him that I was only answerable on matters of security and law and order. He did not even raise the killing of eleven people during the elections. Upon Kulmiye's return to Mogadishu my two assistants (the division commanders of Burao, Col. Belel and Hargeisa, Col. Omer) and myself were immediately transferred. I was posted to the Police Training School in Mogadishu. Mohamed Siad Barre said to me on many occasions, after his coup, that Egal had wanted to dismiss me before Kulmiye's inquiry, and he, Mohamed Siad, had happened to be present during a discussion and advised that an inquiry should precede a dismissal. I did not take much stock of that story.

Those days, I would not have minded a dismissal. When a policeman's job becomes politicized, I have little love for it. One of my former Somaliland police colleagues, Aideed Abdullahi, who had taken the Somaliland law examination well after me, had since been awarded a UN fellowship to study law in London. He was accepted and classed as equivalent to a Bachelor-of-Law (LLB). He studied further and eventually passed the Bar and has become an excellent lawyer. At that time I also had similar opportunity to study law in the Sudan. I wanted to resign soon after I reported to Mogadishu and in retrospect, I should have done so. However, other developments were to determine the course of my future.

During my last assignment in the North (1966–69) western diplomats, always suspicious of Soviet activities and intentions in Berbera, paid frequent visits to the North. They would mostly be governor's guests at State House, except for the Americans who had a consulate there. But I would be asked by the police headquarters to receive and look after military attachés who, apart from making a courtesy call, could have no amicable relations with the army because of the presence of Soviet advisers. One such guest was the Italian military attaché. He happened to know of my interest in Italian from

Signor Sestini, the Italian Consul, in Hargeisa. I had already taken some elementary language courses in Mogadishu, considering it necessary since the unified administration was bilingual, using both English and Italian. The attaché offered me the possibility of studying in Italy, and he was confident that his ambassador would approve.

Approval came through in mid 1968, but Abshir asked the Italians to postpone it until after the March 1969 elections. On my transfer and arrival in Mogadishu I found the Italian language scholarship still available. I resolved to postpone law studies and take up the Italian language course. I attended Perugia University for Foreigners, *L'Universita Per Gli Stranieri,* from June to September 1969. Apart from a dozen or more Somali students in the main Perugia University, I made many friends of different nationalities from amongst the foreign students. Our University was allocated some rooms in the main students' boarding quarters and the administrator assigned me a convenient room, only five minutes' walk from the school and near sports facilities. I played a lot of tennis.

The Italians were not only hospitable, for since Perugia has long attracted tourists, they anticipated that many foreigners would not speak their language. Everybody was cooperative and helpful in explaining whenever one had a need. My closest friend among the foreigners was a Ghanaian medical doctor, Richard Berko, married to a Swiss wife and practising in the Italian-speaking part of Switzerland.

The new Somali script, first introduced in the early 1970s, permitted the adoption of Somali as an official language, effectively retarding any improvement by frequent use to my beginner's Italian, but I later made a study tour with the Italian Carabinieri in Rome during October 1969, staying at a guest apartment in the headquarters of the Lazia Group in the Piazza del Poppolo. I made a courtesy call on Colonel Dalle Chiesa, the Group Commandant, the evening of my arrival. A very pleasant man, he served me some coffee and wished me a good stay in Rome, *"Buon soggiorno Romano."* I was distressed to hear later that he had been murdered by the Red Brigade.

In the daytime I took my meals at the *Scuola di Applicazione* in the south Teveri beside the Garibaldi Square where the mid-day cannon had been fired every day since the time of Garibaldi to underline,

I was told, the presence of the Italian Government. This was where General Abshir and his group had stayed during their officer training. The school commandant, General Marcos, had been in Somalia during the trusteeship. I made daily visits to several Carabinieri Units within Rome, and well recall the unique traditional Carabinieri coat of arms displayed at their respective entrances, with the words, "*Nei Secoli Fedeli*" (Faithful through the centuries).

I was just about to conclude the study tour when I learned that President Abdurashid Ali Shermarke had been assassinated and that five days later, on October 21, 1969, General Mohamed Siad Barre had seized power in my country. This event marked the beginning of twenty-one years of totalitarianism. About four months after my return from Italy, on February 22, 1970, I was appointed commandant of the police force, becoming the fourth head of the Somali police force in ten months! It was only because of its well-founded traditions that the force withstood the confusion resulting from such frequent and sudden changes of command.

The Somali police force had humble beginnings. In the former British Somaliland (the North) an armed constabulary a few score strong was formed in 1884 to patrol the coast. This force was later strengthened by the formation of a heavily armed Camel Constabulary in 1912 to operate further inland against the forces of Seyyid Mohamed Abdille Hassan, known to foreigners as the Mad Mullah. At about the same time, the Italians formed the Somaliland Coast Police in Somalia. In 1927 the Somaliland Police Force was more properly organised under British officers and with Somali inspectors and other ranks. District Commissioners remained responsible for the tasks of law enforcement until the 1930s.

Likewise, in the former Italian Somalia to the South, small armed contingents were formed in 1889 to patrol the eastern coastal strip along the Indian Ocean. In 1911, an Italian Somalia Police Force covering the southern coastland was formed, followed in 1916 by the setting up of another force called *Banda di Nugal* and the formation of a Somali force known as the *Corpo Zaptie,* commanded by officers from the Italian Carabinieri. After the second World War a gendarmerie was established which, in 1948, was reorganised as the Somalia Police

Force. The two forces were merged soon after the independence of the two territories and their union in 1960.

The probable reason for my appointment was Siad Barre's knowledge of my disagreement with the previous regime. Other senior police officers who became members of the newly established Supreme Revolutionary Council (SRC) had not been privy to the conspiracies which preceded the *coup d'etat,* but were co-opted because the cooperation of the police force was needed to ensure the overall success of the 'New Order.' Nor had they, unlike myself, any apparent differences with the former regime. Siad Barre did not therefore trust any one of them, at least at that time, to head the Police Force. During the first four months after the coup, and prior to my appointment, Hussein Kulmiye had served in a temporary capacity.

Whilst commandant, I managed to arrange our membership in the International Police Association (Interpol); to successfully switch road traffic to the right and enact a comprehensive Police Law for the first time since independence. My subsequent replacement as commandant of police, and appointment as minister of the interior in December 1974, resulted from marked disagreements between Siad Barre and myself over the establishment of various security organs which overlapped the normal functions of the police and in fact conflicted with them. However, Siad Barre did not find it convenient to dispense with me altogether at that time.

In self defense perhaps, I took more interest in leisure activities and events in the wider world. One factor that had helped both my work and my studies during the early years was that I lacked any other pastime, even sports. The most commonly played sports in Somaliland were hockey and football and I didn't play either. Nor had I any great enthusiasm to watch them. In the days of the Protectorate, Europeans would play polo and cricket, but only on a few occasions each year. A few played golf and I have recounted how I caddied for one such player under whom I worked, not really for sport; the caddy fees were more important.

Nor did we frequent the cinema much in those days. The first commercial film shows in Hargeisa came into being in the early fifties. Radio entertainment in the form of folklore programs, songs, advertisements and other announcements were also of the same era, though the broadcasting of poems and topical discussion panels were a decade or more older. The Government Information Office would show films on street walls for the general public, but not more than once a year. Europeans and other officials — Indian and Somali — could be issued passes to go to the army cinema, but that was not for the general population.

Only after I resumed work at police headquarters after independence as the second-in-charge did I develop my own appreciation of sports. Contrary to my earlier negative attitude I began to find sport a source of relaxation and mental creativity. Luckily I had a neighbor, Musa (Moses) Gul Mohamed, a Somali with an Indian father, who was a senior civil servant and an active all-around sportsman. In his youth he had played both football and hockey, but at the time played golf, squash and tennis almost every other day. I would accompany him in the afternoons after the office closed at 4 pm, watching at first and then taking a more active interest. Moses would take me on for single tennis games until I became a regular player; I later started playing golf too.

All my nine children, except one, learnt to play tennis, with my second daughter Faiza becoming a serious competitor, winning many prizes including free air tickets to Europe and the Gulf and numerous trophies. Both she and my third son, Mohiedden, would beat me. Meantime my eldest son, Saeed, became a good golfer. I also developed a deep appreciation of indoor games, playing table tennis with all my nine children at home; Saeed, Faiza and Mohiedden being the best players. We enjoyed the variety of dominoes, scrabble, cluedo and finally cards, with a preference for bridge, in which I found a family partner in my son, Mohiedden. Together, we once won first prize in an Italian Club Bridge Tournament in Mogadishu during his summer vacation from university in 1988. My two younger daughters, Yasmin and Suad, played scrabble with me, while my second son, Khidar, played chess, which was not my favorite, although I had tried to learn it well at the police college in England back in 1962. Looking back, I feel most indebted to Moses for the enjoyment of sports that enriched years of my life, as I took time to relax and examine the world around me.

CHAPTER NINE

Djibouti's Independence

O F PARTICULAR INTEREST and importance to all Somalis is our northeastern neighbor, Djibouti. Inhabited by the Afar and the Issa Somalis its controlling position at the southern end of the Red Sea had attracted the interest of the French quite early in the nineteenth century. Known for years as the French Somaliland Coast, in 1968 it was redesignated the French Territory of the Afars and Issas and then simply Djibouti, after the capital city and ocean terminus of the railway route up into the Ethiopian highlands, built between 1897 and 1918.

The colony was not unaffected by the tide of Somali nationalism which swept across the horn of Africa during and after the Second World War but its ties with France were deep and independence was not achieved until 1977. The independence of the British Protectorate and the Italian administered Trust Territory had a profound influence on the course of events in Djibouti.

On the other hand, there was fear that it might not survive as an independent entity. The French were very conscious of the ethnic division in the territory and even the inhabitants feared that Ethio-Somali rivalries and territorial claims might make the country an arena of conflict. Many believed that but for this factor France might have acceded to Djibouti's independence demands much earlier.

The Somaliland Protectorate government had an extradition treaty with French Somaliland, which provided for the handing back of common criminals at the border. Upon independence, all laws in force in the country were inherited by the new state of Somaliland by the enactment of a law for the transfer of statutory functions, which of course implied corresponding obligations. Upon that assumption, and as the senior police officer in the police headquarters, Hargeisa, it fell to me to hand back to the French a man wanted for bank robbery in Djibouti. He had been arrested at the request of the French authorities and was being held on our side of the common border.

There was an outcry from some of the local political parties against my action and the matter became a subject of debate in parliament, followed by official enquiries. The outcome was a ruling that no more Somalis should be handed over since France had not established any extradition treaty with the new Somali Republic, which the latter would not have accepted in any case. This marked the beginning of seventeen long years of non co-operation at the common border until Djibouti's independence in 1977. The soldiers of the French Foreign Legion stationed in Djibouti, exploited these strained relations and there were frequent desertions to our side. Those early deserters were passed to Mogadishu and some of them took up work on the Italian owned banana plantations. Many, however, emigrated to South Africa to increase the white population there, a process of which I disapproved and to which Somalia's foreign policy was opposed. Eventually, however, it was decided to turn them back without any reciprocal benefit. We knew the Foreign Legion did not treat Somalis in Djibouti with much respect.

Our new Somali Republic committed its foreign policy to the encouragement of the decolonisation of Djibouti. This not only strained relations with France, but also became a source of constant clashes between Somali and Ethiopian officials at international fora and in particular at conferences of the OAU and the United Nations, where that issue was to remain on the agenda for more than a decade and a half. Ethiopia considered the railway a vital interest and feared that Djibouti might opt for unity with the Somali Republic. She was prepared to occupy the enclave if the French left.

Ghana was to host the Third Summit Conference of the OAU scheduled for Accra in September 1965. Some moderate African leaders—from the so-called Monrovia Group, mostly from West Africa—had accused President Kwame Nkrumah's government of subverting their regimes and had voiced their intention of boycotting that summit. Ghana responded by inviting all OAU member states to send their chief security advisers to a meeting in Accra in April, there to be free to make any desired recommendations. I was sent to represent the Somali Republic. The meeting was held in Christianborg castle in Accra April 12–14.

My Ethiopian counterpart, a certain 'Daniel', and I soon clashed over the impending attendance at that forthcoming summit conference, of the Mogadishu based *Front for the Liberation of the French Somali Coast,* FLCS. Ethiopian policy was to support continued French presence and control of Djibouti. To that end, Daniel opposed FLCS attendance, accusing it of being likely to disturb the conference. I pointed out that any decision about the attendance of individual liberation movements, of which there were very many in those days, was the sole responsibility of the OAU foreign ministers. Daniel knew that very well, but he wanted to use the security meeting as a platform.

The Ghanaian representative took note of all the proposals and, the following day, confirmed my view as to procedure. Daniel threatened to report to his government that his proposal had not been given due consideration, but the Ghanaians ignored him. We were to meet again years later. Daniel became the deputy chief of Ethiopian intelligence and visited me in my capacity as Somali commandant of police when he led the advance security party for the late Emperor Haile Sellassie's first ever visit to the Somali Republic in 1971. Somalia was also the last foreign country which Haile Sellassie visited. He attended the 1974 OAU Summit, but, as mentioned earlier, was arrested by the *Derg* shortly after his return to Addis Ababa and he died a year later. Daniel had a pleasant personality. Despite our mutual differences, he asked me if I had a photograph taken of us in Accra with Kwame Nkrumah but unfortunately I did not. Daniel was amongst many senior officials of the late emperor's government executed by the Derg.

Divisions between the inhabitants of Djibouti along ethnic lines—between Afars and Somalis—were always a stumbling block retarding independence. The Afars, fearful of domination by the Somali majority were long opposed to independence. The French colonial power exploited such sentiments. Elections were frequently rigged in favor of the Afars. Many Somalis entitled to vote were disenfranchised while non-Djibouti Afars were permitted to enter the territory from Ethiopia merely in order to vote. Then, in 1966 for the first time, several Afar politicians led by a certain Haji Kamil, showed interest in supporting demands for independence. This information was communicated to the Somali government by Abdurahman Jama Adhoule, a trade union leader in Djibouti, and Abdurahman Ahmed Hassan 'Gaboud', a former Djibouti politician, then in exile in Somalia. The Afar politicians were afraid to go to Mogadishu for fear of eventual French reprisals, and arrangements were made for them to meet Ahmed Yusef Dualeh, then Somali foreign minister, in Lahaj near Aden. Abdurahman Jama also participated. After that meeting, Somalia dropped any territorial claim to Djibouti, but her foreign policy with regard to the territory's decolonisation remained unchanged.

In the summer of 1966, the French colonial minister visited Djibouti to pave the way for a visit by President Charles De Gaulle. The Somalis living in Djibouti decided overwhelmingly to seize the opportunity to greet De Gaulle with peaceful popular demonstrations and demands for independence. I was informed of that secret decision by Ahmed Mohamed Hassan, who later became a practising physician in Djibouti and was better known as 'Dr. Djidji', and another young man from the *Party of Popular Movement* (PMP). De Gaulle's arrival on 25 August 1966 was accompanied by riots: we were closely following those developments but strangely enough the French authorities in Djibouti had not. Despite their ever vaunted intelligence, they were taken by surprise. The result was the immediate dismissal of the French governor and Djibouti Somalis were subjected to an unprecedented level of brutality, culminating in the cold-blooded murder of Abdurahman Jama Adhoule and several other pro-independence activists. We suspected that Abdurahman Jama may have been betrayed by Haji Kamil and other Afar politicians who had earlier pledged to support demands for independence, but later closed ranks when the Afars again unanimously took a pro-French, anti-independence stand.

The French colonial authorities had a record of physically liquidating political activists whom they considered to be the brains behind moves detrimental to French interests, as they did in Algeria. Thousands of Somalis were deported, including many who were born in Djibouti but whose birth certificates and citizenship documents were confiscated. Many accepted deportation rather than have to risk their documents so that they could claim their citizenship in the future. Such claims still occur in Djibouti on the part of Somalis who were deported during that time, or their offspring.

The French shortly afterwards announced the holding of a plebiscite by March 1967 which, absurdly we felt, was to demonstrate whether or not the people wanted independence. The authorities had, however, already decided what the outcome of that plebiscite should be. They employed whatever means necessary, including various methods of gerrymandering and the denial of voting rights to many Somalis, etc. Perhaps at French urging, Ethiopia for the first time made public her territorial claims to Djibouti in order to create fears of possible Ethiopian invasion if the French were to leave. Once again the Afars took a pro-French stand in opposition to independence, with the sole exception of a young man named Mohamed Ahmed Issa 'Sheikho' who was put in jail for his views. He went on a hunger strike for some time.

The Somali government of Prime Minister Abdurazaq Haji Hussein established a task force under the chairmanship of the parliamentary under-secretary of the ministry of the interior, based in Hargeisa to keep the government fully informed of any developments. I served in that task force and we paid frequent visits to the border at Loyado. We would exchange coded verbal messages with prominent pro-independence nationalists including Hassan Gouled, former Deputy Musa Ahmed Idris, and Mohamed Jama 'Jujule.' The last made several trips to Hargeisa on business pretexts, in order to meet members of the task force.

As anticipated, the French later announced that the majority of the people had voted in favor of "Continued association with France." They also renamed the country as "The Territory of the Afars and the Issas." Nearly all non-Issa Somalis were reclassified as aliens and only a few would henceforth be allowed any voting rights.

Results of the 1967 Referendum

District	Registered Voters	Number of Voters
DJIBOUTI*	10,920	9,670
ALI SAUEH	4,976	4,740
DIKHIL**	9,526	9,557
TADJOURAH**	9,121	10,981
OBOCK	4,481	4,273
	39,024	39,221

*UN documents gave the territory a population of 125,000 in 1967.

*In Djibouti, where more than half of the population lived, the majority of inhabitants were prevented from registering for the referendum.

**Note that the number of alleged actual voters exceeded the number of the registered voters.

(Sources: *La Dnomme Somalie Francaise* — '*Commandement Revolutionnaire*')

Somalia appealed to the United Nations, with the support of the overwhelming majority of the member states of the Organisation of African Unity (OAU) and the Non-aligned Movement, that the territory's name be not changed. Ethiopia found herself in an embarrassing position. She could neither oppose the motion in the face of the other Africans nor support a Somali sponsored motion of such importance. The head of the Ethiopian delegation to the UN General Assembly, Lij Endalkachew Makonnen, a seasoned diplomat who later became one of Emperor Haile Sellassie's last prime ministers, made a bold move. He approached the Somali delegate at the UN Decolonization Committee which was debating the matter, and offered him a compromise.

Endalkachew said unexpectedly that he would support the Somali motion, but asked for a small concession: that the name of Djibouti be added and bracketed after the words "French Somaliland". The committee chairman announced to the committee that the representatives of Ethiopia and Somalia had agreed that the name of that territory should be "French Somaliland (Djibouti)" which was accordingly approved by the UN Decolonisation Committee, thus ending in a few minutes what could have taken many long hours and perhaps several days of debate.

I have no knowledge whether the French representative voted against the motion or abstained, but despite the international stand that the name of the territory should remain unchanged, France continued to refer to "The Territory of the Afars and the Issas" up until Djibouti's independence in 1977. If, as with Endalkachew, other Ethiopians and Somalis had been able to work together, the horn of Africa would have been a more peaceful place but Endalkachew too, was amongst the many Ethiopian senior officials who were executed by the Mengistu regime.

The usual colonial behavior was to find a scapegoat for problems the authorities were unwilling to face. Not surprisingly, the French believed that any show of support for independence was inspired and engineered by the Somali Republic. That was never the case. I had, from the time of Somalia's independence, been either a key player at various levels or had been in a position to be knowledgeable about all Somali policies towards Djibouti, although Siad Barre tried always to exclude Isaaq officials, such as myself, from involvement in Djibouti affairs. Somalia consistently supported the legitimate demands of pro-independence groups and individuals, but would seldom initiate any such moves.

No Somali government could remain in office if it failed to support legitimate demands for Djibouti independence, whoever might present them, because of very strong domestic pressure. This came especially from the people of the North who were always the first contact with those expelled from Djibouti. Most of the people whom the Somali officials were dealing with were exiles, including some without much political experience in Djibouti itself. Somali leaders always discouraged the people of Djibouti from resorting to the use of force or violence and condemned the smuggling of arms. This is true even in the famous case of the late Mohamoud Harbi who clearly sought to destabilize Djibouti.

Arms were shipped on an Egyptian commercial vessel named *Rastanura* which was carrying an ordinary cargo of cement to Berbera. The arrangement seems to have been that agents would meet the ship's captain in Berbera with pre-arranged bona fides.

After discharging her legitimate cargo the ship remained at anchor in the port of Berbera for one or two more days. In the meantime, a Somali passenger, who had travelled on the ship from Egypt and knew about the arms shipment, flew to Mogadishu without saying a word to the authorities either in Berbera or Hargeisa and informed the prime minister — perhaps he was looking for the highest price for his information. When the anticipated claimants of the arms failed to turn up, the ship slipped anchor early one morning and moved out of sight of the mainland and dumped the arms into the sea before returning to its berth.

The prime minister passed information to General Daud who alerted us from Mogadishu, but it was just too late to seize the smuggled arms. I was in charge both of the investigation and the prosecution and preferred two charges under the Customs Law against the captain of the ship for moving the vessel without the prior permission of the port authorities (even a change of berth within the harbor area would require such permission) and against the ship for having a concealed device in which something could be hidden, which was not shown on its plan, but which was detected during a police search. The captain entered a plea of not guilty, but both counts against him were proved and he was fined a total of forty-two thousand Somali shillings, at that time equivalent to about seven thousand US dollars.

The French colonial authorities in those days forbade any contacts by Djibouti politicians with any foreign power, a policy aimed primarily at contacts with Somali authorities. Our Somali officials were therefore frustrated at not being able to get the first hand views of politically experienced nationalists from Djibouti; they could not come to Somalia, short of taking lengthy involuntary exile. For that reason, Prime Minister Mohamed Ibrahim Egal decided to seek the views of Hassan Gouled (later the president of the independent Republic of Djibouti) before he saw President de Gaulle in March 1968. In my police office at Hargeisa, one morning I received a large envelope with an official heading written in Italian, "REPUBBLICA SOMALIA" addressed to Hassan Gouled. It was sent to me through the police headquarters, Mogadishu, together with a brief explanation of its contents and purpose, and with instructions that I should endeavor to arrange its delivery and get Hassan Gouled's reply before the prime minister's departure for Europe on 1 March. For more than a week I pondered how I could arrange its safe delivery to Hassan Gouled who, according to the information I had, was under constant watch by French security. I was excited by the challenge and determined that it would be delivered somehow. I needed a willing and trustworthy courier. I soon found one in the person of Issa Gaboube, a retired pensioner from the French forces who would shortly be going to Djibouti to collect his pension.

According to the information I had, Hassan Gouled mostly stayed at Arta where he owned a private bungalow facing a French Gendarmerie post which easily kept his movements and those of his visitors under close surveillance. (I was later a guest at that bungalow on Djibouti's independence and found that my information had been absolutely correct.) The French security at the border crossing point at Loyado were also very strict for people coming from the Somali side, though they would only be citizens of Djibouti returning from normal visits to Somalia. My devised scheme, therefore, had to be absolutely watertight. If caught, Issa Gaboube would not only be imprisoned, he would certainly lose his pension, if he did not die under torture.

The device was that I would have a pair of sandals made for Issa Gaboube and that the letter would be folded up and concealed in the sole of one of the shoes. The large envelope was discarded. There were some shoemakers who worked in the Save the Children's Fund camp in Hargeisa as trainers for the handicapped. I knew the camp administrator, Ismail Haji Obali, a retired former civil servant, very well. I called on him and he reported that the work could be done in one or two days as soon as I delivered the measurements; and he chose the shoemaker. Although the shoemaker would be far removed from any contact with the distant French security, nevertheless, I had to give some reason for wanting to put paper inside the shoe in order to negate any suspicion. People normally talk if they are suspicious. Ismail found the answer. He told the shoemaker that I had an uncle who had been suffering from some undiagnosable sickness for a long time and that I had been advised to make him a *Qardha'as* (a piece of paper on which prayers from the Holy Quran — Hejab — are supposedly written and then wrapped up in a piece of skin or cloth). The sick man could even wear the charm without knowing about it.

Having settled all the above, I went one evening to Issa Gaboube, brought him to my house, took tracings of his feet on a foolscap sheet of paper, and asked him to get ready to leave for Djibouti within the next two days. I then drove him back to his place and delivered my order at the Save the Children's fund camp the very same evening.

Ismail Obali contributed another important suggestion and he had even given the necessary instructions to the shoemaker without waiting for my consent. Ismail knew that the letter would eventually have to be removed from the shoe. So he told the shoemaker to stitch the edge of the sole of the shoe in which was the *Qardha'as,* with twine and not with leather stitching, so that it would be easier to cut.

The shoemaker reduced the amount of leather in the sole of the shoe at the exact spot which would contain the *Qardha'as* by an amount equal to the weight of the folded paper, a few inches in diameter, in order to balance the two feet. The prime minister's letter never left my custody and Ismail had to bring the shoemaker to my house at the last minute and finalise his work of putting it into the sole of the right shoe, hammering it smooth and then stitching the border, in my presence. I then drove them home and proceeded to the town to bring Issa Gaboube to my house again for him to try on the shoes. They were perfect. He said he was ready to leave the following day, but the trade truck that he had intended to go with was delayed. I needed to find some alternative transport. Meantime I kept the shoes with me.

I contacted a businessman, Mohamed Idd, later murdered by Siad Barre's men during the destruction of Hargeisa in 1988, who owned a new pickup Land Rover and I asked him to lend it to me with a driver for two days. He agreed and sent it the following morning. I filled it with petrol and contacted Issa Gaboube at our rendezvous. He said he could leave in a few hours' time. Only then did I inform him that I would follow him to Loyado and would still carry his new sandals. It was 16 February 1968, with barely two weeks to go before the prime minister's departure. The *Gu* seasonal rains which usually fall at the end of March or early April had already started, causing fear of delay due to roads becoming impassable. I wanted to receive Hassan Gouled's reply as soon as it crossed the boundary line.

Issa Gaboube and I parted in Hargeisa and next saw each other when we reached Borama 78 miles away. After that, we met intermittently at teashops en route. Whenever I passed him I would pause unobtrusively at the next village just in case there might be an unexpected breakdown. We finally reached Loyado at about 5 P.M. and Issa joined me upstairs above the Customs/Police border house. He put on his new shoes and left his old ones there. Just to take the last possible precaution, I asked him to walk through some muddy sand downstairs to blur the new stitches. I then wished Issa good luck and he crossed the border, leaving the vehicle on our side. After the usual search he passed through freely under the nose of the French security.

Issa promised me he would be back within three days which was a big sacrifice on his part because he had a lot of personal affairs to attend to in Djibouti which was partly his home. I found it hard to spend the next three days idly waiting. I kept shuttling daily between Loyado and the ancient port city of Zeila only 39 Kms away. Issa showed up again on the fourth day at about 5 P.M. and came alone to me upstairs. He exclaimed, "Here it is", and pulled Hassan Gouled's reply from inside the shoe which had not been restitched. I was shocked to see so wide an opening at the edge of the shoe. If the 'very vigilant French security' had just looked down at Issa's shoes that could well have spelt disaster. I would never know what Hassan Gouled's reply contained for it was handwritten in French which I did not read. Sadly, Issa Gaboube was not given due recognition after Djibouti's independence and has since died. May God bless his soul.

Up to that time I had not seen Hassan Gouled personally — only his photographs — but in 1975 I met him at Mogadishu Airport VIP lounge as he and Ahmed Dini were leaving for Kampala to attend an OAU summit conference to plead their case for Djibouti's independence. I introduced myself to him, and we talked about Djibouti's current situation and the years of struggle.

Although colonialism in Africa was on the way out there were two main factors which finally determined the independence of Djibouti: the first was the role played by a vital segment, if not the majority, of the Afar community led by Ahmed Dini, a long time Djibouti politician and men like Ismail Ali and of course 'Sheikho' who closed ranks with the pro-independence Somali majority (Issa and others); the second was the internationalization by Somalia of incidents in the struggle culminating in the daylight abduction of French school children in Djibouti. Similar events in that territory continued to discredit French government claims that their presence was only in response to the wishes of the local people. Somali diplomacy always played an important role in highlighting the day-to-day state of affairs which helped to intensify international awareness of the overall situation. This Somali policy of encouraging the struggle for the independence of Djibouti was consistently followed by successive Somali governments including that of Siad Barre.

Once the solidarity of the two communities, Afars and Somalis, strengthened, the trend towards independence became irreversible, a process which caught Ali Arif, a long time prime minister of non-independent Djibouti, by surprise. He always believed that his French support was absolute, and it would ward off any rising tide of nationalism. He once boasted to a friend that the French had never left a colony before installing their own choice as leader and that they had chosen him to become the future leader of Djibouti. However, I had reason to believe that that remark was relayed to me because I was head of intelligence, in an attempt to influence Somali government policy towards Ali Arif, so it was not passed on.

As the clock of freedom ticked on, Ali Arif made a last minute desperate but futile attempt to turn the rising tide. For the first time he called for independence, but simultaneously tried to delay its realization. He sent one of his ministers, Mohamed Jama Elabe, an Issa Somali, to attend a meeting of the African Decolonisation Committee in Dar-es-Salaam, the latter visited Mogadishu and implied a belief in independence. Ali Arif himself later attended a meeting of the OAU foreign ministers held in Addis-Ababa. He was very strongly supported by the Ethiopians, who saw him as the logical successor to the French. They still sought to prevent the birth of any future government in Djibouti which could be friendly with Somalia. They were able to muster some other African support for him, though a minority.

Ethiopia published a pamphlet, *Who is who in Djibouti,* listing the names of all important political personalities since that country's inception which was distributed to the conferees to suggest that Ali Arif had as good credentials as anybody else — particularly Hassan Gouled and Ahmed Dini who were then championing independence. After several humiliating objections and interventions by several African ministers, who saw him as a foreign stooge, Ali Arif was at long last given the floor to address the African foreign ministers. It was his first and last opportunity, and he defeated his own case, when he failed to call for immediate independence, to the utter disappointment of the few African ministers whose support was rallied for him by Ethiopia. In the meantime international pressure mounted on the French government to admit an observer group of African officials to visit the territory. At last France acceded and the visit took place during April and May of 1976.

The African envoys were surprised by the large numbers of French troops and appalled by the sight of a capital city totally encircled by barbed wire. Some African diplomats privately talked of the 'concentration camp!'. Their report marked the final death knell of colonialism in Djibouti and the dawn of freedom for the people. When interviewed by the OAU Fact Finding Committee, Ali Arif clung to his conviction that he would be the key player in shaping the country's future destiny. He also denied the existence of refugees who had been living outside the territory ever since their deportation during the March 1967 rigged plebiscite. When pressed if he was prepared to participate in efforts for the attainment of the country's independence, Ali Arif answered in the affirmative. However, he admitted his inability to command the respect and trust of opposition parties which in fact were championing immediate independence.

Thereafter, most African governments became as vocal as Somalia and Ethiopia too had to jump on the bandwagon at the last minute and support Djibouti's independence. France lost no more time and started the process of decolonisation by negotiating with the leaders of the opposition. They dumped their long time protégé, Ali Arif, and replaced him with Abdalla Kamil who was proposed by the opposition as an interim prime minister, pending general elections.

The opposition alliance, the *African Popular League for Independence* (LPAI), led by Hassan Gouled, agreed to the distribution of seats and presented a single list of candidates for all constituencies. Ali Arif could not even run for his own seat as an independent candidate, so much had his political following waned. The opposition Alliance candidates were all elected.

Djibouti politicians, both Afars and Somalis alike, wisely refused to yield to overtures from Siad Barre to unite with Somalia immediately after their independence. He even offered Hassan Gouled the Presidency of a Greater Somalia, but Hassan Gouled would not buy it and ignored him without even a formal, yes or no, answer.

However, the stand of Djibouti leaders reflected the wishes of most of their people who wanted to stand alone, in part because of their awareness of the disadvantaged position of the people of Northern Somalia after they had brought about the Union, and because they had no desire to be drawn into any future Ethio-Somali conflict. The governor in Hargeisa imprudently sent hundreds of people from his social organizations to Djibouti, not merely to help and participate in the celebrations, but to show off Somalia's achievements in mass organization. They were many more than the new Republic was prepared to accept because of limited facilities. While officials remained courteous, one could sense popular resentment in the non-official circles against so many people imposing themselves upon the local populace.

On the eve of independence Hassan Gouled was unanimously elected by the National Assembly as President of the Republic of Djibouti and he appointed Ahmed Dini as Prime Minister. I was a member of the Somali delegation to Djibouti's independence which was led by Hussein Kulmiye by then a Vice-President. The reception continued until the early hours of the following morning: except for me, all the members of the Somali delegation retired soon after midnight: I met President Hassan Gouled who recognised me and we enjoyed a warm and friendly discussion.

On his first visit to independent Djibouti soon after the country's freedom, Siad Barre was less than diplomatic over Djibouti's close attachment to France and the continued presence of French forces. He said to Prime Minister Dini over lunch, "You cheated us, because you could always have had your independence if this was all that you wanted".

Before many years had passed, the direction of refugee flows reversed and more recently, after the savage repression in the north and the collapse of the Somali state, the people of Djibouti made great sacrifices to help both individuals and the country. Many Somalis had cause to be grateful that Djiboutians had opted for full independence on their own, in 1977.

CHAPTER TEN

PROBLEMS WITH NEIGHBORING COUNTRIES – ETHIOPIA AND KENYA

THE SOMALI REPUBLIC HAD, from its inception in 1960 onwards, pursued a foreign policy committed to greater Somali unity: that is to say the liberation and voluntary union of all Somalis divided into alien administrations during and after the scramble for Africa. In addition to involvement in the struggle of the French Somali Coast (now the Republic of Djibouti), Somali diplomats continuously called for the direct decolonization of the Ethiopian held but Somali inhabited territory, the Ogaden, named after one of the Somali clans of the indigenous population, and for self-determination for the Somali people of the Northern Frontier District, later the North-Eastern Province of Kenya (the NFD).

In 1962, in the wake of imminent constitutional changes for the then Colony and Protectorate of Kenya, the British Government organized a commission of enquiry to ascertain the wishes of the people of the NFD, but failed later to honor the result. More than ninety per cent of those eligible to vote, it was reported, would favor secession from Kenya and opt for union with the Somali Republic. The British chose rather to yield to the stand of the more vocal mainstream Kenyan politicians who were opposed to the popular demands of the people of the Northern Frontier. Britain's many vested interests in Kenya were the deciding factor. Somalia accordingly severed diplomatic ties with Britain in March 1963 and maintained that position for the next five years. The frustrated Somali population of the NFD, encouraged and assisted by the Somali Government, saw no alternative other than to take up arms against British and later Kenyan, rule.

In March 1963, the Ogaden people, led by their elders, also rebelled against Ethiopian rule, which led to severe reprisals against Somalia. Border skirmishes developed locally into open warfare between the two countries. Other non–Ogadeen Somali clans did not greatly participate in that rebellion and it was for that very reason that Siad Barre later renamed the disputed territory Western Somalia with a view to involving all Somali clans.

There had been serious diplomatic clashes when the Organization of African Unity was formed and its charter signed in Addis Ababa on May 25, 1963. Emperor Haile Sellassie of Ethiopia and Somali President Aden Abdulla therefore met during the conference and established a personal dialogue which was well documented by the protocol perfectionist Somali Foreign Minister, Abdullahi Issa. He was ably assisted by the Somali ambassador to Ethiopia, Abdurahim Abby Farah, later a senior United Nations official who was well liked and completely trusted by the minister. Abby would always travel with the minister on all missions undertaken and conferences attended and acted both as his speech writer and draftsman.

It was agreed in the meeting between the emperor and the president that as a first step, all hostilities should cease, a media propaganda moratorium would be observed by both sides and settlement of all outstanding claims would be made, including the return of many Somali trade trucks seized by the Ethiopian forces at border crossings. An Ethiopian merchant navy ship was being held at Berbera port, seized by the Somali navy on the pretext of having violated Somali territorial waters. Abdullahi Issa stayed behind in Addis Ababa after the conference for more talks with senior Ethiopian officials and was told by Ethiopian Prime Minister Aklilu Habte Wolde, that the emperor would not want release of that ship to be the least pre-condition for the normalization of relations between the two countries. The ship was however released by the Somali government.

At the request of Emperor Haile Sellassie in a personal telegram to President Aden Abdulla, Somalia voted for Addis Ababa becoming the permanent seat of the OAU. Some sources owned that the Somali vote was a deciding factor to break a tie between Ethiopia and Senegal. President Aden Abdulla acknowledged Haile Sellassie's request in a return telegram and promised him Somalia's support. Prime Minister Abdurashid was out of the capital at that time and Minister of the Interior Mohamoud Abdi Nur, who was acting prime minister ad-interim, rather shrewdly avoided any personal commitment and without comment transmitted the text of the two telegrams to Abdullahi Issa at the OAU Foreign Ministers' conference in Dakar. According to one member of the foreign minister's delegation, the ever careful Abdullahi Issa caused inquiries to be made to ascertain that President Aden Abdulla's telegram was not a forgery.

Improvement of relations between the two countries was aborted by the failure of Abdurashid's government to curb the activities of the Ogaden rebels, many of whose leaders were living in Mogadishu. Some of them were secretly reporting planned activities of the rebellion to the Ethiopian embassy. Mohamed Ugas Hashi one such notorious leader, decided to return to Ethiopia, perhaps after he had felt that he had earned some credentials because of his information. The embassy arranged a taxi to take him to the border at Fer-Fer. We had been following him and knew the taxi's number plates, description and the exact time of his departure — the siesta time which typically followed lunch in Mogadishu. The police reported to the government in time but we were told to let him go. The Ethiopians airlifted him to Addis Ababa where they used him for media publicity. Senior government officials considered that insignificant, but it had some negative repercussions amongst the general public.

When later, Abdurashid Khalif, the former leader of the NFD wanted to return to Kenya, in order to show Somali authorities' disinterest in his movements, he was encouraged to leave openly through the Mogadishu civilian airport and he travelled on an Aden Airways flight to Nairobi.

The 1964 OAU annual Summit Conference of Heads of State and Government held in Cairo adopted an important resolution to the effect that frontiers inherited from the former colonial powers, even

The Fragility of Somali Unity

The Somali Nation, made up of independent minded, clan based Imamates, Chieftancies and Sultanates, sometimes in conflict with one another and without central government, has lived in the Horn of Africa since earliest times. The spread of the Islamic faith apart, influences from abroad have often penetrated but little from the coast. These have included contacts, probably with China and certainly with Portugal (15th–18th centuries); with Oman and Muscat (18th and 19th centuries) and with the Ottoman empire and then Zanzibar from at least 1840. Inland there has been contact, trade and occasional friction with the Abyssinians (Ethiopians), particularly when their Christian emperors were strong, as at times during the 14th, 15th and 16th centuries.

Inheriting the Ottoman mantle, from 1875 the Egyptians pressed inland from the Gulf coast, but were obliged to withdraw by the British, in 1882. From then on, it was the Europeans — and again the Abyssinians — who brought the greatest pressure on the Somali people. The world of the Somalis witnessed much turmoil towards the end of the 19th century and throughout most of the 20th, during the colonial period and its aftermath. There have been large scale interventions, in 1941–50 by the British; in 1978 by the Soviet Union and in 1992–4 by the United States and its allies. The United Nationals too has been represented by an Italian trusteeship over Somalia, 1950–60, and subsequently in different capacities during refugee crises, famine and the breakdown of civil order in certain areas of the Horn right up until contemporary times. Since any Somalis have sadly been obliged on occasions to become refugees in neighboring countries (and elsewhere), the presence of large refugee communities is represented on the chart on the opposite page, by the letter 'R.'

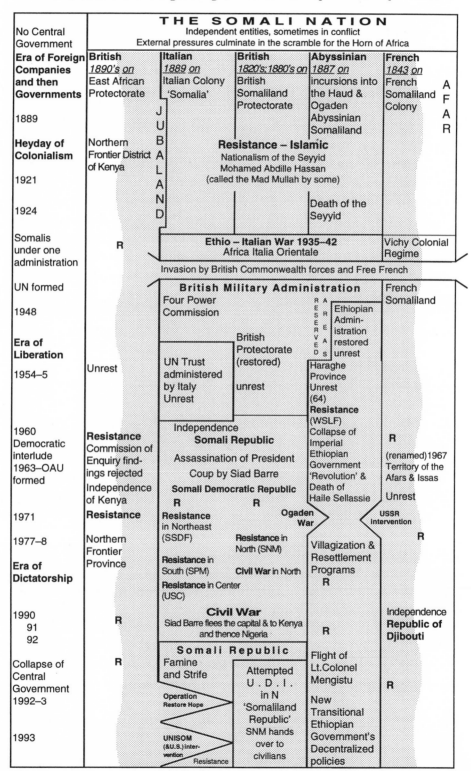

THE SOMALI NATION
Independent entities, sometimes in conflict
External pressures culminate in the scramble for the Horn of Africa

No Central Government	British	Italian	British	Abyssinian	French
Era of Foreign Companies and then Governments	British *1890's on* East African Protectorate	Italian *1889 on* Italian Colony 'Somalia'	British *1820's;1880's on* British Somaliland Protectorate	Abyssinian *1887 on* incursions into the Haud & Ogaden Abyssinian Somaliland	French *1843 on* French Somaliland Colony

A F A R

1889

Heyday of Colonialism — Northern Frontier District of Kenya

JUBALAND

Resistance – Islamic
Nationalism of the Seyyid
Mohamed Abdille Hassan
(called the Mad Mullah by some)

1921

1924 — Death of the Seyyid

Somalis under one administration

R

Ethio – Italian War 1935–42
Africa Italia Orientale

Vichy Colonial Regime

Invasion by British Commonwealth forces and Free French

UN formed

British Military Administration
Four Power Commission

French Somaliland

1948

RESERVED AREA

Ethiopian Administration restored unrest

Era of Liberation

British Protectorate (restored)

1954–5 — Unrest — UN Trust administered by Italy Unrest — unrest — Haraghe Province Unrest (64)

Resistance (WSLF)

1960 Democratic interlude 1963–OAU formed

Resistance Commission of Enquiry findings rejected Independence of Kenya

Independence
Somali Republic
Assassination of President
Coup by Siad Barre
Somali Democratic Republic
R   R

Collapse of Imperial Ethiopian Government 'Revolution' & Death of Haile Sellassie

R
(renamed)1967
Territory of the Afars & Issas

Unrest

1971 — **Resistance** — **Resistance in Northeast (SSDF)** — **Ogaden War** — USSR Intervention

1977–8 — Northern Frontier Province — **Resistance in North (SNM)** — Villagization & Resettlement Programs — R

Era of Dictatorship — **Resistance in South (SPM)** **Civil War in North** — R

Resistance in Center (USC)

1990
91
92

R

Civil War
Siad Barre flees the capital & to Kenya and thence Nigeria

R

Independence
Republic of Djibouti

Somali Republic

Collapse of Central Government 1992–3

R

Famine and Strife

Operation Restore Hope

Attempted U.D.I. in N 'Somaliland Republic'

Flight of Lt.Colonel Mengistu

New Transitional Ethiopian Government's Decentralized policies

R

1993 — **UNISOM (&U.S.) Intervention** — Resistance — SNM hands over to civilians

though they were arbitrary and disregarded ethnic boundaries, were inviable. Ironically, the sponsor of that Ethiopia-inspired resolution, was former President Julius Nyerere of Tanzania who would later recognize secessionist Biafra and support the abortive attempt to divide Nigeria, demonstrating the non-sanctity of the resolution itself, as far as he was concerned. At the time, however, only Morocco and Somalia opposed and submitted official reservations. Morocco later renounced her territorial claims against Algeria, and Somalia would have been well advised to follow suit as far as the NFD and Kenya were concerned, because that was a typical case identical to many similar African cases. That did not happen until three years later when Mohamed Ibrahim Egal became the Somali Prime Minister and came to an agreement with the Kenyan leaders during the OAU Summit conference in Kinshasa in 1967. Former President Kenneth Kaunda of Zambia had been the quiet intermediary. Egal's government later cut off assistance to the Somali liberation movements directed against both Kenya and Ethiopia but he failed to seek parliamentary ratification for his actions. Siad Barre, upon seizing power in October 1969, revised that policy and reactivated the movements, but he contained them until he had consolidated power. Perhaps he would not have done that if Egal had processed the necessary ratification by parliament.

Haile Sellassie was prepared to symbolically surrender a strip of territory to Somalia, as a border readjustment arrangement, without acknowledging Somali claims, but only to buy the Somali government's agreement for a permanent boundary demarcation line along the still unmarked former Italian Somaliland border. When talks on the issue finally failed, Somalia took the case to the OAU Summit Conference held in Addis Ababa in 1973. It was the first time ever that Somalia was able to secure consensus within the OAU for any discussion on the Somali-Ethiopian dispute. Before that, Ethiopia, who dominated the OAU secretariat, had been capable of effecting the total exclusion of the issue from the agenda. It was a credit to Foreign Minister Omer Arteh, who had earned some popularity among Africans for his mediation efforts between Tanzania and Idi Amin's Uganda, but the success aroused the jealousy of Siad Barre and appears to have prompted him to replace Omer Arteh, at first honorably by nominating him as a candidate for the OAU secretary generalship and then for the corresponding post in the Organization of the Islamic Conference. When both attempts failed, he replaced him and kept rotating him from one nominal position to another until his arrest in 1982.

The OAU appointed a committee of eight member states to mediate between Ethiopia and Somalia and to report their findings to the heads of states and governments in due course. Meantime, Haile Sellassie was overthrown by the Mengistu led Derg on his return after attending the OAU Summit Conference of 1974 held in Mogadishu, and he died a year later. General Aman Andom, who succeeded him, and some seventy of his senior officials were executed and many others were either interned or fled the country. Ethiopia was clearly in disarray and Siad Barre felt that the right moment had arrived. Since 1975, he had been actively preparing the Western Somali Liberation Front (WSLF) and it launched a big offensive in June 1977. With the direct involvement of Siad Barre's army, the WSLF soon overran all the Ethiopian garrisons in the Ogaden and reached the suburbs of the cities of Harar and Dire-Dawa.

Alarmed by the scale of the fighting, the OAU Good Offices Committee composed of the foreign ministers of the eight member countries, met for the first time in Libreville, Gabon, on 5–8 August 1977 inviting both Ethiopia and Somalia to attend. Abdurahman Jama Barre, Siad Barre's inept cousin, the newly appointed foreign minister, represented Somalia. Blinded by the early Somali success on the war front, he insisted that the committee invite the WSLF to participate as a liberation movement and when that was not accepted, he disdainfully walked out. Despite repeated appeals by the committee members he left the meeting and thus earned for Somalia the permanent wrath of the OAU. In the meantime the Kenyans in particular, were flustered, for Soviet-equipped Somali forces were by then beyond the furthest end of the Somali inhabited territory at the gates of the Ethiopian highlands. No one knew the limit of their ambition. President Carter received Kenyan ministers, led by Vice-President Daniel arap Moi, urging western countries not to sell arms to Somalia, and Carter, whose attitude was never very consistent, at the time denounced the

Somali Democratic Republic as an aggressor.

I suggested to Siad Barre that he should renounce any territorial claims against Kenya there and then, and if he could not go himself, should send a goodwill mission to Kenya at once. I argued that involvement in the Ogaden was the major stake and that he stood no chance at all of success without making a significant concession elsewhere. Moreover, while the Ogaden was an ill-gotten acquisition by Ethiopian Emperor Menelik during the scramble for Africa — for Ethiopia had participated and shared the spoils of the division of Africa with the European colonialists — and as such was unique and a pure case for decolonization, the Northern Frontier District of Kenya was only one among many similar African cases where ethnic groups were divided. It was therefore subject to the collective African stand of the 1964 Cairo summit resolution on the inviolability of boundaries inherited from colonial powers. The Moroccan and Somali reservations had carried little weight and we also had to face the fact that Somalis in capitalist Kenya no longer wanted to rejoin his socialist Somalia. I had gone too far. Siad was annoyed by my last comment and cut the discussion short.

In the event, the following year saw the Somali forces and the WSLF driven back by a Soviet led coalition of Cubans, South Yemenis and Ethiopians. Then the OAU Good Offices Committee in one of their subsequent meetings held in Lagos, Nigeria, 18–20 August 1980 at foreign ministerial level, came to an (according to *West Africa* 'surprising') conclusion, and advised that the Ogaden was an 'integral part' of Ethiopia. These were national and moral disasters, the effects of which are still with the Somali nation.

In 1979/80 the government of the Kingdom of Saudi Arabia offered to mediate between Kenya and Somalia over the latter's territorial claims. Siad Barre accepted at the level of his own personal diplomacy. The Saudis then committed their full weight and prestige and there was a great deal of behind the scenes diplomatic effort spent by their very able and seasoned diplomat Sheikh Taha Al-Dugheyther, a long time Saudi Ambassador to Somalia. For several months he kept shuttling back and forth from Riyadh to Mogadishu, Riyadh to Nairobi, and vice-versa. Finally, a tripartite summit was arranged at the Saudi summer resort city of Da'if which failed before it even started, simply because Siad Barre had changed his mind. In fact the two sides only met at a banquet held in their honor by the Saudi monarch.

On his return to Mogadishu, Siad Barre reported to his officials that he had been misunderstood by the Saudis. Nobody believed him, because all knew that he and Sheikh Taha had met so many times that there could hardly have been any room for ambiguity. What nobody understood then, and not even today, was the reason he changed his mind, since he had to settle later for much less. The Saudis at least would have compensated him financially for concessions.

Tension with Ethiopia continued at every level. There was little one could do. During an OAU/UNHCR sponsored conference on African refugees held in Arusha, Tanzania, in 10–17 May 1979, the Ethiopian delegation anticipated that we would make a strong attack against their regime regarding the influx of refugees who had crossed over into Somalia after the Ogaden war. They wanted to hear our statement early so that they could prepare a strong right of reply in time. As the minister responsible, I was fully aware of their intentions and we purposely registered ourselves as one of the last speakers. Every day the conference secretariat would update the list of speakers for that day and the Ethiopian girl typists of the OAU staff, acting upon the instructions of their government delegation, would include us in the list of speakers. We would simply refuse to take the floor before our registered time and invariably drew the attention of both the conference chairman and the secretariat to the situation and the poor girls were always embarrassed. The Ethiopians finally had to prepare their speech without foreknowledge, as time was running out for them: they based it on the assumption of an attack from us. When finally delivered, our speech was very mild, to the acclaim of all the participants of the conference. It took the Ethiopians by surprise and caused them to abandon their prepared text and handwrite a different speech in a rush.

The presidency did not give detailed instructions for every event and I was able to present the views of more balanced Somalis on occasions. At Arusha, the Ethiopian delegation at the outset, strongly

supported by Algeria and Angola, had proposed the exclusion of the
U.N. Human Rights Commission, Amnesty International and some
other human rights observers. Refugees were our 'African' or 'family'
concern, they argued. Although we ourselves represented a totalitarian
regime, we joined those delegations which opposed this proposal and
I was glad it was defeated. I never condoned playing politics with
human suffering. In the summer of 1981, after attending one of the
Geneva held *International Conferences for Assistance to Refugees in Africa*
(ICARA), I visited the United States and was met by Dr. Chester
Crocker, the Assistant Secretary of State for African Affairs. I discussed
with him the danger posed by the presence of Cuban forces in the
Horn of Africa, as being one of the root causes of the flight of refugees
from Ethiopia to Somalia.

In the course of our discussion, Dr. Crocker commented, "We
would like to help you, but you should at least find one friend among
your neighbors." It was true that besides Kenya, with whom we had
very cool relations, we had poor relations with Marxist South Yemen,
just across our northern waters, for they had fought against us on the
side of Ethiopia in the Ogaden war because of Soviet pressure. We had
had no relations whatsoever with Marxist Ethiopia since that war. My
reaction was that the USA would have had no desire for us to improve
relations with those two Marxist regimes, at least at that time, and that
Dr. Crocker was only recommending better relations between us and
Kenya. On my return home I briefed Siad Barre unequivocally and also
later addressed the council of ministers during its weekly meeting,
which was chaired by Siad Barre himself. Within a month the OAU
Heads of State and Government annual summit conference would be
taking place in the Kenyan capital, Nairobi, and my report aroused
a great deal of interest. But Siad Barre seemed hesitant and would
not permit any debate on the issue. He dismissed it as not being an
agenda item.

The OAU summit was held in Nairobi in June 1981 and it finally
adopted the ministerial report reaffirming Ethiopian sovereignty over
the Ogaden. Incompetent Somali diplomacy in the hands of Siad
Barre's inept foreign minister, Abdurahman Jama Barre, continued to
contribute greatly as it always had to that decision. I was part of the

Somali delegation to Nairobi. Siad Barre always sent Hussein Abdulqadir Qassim to attend important meetings of the OAU because he knew his relative was incapable. Before the adoption of that report, the chairman, President Moi of Kenya, did not invite comments, but simply asked if there were any objections to its adoption. When silence reigned for a second the Ethiopian foreign minister claimed that it had been adopted. Hussein Qassim at once objected and the Ethiopian Minister and Hussein each took the floor twice and the Chairman who was clearly biased in favor of Ethiopia, grew impatient. It was obvious that Somalia would not get the floor for a third time. I whispered to Hussein Abdulqadir and even wrote him a note to warn that he must lose no more time, but ask for a roll call vote on the report. He did not do that and as expected the Chairman took the Ethiopian position. In a matter of seconds, the Kenyan president just hit the gavel on the table and declared the report adopted. Hussein Abdulqadir knew very well that a number, perhaps even a majority, of the OAU member States would have been unwilling to take sides between Ethiopia and Somalia and definitely would have abstained, whereupon the report would not have been adopted for lack of consensus. Many Somalis accused the Ogaden people of not wanting self determination because, the status quo suited their interests on both sides of the border. I had strongly resisted that assumption but Hussein Abdulqadir is an Ogadeen. He had the matter in his hands.

During the Summit, Siad Barre met with Daniel arap Moi and naturally Somalia's territorial claim against Kenya was expected to be high on the agenda. The President called together eight of us: Ahmed 'Silanyo,' Mohamed Adan Sheikh, Mohamed Omer Jees, Abdulqassim Salad, Mohamed Said Samatar, Hussein Abdulqadir Qassim, myself and the ambassador to Kenya, Abdurahman Hussein. He offered the subject for discussion. The ambassador spoke first and recommended a softening of the Somali position to strengthen bilateral relations between the two countries, but he did not come to specifics. I spoke next and reminded Siad Barre of my statement of some years earlier, repeating it word for word, for it was still my point of view. I was supported by Abdulqassim Salad. Mohamed Said opposed, but offered no alternative option. Silanyo felt that we should not negotiate from a weak position in view of the unfavorable ruling on the Ogaden issue and preferred deferring discussion on the subject. Mohamed Adan, Mohamed Omer Jees and Hussein Abdulqadir abstained. Siad Barre made no comments, still playing his cards close to his chest. I learned that he later told his counterpart that he was personally willing to renounce any claims, but by so doing he would face overwhelming opposition from his institutions, meaning the council of ministers and the parliament.

The subject was in fact, never debated by Siad Barre's rubber stamp institutions, the majority of which I believe would have favored the renunciation if they had been allowed to speak their minds. Negotiations continued, but the necessary protocols and details of agreements reached were still not concluded when Daniel arap Moi visited Mogadishu some three years later and the matter remained deadlocked at a technical level. Siad Barre had no desire to go back on his renunciation, at least at that time, but the deadlock was orchestrated by him. He continued to endeavor to convince Moi that he still faced strong opposition which he promised to overcome. The two Presidents then took the matter over from their deadlocked lower echelons and reached a téte-à-té agreement whereby Siad Barre would send his Minister of Information, Mohamed Omer Jees, to Moi to sign the protocols in Nairobi.

Another interesting piece of information was that the Libyan leader, Colonel Qadaffi, was supposed to have written to Siad Barre asking him to join him in a conspiracy to destabilize Kenya: this Siad Barre promptly leaked to Moi in order to gain the latter's full trust. That, if true, is something Siad Barre would have been quite likely to have done and it would help explain the Kenyan leader's subsequent unreserved support for Siad Barre as demonstrated by the deporting of Somali dissidents back to Somalia. It is noteworthy too, that even after the dictator's fall, the Kenyan government tried to offer asylum and rendered Siad's family and supporters considerable logistical and material support. But time was nearly up and toward the end, Siad entered into agreements with Kenya and with Ethiopia with only one aim in mind, to frustrate and isolate the mounting internal opposition to his crumbling regime. These protocols such as they were, were never discussed or ratified either by the council of ministers or by the parliament. Siad would undoubtedly have repudiated them the moment he found it advantageous so to do. But Siad Barre was meantime overthrown by the Somali people and it is time to go back and analyze his years in power.

CLAN DIVISIONS OF THE ISAAQ AND HAWIYE
CLAN-FAMILIES

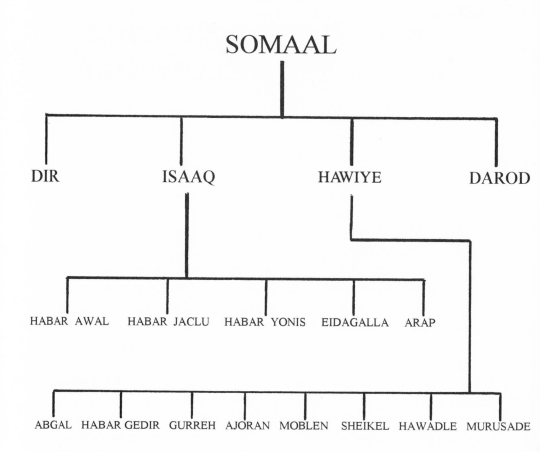

SOMAAL

DIR   ISAAQ   HAWIYE   DAROD

HABAR AWAL   HABAR JACLU   HABAR YONIS   EIDAGALLA   ARAP

ABGAL   HABAR GEDIR   GURREH   AJORAN   MOBLEN   SHEIKEL   HAWADLE   MURUSADE

(The above list is of main groupings, especially those mentioned in the text, and is not intended to be comprehensive.)

CHAPTER ELEVEN

SIAD BARRE AND THE SLIDE INTO DICTATORSHIP

W HEN HE TOOK POWER, Mohamed Siad began for the first time, to use his third name, Barre. It was duly adopted by officialdom and foreigners followed suit, but amongst the majority of the Somali people and especially those of his age group or generation, he remained 'Mohamed Siad,' at least in public, and *Afweyne,* Big Mouth, his nickname, in private.

Like me, Mohamed Siad as a youth had no formal educational background. As an adult and a gendarme he was sent to the Jeans School in Kabetti, Kenya, by the British Military Administration (BMA); that was where he learnt basic English. Both of us had nomadic backgrounds and both had been policemen. Mohamed Siad always felt very proud of his personal achievements particularly his initial promotion to First Gendarme. I heard him tell the story many times of how this was achieved. He said that he was charged for a minor default by a non-commissioned officer (NCO) who was among a group of instructors seconded from the King's (East) African Rifles (KAR) to instruct the Somali gendarmes during the BMA. He cunningly made a deal with the British officer's Somali interpreter and took care to starch his uniform and polish his shoes very well. When he was brought before the officer-in-charge, the interpreter immediately commented, "Very smart," before the NCO had time to explain any charge against the defaulter. The officer, influenced by the interpreter's remark, looked Siad up and down and without asking the NCO anything simply pulled open his desk drawer, picked up a First

Gendarme's badge of rank and pinned it onto Siad's right arm. The astonished NCO refrained from reading out any charge and marched the new 'First Gendarme' out of the office. Siad took care thereafter, to strike a deal of friendship with the NCO since he could not afford to endanger that craftily earned promotion.

Another incident which Mohamed Siad enjoyed recounting was that when he and other young gendarmes were about to depart for school in Kenya, after they had received their final instructions from the Officer-in-charge, someone cried out that his hat had been stolen. He wanted the interpreter to inform the officer so that all kit boxes could be searched. The interpreter, without informing the officer replied, "Let the clever man have two hats while the fool goes without," and signalled to the driver to leave. I could never bring myself to ask Mohamed Siad if he had been the clever man with two hats!

Years later, however, when Mohamed Siad Barre was planning his coup, he did not go undiscovered. In retrospect it is interesting that, although not among the conspirators, a certain army colonel, Mohamed Farah Aidid, came to know of it. According to former prime minister Abdillahi Issa, Aidid warned Ismail Jumale of the imminent coup of Siad Barre on the evening of October 20, 1969. Ismail, then minister of information in that last civilian government, passed the warning to Egal who in turn passed it on to Musa Boqor, a presidential candidate for a would-be next day election to the presidency (following the assassination of President Abdurashid). Musa passed the information to the powerful minister of the interior, Yassin Nur, who rather disdainfully dismissed it as nonsense.

When Mohamed Siad Barre succeeded in coming to power through his bloodless coup d'etat, on 21 October 1969 — the fact that it was bloodless demonstrated lack of support for the previous regime — there were no shortages of areas to be capitalized on as far as the misdeeds of the old regime were concerned. In contrast to that of the triumvirate, his first government consisted of experienced men of integrity and intellectuals, whose careful appointment immediately paved the way for the restoration of public confidence in the day-to-day handling of national issues. Siad Barre vowed to eliminate rampant corruption, to restore security and stability, and called for public support for a wide range of programs of reconstruction based on self-reliance in order to solve the country's socio-economic ills. Indeed, he was quoted in the *Times* of London (9 March 1971) as saying "Injustice and maladministration, lack of social progress and economic development, coupled with a sinking national morale, compelled us to bring about a change."

There was a genuine and spontaneous response across the country. Self-help projects were launched and implemented at all levels of society: national, regional, district and village levels. Dilapidated schools and hospitals were repaired and made habitable through community labor and merchants made cash contributions for the purchase of needed materials. Road repairs and improvements to other infrastructure were set in process. The salaries of all government employees were reduced by a small margin in order to balance the ordinary budget for the first time since independence. Italy had previously covered the budget deficit, but future Italian assistance was to be development oriented. The salaries of certain higher categories of government officials were subjected to a development levy.

All criminals in custody for alleged capital offenses were immediately brought to trial and those found guilty were executed. In the initial stages, Siad Barre's activities were impartial and the general feeling was one of euphoria. For those who had not previously known Siad Barre, he became a savior, while most of those who had known him tended to give him a chance and support his programs of nation building. This brought about the consolidation of his power base for increasingly totalitarian rule. Ironically, it was eventually to reduce society to the level described in Orwell's *Animal Farm.*

Ideologized school children and those whom he had brought from obscurity, including those of low birth or caste (Somalis have no untouchables, but there are groups with whom ordinary Somalis would eat but not intermarry) called him *Abbe Siyaad*, Father Siad. In later years this became, *Macallimka Ummadda,* the Teacher of the Nation — an amazing title for a man without a school certificate at any level! As a nation, we are fervent admirers of poetry — and our poets began to warn us of what lay ahead.

It was the beginning of the *Gu* season, the best part of the year especially for the rural society. A few months after his coming to power and just after I had been appointed commandant of police, Mohamed Siad wanted to send some of his many children (he is reputed to have about twenty-seven from several wives) to the nomadic areas for a spell, where he owned a lot of camels and cattle. He had always done this in the past perhaps to save money at home. He was, however, concerned for their security and wanted me to arrange a discreet escort. We needed to know when the schools would reopen, for the children would have to be escorted back again. It was an afternoon so he telephoned his house to ask. Whoever answered did not know and he asked for one of his daughters, Faduma, but was told that she was asleep. He ordered that she be awakened. When she answered, I was surprised to hear him question her: "Have you been sleeping?" "Yes." "Then why did they wake you up?" That kind of hypocrisy shook my confidence and was an early indication to me of his character. It put me on my guard.

All people who had undergone special training needed to be handled carefully. But Siad Barre frequently harassed and endeavored to discredit people with credentials. The arrest and detention of Dr. Ahmed Shire Lawaha, a fellow Marehan, almost immediately upon Siad Barre's accession to power, is a case in point. Lawaha suffered from eye disease resulting from his detention and had a stroke but Siad Barre never allowed him to leave the country to get proper treatment and he died. Lawaha, a graduate of Lincoln University, USA, had been a leading member of the youth wing of the pro-independence Somali Youth League (SYL) in the 1940s and had thereafter maintained a sound nationalist record. Siad, on the other hand, was suspected of association with several unsavory activities culminating in the murder in Mogadishu in 1957 of Kamal Al-din Salaah, the Egyptian Representative on the International Control Commission which oversaw the Italian administration of the UN Trusteeship of Somalia. The police guard had been withdrawn from the representative's residence just before his assassination and the killer not only enjoyed easy access but was assisted in his attempt to escape. The assassin was in fact arrested by the Egyptian staff, but on whose orders the guard was withdrawn, and why, remain a mystery even today. Mohamed

Siad was then in charge of the Capital Police and as far I can tell, only he had authority to temporarily withdraw bodyguards.

There occurred in those early days one sharp warning of things to come—a rebellion on the part of certain young northern officers. Many Somalis in both the North and the South, mistakenly believed—and have since maintained—that the rising led by Hassan Keyd on 10 December 1961, was part of a broader northern secessionist manifestation. Although dissatisfaction existed due to the imbalance in power sharing after the Union, I can confirm that there were no wider separatist tendencies. The 'coup' attempt, as it came to be called, resulted only from the young officers' dissatisfaction over the lack of comparable adjustments of military rank upon the integration of the Somaliland Scouts Regiment into the Somali National Army, six months after the Union.

Every uniformed officer and many other government employees in the South had been granted independence bonus promotions en masse on 1 July 1960. Unlike the South, only those senior officials who had replaced departing Europeans on the North's independence on 26 June 1960 were upgraded; there were no such mass promotions. Hassan Keyd, who had graduated with the rank of lieutenant from Sandhurst in the UK, and had just returned on the eve of the North's independence, together with his other colleagues of the Scouts Regiment, discovered that they were junior in rank to their respective southern counterparts, including those who were even then still undergoing officer cadet training. They complained and claimed rank readjustments with retrospective effect and they waited six months without receiving equitable treatment. Sympathy for their plight was widespread—and expressed even in Ethiopia, by Brigadier General Aman Andom, then commander of the 3rd division in Harar and certainly no friend of the Somali nation.

The 'coup' was foiled by the (all northern) rank and file who made up the Scouts Regiment. There was also a lack of public support for the violence of their reaction. The coup makers themselves were not counting either upon the loyalty of the army or the support of the general public, but just gambled with the hope of achieving a *fait accompli*. In order to maintain maximum secrecy, army personnel in

Hargeisa were not redeployed during the initial stages of the coup attempt. Those involved had themselves arrested the senior southern army officers at the officers' mess the previous evening and they kept them hostage in a nearby bungalow. Only then did they order an army platoon from the Goraya-Awl Garrison near Borama to seize control of key targets in Hargeisa during the night. The police headquarters, police station, Radio Hargeisa and the telecommunications system offices were occupied. Early the following morning Hassan Keyd addressed the army personnel in Hargeisa, after everyone had reported for duty and claimed that there had been a military takeover throughout the Somali Republic under the leadership of General Daud. For the first few hours thereafter the army's performance was one of absolute loyalty and devotion to duty.

At 9:00 A.M. Hassan Keyd again gave an address, this time to the various heads of government departments at the high court building. Oblivious to the presence of his army escort who had also attended his earlier lecture, he informed the assembled senior civil servants that the military takeover was limited to the north and that its motive was in reality secession. The warrant and the non-commissioned officers (NCOs) relayed this information and resolved to conduct a secret rescue operation. They discovered the senior officers and released them within an hour, at eleven o'clock.

Meantime, after meeting with the senior civil servants, Hassan Keyd asked the regional governor's deputy, Mr. Mohamed Hassan Kambi and myself, to follow him and his colleagues to the officers' mess. When we entered the club lounge we saw that a large tape-recorder, apparently intended to register our forced declaration of support for the 'coup,' was laid in place and beside it was an automatic gun. Apart from Hassan Keyd, two other young rebel officers, Said Ali Ghir and Mohamed Mohamoud Said *Bidihle* were present. They all looked very tired, especially Hassan Keyd who must have missed a lot of sleep. Addressing me, he said they wanted to return the police premises that they had occupied the previous night but before doing so they needed my declaration of support. I retorted quite frankly that the police were not party to their coup in the first place, and that we would not be involved now. At that juncture, Said Ali Ghir plugged the tape-recorder into a power point: it was a threat of force, but it was not certain how far they intended to go. However, any further escalation was averted in the nick of time by a sentry coming in and reporting that there had been some firing. It was the rescue of the senior officers. The rebel officer who was keeping them hostage, Abdullahi Said Abby, was killed. Hassan Keyd and his colleagues then rushed off toward the army headquarters but Hassan Keyd was shot and wounded in the leg as he attempted to re-enter the army fort. The rebels were arrested later that day in Hargeisa, Berbera and Burao, except for one who absconded.

Despite the seriousness of the case, the political leaders favored the young officers' release unscathed, after they had been in custody for rather more than a year. Their conviction might carry the death sentence which they considered unwarranted, realizing that it could only make the northern people's simmering dissatisfaction brim over. Manoeuvering on the part of the politicians resulted in the dismissal of the case. The only dissenting view was that of the army commandant, General Daud, who told me that there had been fourteen such coup attempts in Syria because, in his opinion, the first case had not been dealt with seriously. The politicians had to act behind his back because they respected him very much, but he undoubtedly felt bitter about their decision.

One of the first actions of Siad Barre's regime's Supreme Revolutionary Council (SRC), was the arrest of members of the former government and their confinement in a detention center in Afgoi or elsewhere for the next three and a half years. To the bewilderment of many, those interned included the first Head of State, Aden Abdulla Osman, who had been defeated in the presidential election of 1967 and who had retired peacefully and the former prime minister, Abdurazaq Haji Hussein, who was then the lone opposition member of parliament. They were the very men who had made Siad Barre. Abdurazaq, with the consent of President Aden Abdulla, appointed him to the post of chief of staff of the national army, thus presenting him with the chance of seizing power. Both had known Mohamed Siad Barre very well and he was probably unwilling to allow them to move freely among the people until such time as he had irreversibly consolidated his power base. Had he not received initial public support they would perhaps have remained in detention much longer. Nevertheless, many people took an interest in the well-being of those two former leaders but whenever Siad Barre was questioned about their fate, he would avoid any clear-cut answer, hinting at their release as soon as the situation became 'normalized.' They did, however, continue to languish in detention with other inmates for far too long. Cases in point include the former police commandant, General Abshir Musa, and a leading lawyer Yusuf Jama Dhuhul, who was also editor of a monthly journal, *Dalka* (The Homeland) which had been critical of the old regime.

Upon his succession to power, Siad Barre arrested and detained for nearly twenty years, Yusuf Isman Samatar *Berda'ad* an avowed communist and the best Russian connection in Somalia. Clearly, he was removing a serious contender for the ear of the Russians. Likewise, upon his rapprochement with the United States, Siad Barre later tried to arrest and detain Omer Moallim, the first Somali ambassador to the USA, again seeking to neutralize a possible serious contender. Omer had been tipped off and left the country in the nick of time never to return until after Siad Barre's overthrow.

Within one year of coming to power, in October 1970 Siad Barre felt secure enough to introduce *Scientific Socialism* which he eloquently preached out of sheer expediency without much knowledge or personal commitment. I can say that, for during my intelligence career I read most of the works of known revolutionaries: General Vo Nguyen Giap, Mao Zedong, Ho Chi Minh, Castro, Che Guevera, etc. I was interested in definitions: what constituted guerrilla warfare etc. Curiously, it was because of Siad's speeches that I read some of Lenin's works. I have also studied *The Craft of Intelligence* by Allen Dulles, sometime director of the American CIA. Most writers agree on one thing: whoever gets the support of the local populace should win. Siad Barre did not understand that; but he must have also read a lot on both sides when he was planning his coup. This was reflected very much in the nature of his early speeches to win public support after seizing power. I once heard him very eloquently lecture in Somali on Allen Dulles's distinction between a coup d'etat and a revolution, but without acknowledging the author. Siad Barre was to purposely ignore the important principle of popular support as soon as he consolidated his power base. Instead he chose to rely on acts of terror against the civilian population among whom not just the activity, but the very presence of opposition group members was reported to him directly.

Thus the scientific socialism of Siad Barre may be said to have rested on two main pillars: mass organization, and a rapidly expanding security apparatus network with unlimited powers of search, arrest, detention without trial and torture. A new National Security Service (NSS) replaced the former police special branch. The promotion of Siad Barre's slogans and the harassment of dissidents, real or imagined, soon became daily routine. This was followed by the creation of a number of other terror organizations including: Regional Security Committees in 1970; the *Guulwadayaal* Militia or so-called 'victory pioneers' in 1972; and Siad Barre's legalized instrument of power, the *Somali Revolutionary Socialist Party* (the SRSP), formed in June 1976. That marked the end of the Supreme Revolutionary Council (SRC) as an institution. It was already an impotent rubber stamp, for Siad Barre had long since usurped its authority.

The creation of the Party in July 1976, which was probably a Russian suggestion, also ushered in the formation of party investigation committees as well as workers, women and youth organizations (the last three were called social organizations) and, later, the *Hangash* or military intelligence was reconsolidated. Each and every one of those terror organizations was part of a comprehensive network, reporting directly to Siad Barre himself from whom they took their orders. All these organizations were legalized as legitimate institutions with the exception of the *Hangash,* the Red Berets, whose role was never legalized despite its being the most powerful and notorious innovation. With the exception of the social organizations, they all had powers of arrest, search and seizure of property, torture and detention without trial. The social organizations fulfilled the role of intelligence gather.

The SRC had been profoundly weakened first in April 1970, by the arrest of General Qorshel, a former police commander, for 'harmful and counter revolutionary behavior,' and then in May 1971 by the arrest of two of its members: General Mohamed Ainanshe and Colonel Salad Gaveire together with another senior army officer, Col. Abdulqadir Del and nearly two hundred others. The first three were eventually executed in July 1972. The formation of the Somali Revolutionary Socialist Party allowed Siad Barre to become the sole ruler of the country, and the execution of those officers, who were from the three main clan groups who had hitherto dominated both the economy and the politics of the country: Mijertein, Hawiye and Isaaq, had been a deliberate test of his strength vis-a-vis the groups concerned. The absence of any reaction encouraged Siad Barre in the pursuit of his goals.

The full weight of the newly formed terror organizations were first brought to bear against the Mijertein clan in the 1970s. Before Siad Barre's coup and ever since independence, they had dominated both the economic and the political spheres of the country — a privileged status which Siad Barre feared would not be easily abandoned by those who had enjoyed it. Through a program of harassment, surveillance, arrests and deliberate restrictions over business opportunities, many important and prominent clan personalities were forced to leave the country and seek refuge in neighboring East African countries and beyond. This unhappy state of affairs ultimately led to a coup attempt, led by young officers in April 1978, followed by the establishment of a movement, the *Somali Salvation Democratic Front* (SSDF) with a military wing based in Ethiopia. Thus was the pioneer movement of direct armed struggle against the regime born.

The response of the regime was direct military action and punitive measures against non-combatant civilian populations throughout their clan homelands in Mudug and Nugal regions, where the capitals were Galkayu and Garowe, respectively. The destruction of water reservoirs in their rural areas was total and indiscriminate. Agents would kill many dissidents by torture or direct murder without accountability. There were neither inquiries nor inquests: just remembered resentment.

In retrospect, Siad's gradual adoption of a disastrous policy to favor his own small clan — the Marehan — and his own extended family against all others, may also be dated from this time. It has been noted that Siad Barre appointed his inept relative, Abdurahman Jama Barre, as foreign minister to replace Omer Arteh. In order to force the acceptance of the new minister who was respected neither by Somalis nor by foreign diplomats, Siad forbade all other ministers from inviting or receiving foreign diplomats working in the country. They were to have nobody else to call on. The prohibition was specifically aimed at the former foreign minister who was popular among the foreign diplomatic community, specially among Afro-Arab ambassadors, whereas Omer Arteh's successor combined incompetence with bad public relations. Yet Siad perceived negative comments or complaints as belittling to himself also.

On the occasion of the national days of the various countries represented in Somalia, Siad Barre would go so far as to nominate who should represent the host country from amongst his most trusted officials. This would be the only occasion on which a minister, even one who held the president's full trust, might accept an invitation from a foreign embassy, even a friendly one, unless one's counterpart was visiting the country, when the embassy concerned might well extend such an invitation. The ban was violated from time to time because it was frequently unworkable.

Very well liked was Ambassador Ali Hussein Miftah, the first ambassador of the State of Qatar to Somalia and dean of the Arab ambassadors. He was leaving the country at the end of a long tour of more than four years. There were numerous invitations and enter-tainment offered by both Somali officials and Arab diplomats. Siad Barre re-issued his banning orders, this time to the extent of instructing his security men to take appropriate action against anyone violating them, which could involve the arrest or questioning of ministers. These new and stiffer orders coincided with the day of a reception by the Sudanese ambassador, one of the countries with whom Somalia was diplomatically close. The reception was thus not well attended by Somalis. I personally attended, defying Siad Barre's orders, because of my deep friendship with both ambassadors, the guest as well as the host. I cannot remember now how many but several such functions were canceled.

There were, in retrospect, discernable patterns in Siad's behavior. Much later, in 1985, the Director of the US Agency for International

Development (USAID), Lou Cohen, organized a party to be a reunion of all Somali participants of USAID sponsored scholarships. The then American ambassador, Mr. Bridges, also attended. Siad Barre posted his own guards with instructions to prevent any Somalis from attending the party. For the first hour or so, to the host's surprise, foreign guests arrived, but not many Somalis, the real guests of honor. Then some of Cohen's Somali staff telephoned and informed him that they had been turned back as had all other Somalis. Both Cohen and the ambassador then came out and witnessed their guests being chased away by Siad Barre's men. The embassy lodged a protest, but received no formal reply.

Some weeks later, Siad Barre, a day or two after his return from a trip to Libya, invited the American ambassador and his seven most senior diplomats to dinner together with some of Siad Barre's senior officials and said that he had heard about that incident and ordered an investigation, but no clues could be found as to who had given the orders. It perplexed many people why Siad Barre would thus antagonize the most important sustainer of his hated regime — the US administration. One theory was that he had wanted to provide Qadaffi with some appearance of anti-Americanism. After the Libyan leader did not respond with generosity — his help fell short of Siad Barre's expectations — the latter might well have had second thoughts about risking the loss of US support.

Siad's conceit, jealousies and underhand tactics were actually pandered to by those close to him, from early times. When Siad Barre's Somali Revolutionary Socialist Party was first established in July 1976, replacing the Supreme Revolutionary Council (SRC), his party demagogues unleashed a campaign aimed at capturing the leading positions in all important institutions of the state. They saw themselves as the legitimate guardians of the newly adopted philosophy of Marxist-Leninist socialism and thus destined to replace the members of the SRC, whom Siad Barre himself was comfortable to dispense with. The rest of us in the government knew we would be the next targets. In the early days of his accession to power, Siad Barre, when commenting upon current developments, frequently boasted that he had predicted one or other prevailing issue. He told me many times

"You can ask Ismail Ali Aboker whether" on such an occasion at such an hour, "when we were planning the revolution I had not told him that would happen." But later, after the establishment of the party and in order to deny the SRC members any legitimacy, Siad developed a new line that the 'revolution' was entirely his own creation and that he had had to summon the rest of the SRC members by telephone at the last minute.

Nevertheless, he kept a close eye on the activities of those SRC members who manifested personal disenchantment with the outcome of the 'revolution' of which they had been the original architects. Siad Barre also made it his practice to attend the most popular functions irrespective of their importance. He would use such occasions as a platform for making speeches. Whenever he was not available himself, he preferred to delegate Vice-President Hussein Kulmiye, his assistant in administrative matters, although Ismail Ali Aboker was also vice-president and his deputy for party affairs, including social organ-izations. In the absence of Siad Barre, party officials reported to Ismail as the protocol incumbent and not to Hussein Kulmiye. On such occasions, Ismail took the opportunity to openly attack the resurgence of corruption and nepotism. Once he disassociated himself from such corrupt practices, claiming a clean record — which in fact was public knowledge — saying that he had even had to borrow from party funds for the burial expenses of his late father. The relationship between the two men deteriorated rapidly. Siad no longer left Ismail behind if he travelled, but would always include him in delegations until his eventual arrest.

Ismail Ali Aboker, a Brigadier-General, had served as military adviser to the OAU Liberation Committee in Dar-es-Salaam and in 1969 had toured all the Frelimo held territory in Mozambique at the latter's request. They sought increased assistance from the OAU for their liberation struggle. General Samatar, whom Siad Barre brought from obscurity to the office of first vice president — because of his low birth he hardly presented a challenge — remained first vice-president for many years. He visited Mozambique in December 1983, as a cover for a subsequent secret arms dealing visit to South Africa. The late respected President Samora Machel received him but had Ismail Ali

Aboker's photograph hanging prominently on the wall in his office. He inquired from the already embarrassed Samatar about Ismail's whereabouts. Samatar remained silent since he could hardly admit that Ismail among other prominent figures had been detained without charge or trial.

Somali groups of low birth (low castes) have frequently allied themselves with one of the major clans, whose identity they also claim for protection purposes. Samatar, therefore, claimed to belong to the Issa Mohamoud of the powerful Mijertein clan. Siad Barre could not have trusted him during his conspiracy but adopted him after the success of his coup d'etat. It was a planned investment and served Siad Barre well. He not only used Samatar's position and his pseudo clan identity to divide the Mijertein; he hoped from the resources of Samatar's position to divide the former SRC members and in particular to drive an irreversible wedge between Ismail Ali Aboker and his own son-in-law Ahmed Suleiman, and between two erstwhile very intimate ex-Sandhurst comrades Ahmed Suleiman and Mohamed Ali Shire, not only relatives but also very close friends. Siad's view of those around him was ever machiavellian.

Both Siad and his cousin Abdurahman Jama Barre were very conscious of their supposed status. Siad journeyed to Washington in May 1981 under the pretext of medical treatment, but in reality since he wanted to get acquainted with President Reagan. He was not received and was bitterly disappointed. It was soon after the American president's recovery from a gunshot wound and he was still following a light schedule. Siad Barre was warned well in advance, but he noted that the prime minister of Japan had been received the week before. He ignored the warning and tried to impose himself which did not work. Siad Barre could not understand that he was not on a par with the prime minister of a leading world economic power. As it was, Secretary of State Alexander Haig took trouble to make a courtesy call on Siad Barre, but the dictator remained disconsolate. He believed only the President mattered, as in his own case — at least as he saw it.

Siad Barre, though ruthless, was of exceptionally strong character, charismatic, persistent and with the stamina to endure setbacks. He also had the capacity to absorb and evaluate almost any kind of information.

Curiously, he would never like false informers to be prosecuted. General Ahmed Suleiman, *Dafle* (the blade), Siad's son-in-law was the head of the National Security Service. He once ordered an arrest for the giving of false information. I remember Siad Barre overruling him and ordering the release of the false informer. He was trying to convince his son-in-law that the false informer could equally well have given true information and that he should never dispense with any informer. He once appointed one such false and unqualified informer as a district commissioner, a promotion I vividly recall, since he had the audacity to remove some bank notes from my wallet while I was having a bath during a tour of his district. Blind loyalty just became a vital criteria in Siad's appointments after his consolidation of power, and some were consequently of the lowest quality. He possessed a shrewd and quite wide knowledge of Somali society, but he also blundered when he ignored the different mentalities and human values particularly of the northerners, whose historical experiences had been different from his. Siad was in all probability capable of himself ordering the physical liquidation of opponents. Cases in point include Ali Sheikh Ibrahim *alias* Ali Heyje; Abdullahi Issa and Mohamed Sudi *Aflaw*.

Ali Heyje was a political lieutenant of the former Djibouti politician and prime minister, Mohamoud Harbi, who was himself killed in a mysterious air crash on the Swiss-French border in 1961. It is sometimes said his death may have aborted a delivery of clandestine arms to Djibouti. During Harbi's struggles in exile, Ali Heyje acted as his secretary. Upon Harbi's death, other Djibouti exiles accused Ali Heyje of keeping Harbi's funds, which he denied, breaking with them and ending his political activities *vis-a-vis* Djibouti. However, he gave the impression of possessing personal wealth, investing in several business ventures and entertaining lavishly. He travelled extensively overseas and associated himself with the foreign intelligence community based in Mogadishu. This drew suspicion during my tenure as head of intelligence and security though he had no known contacts with the Ethiopians. We had opened a dossier on his movements and other activities for future reference. Ali Heyje was known to have once smuggled two members of the Somali parliament into Israel. Not long after the 1961 election, President Aden Abdullah Osman flew via Rome to attend the inaugural conference of the Non-Aligned Movement in Belgrade. On the plane he learned of the unexpected presence of the two M.P.s in the economy section of the *Alitalia* flight which was routed via Aden in the Yemen, Asmara in Eritrea and Khartoum in the Sudan. The president spoke to one of them as the flight left Asmara and inquired where they were going.

Both had voted against Aden Abdullah in the presidential contest, but he had won by one vote, which, although his name was misspelled did not bear the name of any opponent, and so had been declared valid by Jama Abdullahi Ghalib, the President of parliament. Recalling this, they declared not only that their destination was the same as the president's, but that they intended to "declare to the world that his election was invalid."

As the plane neared Rome, the embarrassed president decided to speak with them again there, but he could not, for it transpired they were whisked away that same night to Israel. Somali passports were not valid for Israel, but the immigration authorities did not stamp them, since they were received by Golda Meier, then Israeli foreign minister. Whatever the Israeli motive — and perhaps they were merely establishing contacts as a long term investment — the two M.P.s were clearly seeking financial help with which to ward off any government attempt to supplant them at the next election.

The Somali government was fairly tolerant of this. That it had hoped that Israel would attend the independence celebrations in 1960 has been mentioned. But it was also common knowledge that Israel had supported Somali independence in the crucial General Assembly vote in 1949 and it was believed that Eba Eban, then the Israeli Permanent Representative to the United Nations, had made other valuable contributions to the adoption of the resolution.

However, it was noted that the M.P.s had been met in Rome by Ali Heyje, who had accompanied them and acted as their interpreter in Israel. Through him they were offered an Italian Jew living in Mogadishu, as a contact but they did not trust him and opted for an Israeli diplomatic contact in Nairobi. In the event they decided not to take that up either because of their ignorance of both Hebrew and

English. Unfortunately for such as Ali Heyje, Siad Barre, once he had access to them, frequently misused intelligence files. Solely upon the basis of what was a rather flimsy dossier, immediately upon his accession to power, he ordered Ali Heyje's arrest.

Because of the recognition in those days of the legal concept of 'habeas corpus,' Ali Heyje was acquitted outright, only to be rearrested on Siad Barre's orders before he could even leave the court house compound. Siad then repealed the legal provision of 'habeas corpus' in the criminal procedure code, and Ali Heyje remained in detention until his final and total disappearance. He was apparently executed prior to, or during, September 1975, at the maximum security prison of Labaatan Jirow, thirty miles north-east of Baidoa. Ali was believed to have had Swiss bank accounts which might have contributed to his fate. I personally heard about his liquidation only several years later, despite being the country's minister of the interior at the time. Meantime, the president of the supreme court, Mohamoud Sheikh Ahmed, resigned in protest against the repeal of the *habeas corpus* legal provision and sought residence abroad.

Abdullahi Issa, a close relative of Colonel Salad Gaveire, was arrested in 1971 as his imagined accomplice. A member of the SRC and a former minister of defense, the colonel was considered a rival to Siad Barre. Abdullahi was tortured to death. A number of Marehan officers were also tortured to death by Siad Barre's agents: these included Captain Hassan Halane *Afdhuub,* also known as *Haruuza* or as originally written *Hariisa* and Major Hussein Dirie Shire, also known as Hussein *Aabi.* Then there was Mohamed Sudi *Aflaw,* first arrested after a civil case between himself and an Italian businessman, allegedly over the sale of a consignment of ivory which was transacted through false bank checks during the mid-seventies.

The corrupt story of massive ivory poaching and smuggling — rife in Siad's time — has yet to be told. Mohamed was detained but escaped from Mogadishu prison to neighboring Kenya. Siad Barre's agents tried to smuggle him back from Nairobi with the co-operation of the Kenya security. In the meantime, he obtained a forged Tanzanian passport and claimed citizenship of that country to which he was deported by the Kenyan authorities. Siad Barre later met him in Dar-es-Salaam, treated him kindly and gave him a letter of pardon, to tempt him to return to Somalia. He did that and lived freely only for a few months. In 1979 he was included in Siad Barre's annual pre-October celebrations round-up arrests of those not to be trusted. He remained in detention until his execution, probably in 1984. His earlier arrest and detention may have been a facade for he might well have known too much of the involvement of Siad Barre's senior wife, Khadija, in elephant poaching. The elephant population in Somalia had been all but exterminated and Khadija and other family members are known to have long directed poaching operations, in Kenya and elsewhere. After the successful rising in the North, containers of ivory were noted stranded at Berbera port, marked for shipment to Abu Dhabi. On the other hand, Dallaayad, another of Siad's wives, was never accused of any involvement in corrupt practices, to my knowledge.

Mohamed Siad was an insomniac, staying up almost all night, from sunset until the following morning. He would be asleep most of the day, in the mornings and in the afternoons. Moreover, he would not receive foreigners, including accredited ambassadors, in the early evening and in most cases not before midnight. He considered keeping such hours was a safeguard for his regime and himself and he liked to fish for compliments concerning his long and late working hours. On one occasion in response to Siad Barre's appeal for help, an Arab League delegation visited Somalia to study the refugee situation. They toured all the camps and on their last day were required to make a courtesy call on the President. They were tired and asked if they could be received early that evening. I reported that to Siad but he retorted "Let them know how we work." He wanted to see them at exactly midnight.

I took them for a late dinner at the Azan Roof Garden Restaurant, but could hardly keep them awake even until 10:30 P.M. Thereafter they excused themselves and retired to their rooms in the Hotel Juba. I also went to my house and slept. After I failed to turn up with the delegation at the expected time, the president's guards rang me up after midnight to deliver the message that I should bring the delegation. I had to bluff, saying they had gone out of their hotel with some other Arab diplomats and I did not know where they were. Had I not said that, Siad would have ordered they be awoken even at such a late hour. Before his head injury in 1986, Siad Barre retained the stamina to go without sleep for two or three days. After that he would receive only a limited number of people in the evenings, as his doctors forbade him to work under stress.

Siad lacked many positive qualities of leadership; self discipline among them. A chain-smoker, he always threw cigarette butts on the floor of his office despite the availability of ash trays. His lack of discipline came to be reflected in his system of government and eventually was to bring about the disintegration of the army, formerly the strongest pillar of his power structure. Soviet Ambassador Pasiutin used to ridicule army discipline. After he visited me in my office at police headquarters I took him down the stairs. He commented upon the cleanliness of our corridors and suddenly said, "Army Head-quarters, ah — discipline." Pasiutin deviously played down his country's closeness to Siad Barre when he said to me on another occasion — and not entirely accurately — that all the ongoing co-operation agreements had been signed with the previous civilian governments.

As the years passed, in the absence of any challenge to his actions, Siad Barre reverted to his true character and resorted to unlimited acts of nepotism and corruption. He felt so resourceful that he believed his popularity was inexhaustible. In fact he enjoyed only the semblance of a popular power base being insured against internal criticism by his formidable security apparatus. He retained this overconfidence up to and after his downfall.

But to return to earlier days, the execution of senior officers and detention of potential opponents assured Siad Barre of the absence of serious challenge to his one man rule. The members of the SRC had already been pushed to the sidelines, some driven even to soliciting protection and other favors from rising Marehan figures.

Siad soon felt strong enough to embark upon a policy of controlling — even monopolizing — the national economy. Measures were specifically aimed at crippling the economic base of previously favored groups. He nationalized all banks and private industries and restricted the issue of all important export-import licenses. Out of obscurity, he created a new type of entrepreneur from his own clan.

Abdi Hosh, a government driver when Siad Barre seized power, is one example. But despite all their political access and support, the likes of Abdi Hosh could not compete with experienced businessmen. Siad Barre therefore adopted a system of naked harassment meted out by his security agents against the traditional business community. The latter found themselves unable to contact visiting foreign principals. They could not meet them at the airport nor could they visit them in their hotels. Likewise, they could not visit foreign embassies, even to secure visas, without first going through a security interrogation. Meanwhile Siad Barre's newly created novice businessmen were free to do all that was denied to the ordinary businessmen. All tendering for government purchases was restricted to the novices and a new Chamber of Commerce established to implement Siad Barre's economic policies. Some businessmen fled the country; others gave up their businesses, but many fought the system and eventually rendered it ineffective, mainly by bribing Siad Barre's security agents. Many leading businessmen felt obliged to pay to retain the protection of top security officers.

In 1982, two ministers, Ahmed Mohamed 'Silanyo' (Commerce) and Ali Khalif Galayd (Industries), in their capacities as members of the Cabinet Economic Committee, objected to the award of a fuel import contract to Abdi Hosh, considering his bid was far from the best offer. Siad Barre then canceled the whole tender. It could not then be awarded to the lowest bidder. A few days later, he dropped the two ministers in a government reshuffle and Abdi Hosh was then granted a permanent franchise for fuel imports which remained in force until Siad Barre's fall, after which Abdi sought refuge abroad.

Siad Barre continued to promote the worst kind of economic practices, the consequences of which he should have foreseen could only lead to disaster. In the late nineteen seventies, when the rate of inflation, which had been inconsequential before he seized power, began to rise alarmingly, Siad Barre simply ordered the banks to change his protégés Somali shillings into US dollars at the official rate of six point three to one US dollar. Those involved were often not even superficially engaged in commercial transactions or other legitimate business activities. Afterwards they would change their newly acquired

US dollars on the black market back into shillings again at a rate of twenty or more. Those Somali Shillings could in turn find their way into the bank to buy yet more dollars. Indeed, that was often how Siad's novice entrepreneurs came into the business world in the first place. Well connected but totally inexperienced youngsters, office clerks and the like, could obtain foreign exchange in order to take holiday trips or to buy cars in Europe. At one time beneficiaries included prominent former political detainees — including some northerners — who had mended fences with Siad. General Mohamed Abshir was so invited, but refused. It is hardly surprising that in due course the black market exchange rate rose as high as several thousand Somali shillings to one US dollar.

Successive ministers of finance shamefully and immorally seized foreign exchange holdings from the private accounts of bank clients, including the United Nations agencies and other international organizations, in order to finance Siad Barre's extravagances: the maintenance of an unnecessarily large number of sometimes over-staffed embassies; spurious official trips abroad and his insatiable purchase of arms on the black market. The nation became debt-ridden, bankrupt, and totally bereft of foreign exchange reserves. Meanwhile numerous secret foreign accounts were privately operated by Siad Barre's family and cronies. He and many of his ministers would even divert Somali shillings from various private accounts without the depositors' knowledge, let alone consent. In the late 1980s, the public stopped depositing money into the banks, resulting in serious cash flow and availability problems and their eventual collapse. The Commercial and Savings Bank of Somalia was a case in point.

CHAPTER TWELVE

NEW POLICIES
AND DECISIONS

A PART FROM HIS ATTEMPT to introduce 'scientific socialism,' which was bound eventually to fail in as deeply a religious and individualistic society as that of the Somalis, Siad Barre did effect some innovations of lasting importance. One of them was quite positive: the writing of the Somali script. The other was Somalia's membership of the Arab League. Neither could have been realized without a dictatorial regime, for both lacked any common parliamentary consensus during the previous civilian governments.

With regard to the writing of the Somali language, the whole nation had long been aware of its desirability, but remained divided on specifics at all levels of society. Some groups favored Arabic characters, others favored Latin, while a third were in favor of a new script. The political courage to make a decision was lacking. The Supreme Revolutionary Council (SRC) led by Major General Mohamed Siad Barre committed itself to addressing this important issue and in fact it was one of the thirteen points of the Revolutionary Charter. After interviewing various researchers and promoters of the alternative scripts, the SRC debated the subject, but found itself as divided as its predecessors. Siad Barre had to shelve the issue for almost two years.

In 1971, an SRC delegation visited China to discuss the building, by the Chinese, of 962 kilometers of tarmac road linking Belet-Wein and Burao, in effect the South and the North of the country. Siad Barre had asked for Belet-Wein to Bosaso and the current road was only made possible by the presence of a northern economist among the Somali delegation who argued the economic advantage of a link with Burao. The Chinese Government had sent a survey team who examined the alternatives and opted for Burao. Much the same thing applied to the Burao-Berbera road financed by the United Arab Emirates which not only shortened the distance to Sheikh Pass, but also realigned the entire route and widened it to two lanes in order that it could be used by traffic in both directions without any time restrictions. This too was only made possible by the fact that the Somali negotiating team was led by a northern minister. Anyway, at the end of its visit to China the delegation was received by Chairman Mao Zedong, who must have been following developments in 'Revolutionary Somalia' for he questioned delegation members on when they were going to introduce a Somali script, and with what characters. They had no answers and Mao realized that the decision would be reserved for the 'Revolutionary leader.' He then remarked, "whatever you do, do not make the same mistake we made. After all these years, China is now considering transcribing its script into Latin in order to share technology with the advanced world."

Upon its return, the delegation reported Mao's remarks and there and then the SRC decided on the Latin script, but announcement was deferred until October 1972. Mao Zedong should perhaps be given the credit for enabling the Somali language to be written at so early a date, rather than Siad Barre, but nevertheless it remains the greatest achievement of the latter's regime. Another important factor which may well have contributed to the choice of the Latin script was the opinion of the Soviets, who also favored it. They had great influence upon Siad Barre despite his stubbornness. Soviet Ambassador Pasiutin once advised me at a North Korean embassy reception, that it would be very difficult for them should the Somali language be written in Arabic or in any script other than Latin.

With regard to membership of the Arab League, another of Siad's innovations, many Somalis questioned whether it was at all necessary to join. Had the Arabs themselves ever accepted the Somalis as genuine Arabs? The Charter of the Arab League itself defines Arabs as those bound together by a common culture, not necessarily Islamic, because many Arabs do not subscribe to the Islamic faith, and having the same language (Arabic) as their mother tongue. Although the Somalis probably provide the greatest number of Arabic speaking people of any non-Arab nation, not counting Sudan or Egypt, Arabic is neither their native language nor do the majority speak it at all. Some of the Somali vocabulary derives from roots in ancient Arabic — a fact sometimes cited to support the legendary origin of the patriarchal ancestors of leading clan families such as the Darod and the Isaaq — but linguists do not classify Somali as a Semitic language.

Furthermore, Somalis do not fully conform to the common Arabic cultural heritage. Jihan el-Sadat, the wife of the former Egyptian president states in her book, *The Woman of Egypt* (page 470) ". . . that every Arab country except Oman and the Sudan having severed diplomatic relations with Egypt." She refers to the period following Egypt's peace agreement with Israel. She makes no mention of Somalia, the third member of the Arab League that did not sever diplomatic relations with her country. She was complaining about the actions of fellow Arabs and it follows therefore, that to her, being Arab is one thing, while membership of the Arab League is another. She did not equate being a member of the Arab League with being Arab, seeing Somalia as just one of the many countries with which Egypt had friendly relations.

However, every Arab leader enthusiastically embraced and supported Somalia's application for membership in the Arab League in 1974 and acceptance was unanimous. That did not reflect a sense of Arabness on the part of the Somalis, but rather a reflection of a common destiny of two peoples, the Arabs and the Somalis, as a result of historical bonds, geographical proximity, trade connections and of course the bond of Islam. These affinities which tie the two peoples together would always be there whether or not Somalia had joined the Arab League. Such interrelationships between the Somalis and the Arabs, and particularly with countries like neighboring Yemen, are as old as history itself. They remain natural and have worked through the centuries to the mutual benefit of both sides. Similar particular relations have always existed between the Somalis and the Arabs in the Gulf.

The beneficiary from membership of the League of Arab States was Siad Barre himself rather than the Somali people. Most Arab leaders adopted him and sustained his totalitarian regime at the expense of the Somali populace. Support from many Arab governments for the repressive regime of Siad Barre, both financial and military, was to be mercilessly used against the civilian population particularly during the destruction of the northern cities and settlements.

Egypt too had especial historical ties with the Somalis in the North, withdrawing as a colonial power as late as 1876. Egypt also contributed greatly to the realization of Somalia's independence, especially in the South, during the United Nations Trusteeship era. She later provided a great deal of military training. Perhaps that explains the reasons why the Egyptian leader of that era, former President Gamal Abdel Nasser, is still held in very high esteem in Somalia. Egypt also provided large-scale educational assistance to Somalia from the pre-independence period continuously until the country's recent disintegration.

Consequently, few issues have ever been more hotly debated by Siad Barre's rubber stamp institutions than that of whether or not to break diplomatic relations with Egypt after Camp David. The Soviet Union wanted to seize the opportunity of settling scores with President Anwar el-Sadat for having ended their political influence over Egyptian affairs. The whole eastern bloc were supporting a general Arab boycott of Egypt. The majority of the members of the relevant Somali institutions belonged to the younger generation and those Siad Barre had brought from obscurity. They had all acquired their political orientation in or from the Soviet Union or other eastern bloc countries. When Siad Barre adjusted his relations with those countries during and after the Ogaden war, many members of his 'new society' abandoned him. Anything not approved of by the Soviet Union was to those people anti-socialist — and that included some of the actions of China, the largest socialist state.

It was at a central committee meeting of the Somali Revolutionary Socialist Party, chaired by Siad himself, that members of his 'new society' attuned to the communist music against President Sadat's Egypt, called for the breaking of diplomatic ties on the pretext that Somalia could not afford to lose the support of the overwhelming

SOMALI DEMOCRATIC REPUBLIC

BAR COUNCIL
(Commissione Forense)

CERTIFICATE OF ENROLMENT OF ADVOCATE

(Articles 95 and 96 of the Organisation of Judiciary Law, 1956)

This is to certify that ____ MR. JAMA MOHAMED GHALIB ____

whose photograph is affixed to this certificate has been enrolled in

the ~~ORDINARY ROLL~~ ~~OF ADVOCATES~~ with effect from ___ 2nd July, 1970
SPECIAL ROLL

Mogadiscio, ___ 5th July, 1970.

Chief Registrar, Supreme Court
Secretary, Bar Council.

(Mohamoud Sheikh Ahmed)
President, Supreme Court
Chairman, Bar Council.

The author today, his first
qualification as a lawyer, and the
identity card which he was issued as
Commissioner of Police, back in
1969.

The camel herds I left behind but never forgot.

Most of my country is a dry, sunny and beautiful savanna, suitable for pasturalism, but lands near the rivers, the Webi Shaballe, seen here N.N.E. of Mogadishu, and the Juba, can support quite rich agriculture, harvesting crops such as paw–paw (as below), sugar, bananas, etc.

Elders and children in the north, not far from Berbera.

Traditional Somali culture is rich in poetry, oral tradition and dance.

GOVERNMENT INSTRUCTIONS

Issued under the authority of the Acting

chief Secretary to the Government.

HARGEYSA   31st   JULY, 1957

_____

NO. 52/57   CURRENCY

    The last date notified in Government instruction No. 29/57 Concerning
the withdrawal from circulation of the state notes for 100 and 50 lire has
been extended and they Should now reach Rome not later than 30/9/1957 and
31/12/1957 respectively.

PART II

LAW EXAMINATIONS

    The following passes were obtained in the law Examination held in Hargeisa
on 22nd and 23rd July:-

    Sub-inspector jama Mohamed khalib (with credit)

    Mr. G.F.D. Hazlewood

    Sgt. ali Haji Adan

    Mr. D. Jacob

PART III

NIL

(I.G. COGHILL)

For ACTING CHIEF SECRETARY TO THE GOVERMENT.

Not all of even the flatter plateau country is hot semi-desert. A pass, part of which is to be seen above, leads up to Sheikh, where I studied in 1956; it is a very steep climb and I found the college extremely cold at night. The following year, down in the often humid warmth of Berbera, I learned with delight that the then colonial government had announced my success in the law examinations.

A Somali artist's portrayal of the controversial Somali nationalist, Seyyid Mohamed Abdille Hassan, the "poor man of God," who was dubbed the "mad mullah" by the British imperialists. His monument (below left) recalls his fortress at Taleh (below right). The statue was knocked off its plinth, one night in March 1991, smuggled out from the chaos in Mogadishu to the United Arab Emirates and sold as scrap metal.

Abdurashid Ali Shermarke, pictured above when he was prime minister (1960–64). He stood successfully in 1967, for the office of president, only to be assassinated by a policeman, on 15 October, 1969. Right is the "official" picture of Major General Mohamed Siad Barre who led the so-called "bloodless coup" to seize power, a few days later, on 24 October, 1969.

In the north, the fine city of Hargeisa, former capital of the British Protectorate, was soon neglected, international assistance was discouraged and even self-help frustrated. Pictured is a Somali doctor and an international colleague, in this instance from China. Eventually, all the terrors of modern warfare — including mercenaries — were unleashed upon it and it was razed almost to the ground 1989–90 as well as infested with landmines and anti-personnel devices. Meantime Mogadishu was beautified and received grossly disproportionate effort and investment, only to suffer similar destruction in the uprising of 1990–91, the ensuing civil strife and international intervention in 1993–94.

The Western Somali Liberation Forces, even with the full support of the Somali Armed Forces, were no match for the Soviet equipped and led Ethio-Cuban armies they had to face. They are pictured here in Jigjiga in 1977 and early 1978, just before their defeat later that year.

Omer Arteh Ghalib, the most successful Somali foreign minister, for years held as a political prisoner, and his successor, Abdurahman Jama Barre, a cousin of the dictator.

In 1979, surviving Russian-built tanks rumble past huge posters of the junta — the SRC — marking the tenth anniversary of the coup d'etat (by then termed a "revolution").

A view over the city center of Mogadishu. On the right is the Roman Catholic cathedral, inside which the Italian bishop was murdered by an assassin who fled to the presidency. The cathedral was fired during the 1990–91 popular uprising and later bombed during civil conflict in 1993.

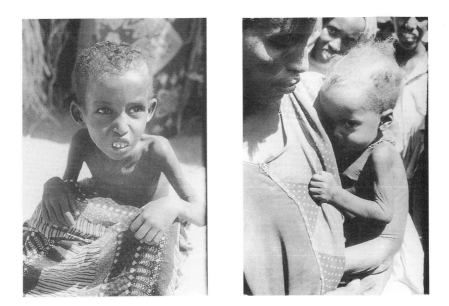

Despite the distressing plight of the refugees who flooded into the country in the wake of the Ogaden debacle, the regime sought to exploit the assistance provided through international goodwill, by conspiracies to falsify their statistics, by diverting their food, arming them and encouraging them to oppose and dispossess disquieted sections of the population.

At home, children and youths, inspired by patriotic fervor, were indoctrinated with "scientific socialism," atheism and the dictator's own vain personality cult. However, abroad, beyond the reach of the regime's several "security" organizations, students — even some from leading families and the dictator's own clan — and other emigre Somalis, took to the streets. Below, they are seen peacefully demonstrating outside the White House, during one of the dictator's visits to the US capital. Opposition escalated throughout the 1980s and responsible ministers and diplomats defected.

Siad Barre at home and abroad, haranguing the citizens of Mogadishu and attending the OAU Summit in July 1979, held that year in Monrovia, Liberia. (picture courtesy of *Africa Report*).

On March 6, 1991, a tank, knocked out before the dictator's flight to the south, still lies abandoned near the 1971 pedestal from which the statue of Hawa Osman Tako — a girl killed by an arrow during riots which accompanied the visit of the Four Power Commission in 1948 — had been looted in the confusion. In 1992, the less accessible Degahtur monument of a patriotic stone-throwing youth, erected in 1970, suffered a similar fate.

The new French and US embassy compounds were sacked and local employees of the British embassy, who stayed at their posts for months after the diplomats had departed, are seen indicating the spot from where looters dynamited their way into the top-secret area. They dragged the safe into the compound and blew it up, only to find it empty. They then tore down all the embassy ceilings in a vain search for hidden money.

The central stores of the police, completely stripped by looters in early 1991. Even so, the damage to the city, though extensive, did not equal that caused in 1992 by conflict between factions of the USC or during the 1993 resistance to the attempted arrest of Brig. General Aidid. Below is the Mogadishu residence of Ali Mahdi Mohamed, destroyed after he was declared interim president without the full agreement of all parties.

Former ambassador and Brigadier General Mohamed Farah Aidid is seen in a neighborhood in southern Mogadishu in November 1992, before its destruction by US Special Forces during the ill-advised manhunt for him mounted by the United Nations in 1993.

With the destruction of the infrastructure and institutions of the Somali state, a generation has grown up lacking education, direction and appropriate role models, their plight compounded by easy access to an abundance of sophisticated weaponry irresponsibly abandoned in our area by superpowers and others. Who has benefited from the vast expenditures of recent years? Certainly not the Somali people, whether they be in Somaliland or Somalia. The tasks ahead are indeed daunting.

majority of Arab countries by choosing to ally itself with the isolated Arab Republic of Egypt. Ironically, until that time these members had tended to be against the majority of Arab countries (reflecting the overall policy of the Soviet Union).

There was strong opposition to their Communist inspired rhetoric, but specially three of us, Abdulqassim Salad, Omer Arteh and myself, hit them hard. Although we were a minority, we held one important card — Siad Barre himself did not favor cutting off relations with Egypt. However he was worried about losing the support of the wealthier Arabs at a time when his finances were depleted as a result of the Ogaden war. When I took the floor, I argued that no Somali government had a mandate to sever relations with Egypt without going to a referendum. Siad Barre saw a way out and whispered to someone sitting next to him, asking "How long will it take us to organize a referendum?" At the end of the debate, he concluded that we should continue to study the subject. I knew we had won. He would never allow a vote to be taken unless he was sure of winning it but in any case there would be no referendum because he would never want to set a precedent for popular decision making. That was his prerogative and he guarded it jealously.

Coincidentally, Mr. Ahmed Salah Boukhari, the former — in fact the first — Sudanese ambassador to Somalia, then in retirement, paid a visit to Mogadishu. We were very good friends and I visited him in his hotel as soon as I learned of his presence. I invited him to lunch the next day and included some of Siad Barre's top aides to facilitate an early meeting with Siad. I suspected he might have been sent by President Gaafar Numeiri to find out whether Somalia would break relations with Egypt. Not only was he very well known and liked by Somalis, but he had known Siad Barre and worked closely with him during the 1964 Khartoum Peace Agreement, mediated by the Sudan Government of President Ibrahim Abboud, between Ethiopia and Somalia. I spoke with him again before he left: "Look Ahmed, I don't know if it is what you want to know, but I can tell you that we are not going to break relations with Egypt. It is not in the interest of the Somali people." He indicated that he appreciated my remark but did not directly comment — always a shrewd diplomat.

Meantime, Siad Barre sent Omer Arteh to the Gulf countries. Although Omer had already been replaced as foreign minister, the incumbent, Siad Barre's cousin Abdurahman Jama Barre, simply could not be trusted to undertake such an important mission. Omer started with Saudi Arabia and met Prince Sultan. To his surprise not one Arab leader showed any great interest in which way Somalia went. Nor were the more conservative states much concerned by the repressive tendencies of the Somali regime: they just supported the leadership.

Even after April 1988, when Siad Barre concluded a peace accord with Ethiopia which removed any external threat, Arab military and financial assistance from the Gulf continued until late 1989. Likewise, until the last hours of his rule, Libyan military assistance was in the pipeline. Regrettably, no Arab government helped the hundreds of thousands of Somali victims of Siad Barre whose homes were destroyed with Arab military assistance and who were forced to flee their country, crossing the borders into Djibouti, Ethiopia, Kenya and countries beyond, as refugees. Nor did most Arab governments, except Syria, the Yemen and Djibouti accept many of those displaced.

Few Arab countries significantly supported the international assistance efforts for refugees, possibly out of respect for Siad Barre who would always sell the Somali vote to the highest bidder if there was squabbling within the Arab League. One Gulf country paid him two million US$ for the Somali vote during the transfer of the organization's seat from Tunis and he is said to have been paid a further seventy million US$ for the symbolic involvement of Somalia in the Gulf war, on the side of the anti Iraq coalition. Most of this money was deposited in foreign banks by the Siad Barre family.

International aid for the suffering Somalis was mustered mainly by the western Christian powers, people and church organizations. It must be said, however, that the responses of the Arabs to the Afghanistan conflict were the opposite: governments positively supported both diplomatically and financially, the oppressed people fighting a similar totalitarianism. Perhaps they were exhausted—but the whole refugee tragedy became so important, it demands separate examination and this follows.

CHAPTER THIRTEEN

REFUGEES

T HE ORDINARY SOMALI PASTORALIST enjoyed a decent and dignified way of life which reflected his deep rooted values and nomadic cultural background. Always in constant pursuit of a better life, self-confident and fearless, he was prone to impossible ventures and has throughout history taken easily to foreign travel. It follows that the overwhelming majority of such travellers were not literate and they accepted fairly menial employment. It is not hard even today to find Somali seamen on many foreign ships and in many foreign ports. The Somali people were numerically few compared with neighboring populations. They could, however, be found in almost every corner of the globe since well before the turn of the twentieth century—a circumstance somewhat facilitated in the case of nationals of the former British Somaliland Protectorate, by the extent of the erstwhile British empire, as they would carry British passports.

Even before the Second World War, there were established and quite large Somali communities in several countries of the world, in particular, the United Kingdom, the United States of America, the Arabian Peninsula and in neighboring East African countries. Other Somali nationals or persons of ethnic Somali origin were to be found almost everywhere, although in smaller numbers and there was hardly a country that could not claim the presence of some Somalis. There were Somalis too, on the other side of every international 'border', in Djibouti, Ethiopia and Kenya and across the gulf waters in Aden and Socotra.

Being neither literate, nor possessors of a written script for their own language, the Somalis' culturally vibrant oral society was among

the biggest users of the radio, and later also of the telephone. Their
heavy dependency on the radio accounts for Somali being one of only
three African languages on the BBC Overseas Service. The other,
being Hausa, because it is spoken by the majority of Nigerians, the
most populous African nation and beyond and Swahili which is spoken
in some eleven countries in east and central Africa. Today, twenty years
after the writing of the Somali script, when most Somalis abroad
can write their own language, even educated Somalis continue to
prefer to make expensive use of the telephone for even trivial matters.
Others tape live voice messages through the BBC to relatives scattered in many parts of the world rather than send letters or telegrams
which would be much cheaper. The Somali Service, with its daily
variety of programs of world news, comment, condolences, information about wanted relatives, greetings, entertainment, congratu-
lations for marriages and childbirth, etc., is the busiest of all BBC
overseas programs.

Many Somali people, traditionally democratic and fond of their
individual freedoms, were averse to control and management and
found it impossible to co-exist with, or tolerate, the sudden emergence
of a totalitarian regime. Many felt forced or chose to flee their own
country, which transformed the normal Somali travelling patterns into
mass migration. They were often scorned, not unexpectedly, in the
countries of their new asylum. There will always be dropouts, failures,
delinquents and criminals in any society. Somali overseas communities,
before the rule of Siad Barre, exhibited the least number of such cases
in comparative terms. Likewise, foreigners would at one time single
out Mogadishu as the safest city in Africa.

The world had never known, before Siad Barre, the mass
migration of Somali families; women, teenagers and children
unaccompanied by male family heads, in search of sanctuary or
adoption. The world had never seen armies of Somali women,
who out of desperation and humiliation would turn to prostitution
as a last resort to earn a livelihood. The world had never, before
Siad Barre, discovered planeloads of Somalis all carrying forged
passports, nor apprehended Somali travellers involved in the international drug trade. These became commonplace and the world

grew alarmed at the notoriety of the influx, as much as decent Somalis have become distressed. Yet despite the many problems the Somali influx has presented, several countries of the world have generously accepted large numbers of refugees even at the cost of inconvenience to their own societies, the Scandinavian countries, Holland, Germany, the United Kingdom and Canada are cases in point.

Not all countries under dictatorship produced similar influxes and world opinion did not easily understand or bestow any special sympathy on the Somalis, not being familiar with the particular characteristics of our people. While in many societies, at least for a time, repressed people would submit or succumb, Somalis would either resort to violence or leave. The latter signifies admission of defeat. One would be justified in asking why, during 21 years, did not even one of the many oppressed Somalis take the bold step of physically liquidating their oppressor? One reason is that the Somalis are only skilled at guerilla (nomadic) warfare. They lack the patience and perhaps the discretion necessary for planning an urban assassination. Significantly, President Shermarke's assassin was a trained policeman and not an ordinary nomad.

Somali opposition to Siad Barre and his regime, wherever it might be, both inside and outside the country, was unanimous in its belief — and so advised the outside world through international donor community representatives — that the flow of assistance for Somalis which was being donated to the corrupt regime, was just sustaining it and thus was actually undermining the democratic process which the western world championed. The biggest such abuse was of assistance meant for the refugee programs inside the country, channelled through the United Nations High Commissioner for Refugees (UNHCR) and the Somali Government. Siad Barre and his close officials sought always to divert it and to double the actual number of refugees on which it was based so that at least half of the food allocation would go directly to the Somali army.

The distortion of refugee statistics did not go unnoticed by international observers. Norman Miller, writing in the 1982 (Volume 5, number 3) edition of the *Horn of Africa* had this to say:

At all levels, including the top, one practice is universal: over-counting refugees. Whether to get greater inflows of food or other aid, greater sympathy and wider international news coverage, it is apparently expedient for the refugee officers to grossly inflate totals. At the lower levels, for essentially the same reason, camp figures remain overstated and inaccurate.

Moreover, more than half of the supposed refugee community would be armed, many of them by forced conscription, to fight for the regime, not only in Western Somalia but also against other clans who were their host civilian population. This led to many refugees being killed, for years mainly in the north, but later also in the south, in the area of Belet-Wein.

I was minister of the interior, later redesignated minister of local government and rural development, when the influx of Ethiopian refugees started in earnest to cross into Somalia at the end of the Ogaden war early in 1978. Siad Barre quickly posted some army officers of his own clan to the refugee camps to maintain order. These officers would coerce the civilians employed there to double the registered number of the refugees but the suspicion of UNHCR officials, the press and other international observers was soon aroused. Siad Barre's selected men, although they officially reported to me, did not provide me with true and accurate reports. However, I was personally alerted by a German journalist who had visited the refugee camps and made in depth investigations after he had heard rumors of the deliberate inflation of the refugee count. He briefed me in confidence, but admitted he would not want to publish the story because it might restrain or even halt international assistance; there were, after all, many genuine refugees in desperate need who would be affected.

At the same time, I received confirmed reports of the large-scale theft of food rations. In the early stages of the arrival of the refugees, before donated food pledges could be delivered, we were compelled as an emergency step to borrow supplies of rations from the state-owned Commercial Distributing Agency (ENCE). There was to be replacement in kind later. I learned that ENCE officials were properly selling the replaced rations to the public, but with the import markings,

"UNHCR," etc. unobliterated. Siad Barre's officials at the refugee camps then dishonestly took advantage of that arrangement to sell stolen rations on the market long after UNHCR supplied rations in stock were adequate and the emergency replacement exchange with ENCE had ceased. At that juncture, I transferred some of the more corrupt of Siad Barre's men starting with a certain notorious *Irris*, whose name had become a legend among the donor representatives. He was, I learned later, married to Siad Barre's crippled niece. Naturally I clashed with the president and this contributed to the eventual removal of refugee affairs from my ministry. A National Refugee Commission (NRC) was created with ministerial status for its head, entitled Extraordinary Commissioner for Refugees.

I resolved to tackle the problem at source and remove the distribution of food and all assistance to the refugees from control by Siad's corrupt nominees. I did not realize how difficult this would prove and I had little time before the new authority, the NRC, took over. The ministry of planning was the government negotiator with the UN agencies and the donor community. Fortunately I enjoyed the confidence and co-operation of its upright vice-minister Mohamed Omer Jama, known as *Dhigi-Dhigi*. We assisted the UNHCR to seek an outside distribution authority to be known as the emergency logistics unit under international contract. A private United States group CARE which, although it is rarely used in full, actually stands for Cooperative for Assistance and Relief Everywhere, won the contract to deliver food rations to the refugee camps.

Siad Barre was livid and in consequence a UNHCR official, Jiddo Van Drunen of Holland was declared *persona non grata*. I personally took up the latter's case with the UN High Commissioner for Refugees, then Paul Hartling of Denmark, and confirmed my entire satisfaction with Van Drunen's loyalty to his duties and honest performance. Being the minister responsible for refugee affairs I knew well that Siad Barre would resist an independent distribution contract, or for that matter, an independent assessment of refugee numbers, since that, to say the least, would limit his ability to violate the norms of international co-operation. *Dhigi-Dhigi* and I, therefore quietly agreed that the contract be solely UNHCR's affair, so that the regime could be kept at a distance; that way it could all be approved.

It was then the end of March 1981, and I was almost immediately to leave for Geneva, still the incumbent minister, to attend the first large International Conference for Assistance to Refugees in Africa (ICARA I). In my speech I pointed out that the High Commissioner and his deputy had already recognized the refugee problem in Somalia as "the most serious in the world." I called for a long as well as a short-term plan of action and asked that the root causes of refugee flows be addressed and appropriate solutions found "based on respect for peoples rights and human dignity."

After the conference I proceeded to New York to attend the follow up meeting of the Economic and Social Council (ECOSOC) of the United Nations. Then I travelled to Washington and, after a meeting with Mr. Chester Crocker, the assistant secretary of state for African affairs at the State Department, I was asked if I would meet a senior lady official, Mrs. Taft, who was in charge of humanitarian assistance. She asked me if I had known that a US service organization, CARE, had entered into a logistics contract with UNHCR. When I answered in the affirmative, she surprised me by asking what the Somali government's objection was to that contract. Neither of us had an adequate brief but I realized I was entering into another tussle with Siad Barre.

Mrs. Taft suggested that on my return to New York I should see the general manager of CARE, a Mr Philip Johnson. It was a friday and I was going to New York the following day. Ten o'clock on monday morning a telephone in the UN lobby rang for anyone from the Somali UN mission. A representative from CARE wanted to arrange the meeting and learning that CARE's head office was only a few blocks from my hotel, I called there at 5:00 P.M. that same day. I met Philip Johnson; exasperated, I asked him "how the hell did the Somali government come to get involved in a UNHCR contract?" It appeared that CARE, having to take over government owned facilities in the old port from the UNHCR, in order to have a safeguard against later being asked to vacate those facilities, had themselves initiated action designed to make the contract tripartite. Thus Siad Barre got into the picture and the difficulties began. A lot of money was at stake but I remained determined to save the refugees as much as the donors from corrupt exploitation.

Abdi Mohamed Tarrah, the new extraordinary commissioner for refugees, took the draft contract agreement to the council of ministers for approval. Siad Barre burst into fury and rebuked Mohammed Omer Jama *Dhigi-Dhigi,* the vice-minister of planning, for not being open in keeping the president informed of such 'important matters'. The vice-minister defended himself, insisting that the contract was a UNHCR affair and had nothing to do with the Somali government; the recipient CARE's preference for a tripartite agreement which did involve the government was a new development, he added. Nevertheless, Siad Barre used that meeting of the council to reject the tripartite agreement.

Dhigi-Dhigi, along with Ahmed Silanyo, was one of the few remaining intellectuals in Siad Barre's rubber stamp institutions. As such I judged him capable of negating Siad Barre's pretensions if drawn into an argument, recalling that Siad Barre had once proposed, after a rigged referendum over his constitution, to announce that Somalia's population was ten million. Silanyo as chairman of the economic committee challenged him and explained the prerequisites for arriving at any reliable population estimate. Siad interrupted, as he often would when he did not like a speaker, and criticized him for only echoing foreign concepts based upon western-style expensive methodology. Silanyo remained standing, knowing that if he sat down, Siad Barre would not give him the floor again. When Siad's waffle petered out, Silanyo continued, simply stating that he still believed his reasoning was valid, but he added that were he to take the president at his word, it would imply the failure of the 'revolution', because there were not enough schools, hospitals, to serve etc. even a fraction of ten million people. Siad Barre's carefully conceived proposal crumbled to the floor. He sweated and glowered but never raised that subject again; he could not bear any suggested failure of his 'revolution'.

Philip Johnson told me he would be in Mogadishu the following monday but if meantime no agreement was reached he would then pull out the personnel he had already in place. At that time I did not know about developments in the council of ministers so advised him to contact my trusted colleague, the vice-minister of planning in order to discuss his problems, adding that I would also alert him. Before leaving Washington I learnt from the Somali ambassador that Siad Barre was coming to the United States supposedly for medical treatment, but actually because he wanted to shake hands with President Reagan. He was not received and felt terribly bitter afterwards, but nevertheless, the trip paid off in the longer term, as the Reagan administration committed itself to sustaining Siad's totalitarian regime.

I returned to Geneva the following Friday hoping to see the High Commissioner for Refugees before returning to Somalia, but he had travelled to Mexico. Siad Barre was due to arrive in Rome on sunday morning. I went to meet him and to call on certain World Food Program (WFP) officials. I arrived, was met and the ambassador arranged a room on the second floor of the Grand Hotel, all of which was reserved for Siad Barre and his large entourage. Everybody was asleep as they had been travelling throughout the previous night. At last I met one minister who greeted me with the disturbing news that the council had rejected the tripartite agreement for the CARE contract.

The matter was strictly Tarrah's responsibility but the minister briefed me because of my previous involvement with refugee affairs. He recounted Siad's wrath against *Dhigi-Dhigi*. I saw the president later that same evening and briefed him about my trip before raising the refugees logistics contract. Siad instantly shouted, "No contract". I explained to him that the reason which had prompted the UNHCR to enter into that contract in the first place was that there was reasonable suspicion of corruption from which it was in the best interest of the Somali government to distance itself. I also warned that rejection would arouse further suspicion. The credibility of his government was at stake. He kept silent, but I knew that he was not yielding. I resolved to interpret his silence 'legally' — that acquiescence implies consent. He was leaving the following morning for Washington and I excused myself from not being able to see him off at the airport as I had a prior engagement with the WFP. I had a little time, but Philip Johnson was due in Mogadishu the following day and I had still to fulfill my promise of contacting *Dhigi-Dhigi*.

In the morning, I telephoned Ahmed Habib, minister of planning, who was then also in Rome, but staying in another hotel, to obtain the telex number of his ministry, and sent an urgent message to *Dhigi-Dhigi* informing him of Philip Johnson's arrival adding that I had briefed the president. I wanted to encourage *Dhigi-Dhigi* to commit the Somali government to the agreement, but unbeknown to me he had washed his hands of that matter after Siad Barre had blamed him. He only passed on my message to Tarrah, the new extra-ordinary commissioner for refugees.

Habib had been at the airport to see the president off and when I called on him in the evening, he asked me why I had needed his telex number. I told him of the message I had sent to his Vice-Minister. He asked me the president's view but when I said that he had neither agreed nor disagreed, Habib contradicted me. It appears the president had taken him aside and told him to convey to Lieut. General Samatar, the acting president, the message that he should never accept the CARE contract. Furthermore, the president had complained to Habib about his vice-minister's unilateral actions. Both Habib and I were returning to Mogadishu the following Friday and I asked Habib to keep the matter to himself until he had seen Samatar. Next day, Tuesday, I returned to Geneva hoping that *Dhigi-Dhigi* would by then have finalized the contract.

On Wednesday, I met both the High Commissioner and his Director of Finance, Dr. Zolner, who had just been to Mogadishu where he had met Siad Barre who had flatly stated that he would never accept the contract, although neither of the two high UNHCR officials revealed that to me: they only expressed concern and anxiety were the logistics contract not to be approved. I spoke optimistically. But in the afternoon two officials from the US humanitarian office in Geneva, who had heard about my presence there, asked to see me and raised the same subject. When I expressed my optimism, they were quite frank. Unlike the UNHCR officials, they revealed that Dr. Zolner had been to Mogadishu and had seen Siad Barre who had unequivocally rejected the contract. Shaken, I nevertheless told them that Dr. Zolner could not speak for my president and I over-confidently pulled out of my brief case a copy of the telex message I had sent to *Dhigi-Dhigi* which fortunately I had written in English, and gave it to them. They seemed reassured when they read that I had briefed the president.

Two days later on Friday evening, I joined Habib at Rome airport and together we flew to Mogadishu, arriving there at six o'clock the following morning. I rushed to see *Dhigi-Dhigi* and only then learnt that he had distanced himself from the matter. Prospects did not look good. After all, I had already been relieved of my responsibilities in connection with the refugees; was I being too conscientious to fight against Siad Barre's corruption? I was up against very strong odds. I felt very tired and went home to rest. The same evening, my director of the food-aid department, Abdi Aden Noor, came to see me and officially informed me that the tripartite agreement talks had ended in disagreement and that the CARE officials were leaving the following morning.

There was a reception that same evening at the German embassy and there the director-general of the foreign ministry, Hashi Abdulla, was approached by several highly placed western and UN officials who did not like the way the Somali government was handling the matter. They pointedly warned about its eventual negative effects. I lived not far from the German embassy, so Hashi came by to see me. I briefed him and he alerted some members of the former Supreme Revolutionary Council (SRC) which Siad Barre had re-established a year earlier, on the pretext of correcting malpractices. They were meeting regularly every Monday. They were trying to salvage their reputations and were no longer Siad Barre's "Yes" team, (and for that very reason he was soon to disband them again). Meantime, Samatar fell sick and was flown to Rome for treatment. Upon the instructions of Hussein Kulmiye, a former police officer who as second vice president was then acting as president, Hashi contacted the US embassy to help arrange the postponement of the CARE departure. Philip Johnson would not stay, but he agreed to leave behind some of his personnel.

The following Sunday morning, I briefed Kulmiye and a few other SRC members and they met in full session the day after. To my delight, they approved the tripartite contract agreement and left its implementation to the acting president and the extraordinary commissioner for refugees. On Tuesday morning, the US Embassy counsellor called me to enquire if there had been any progress: I said that the SRC had met the day before to discuss it, and promised that I would let him know as soon as possible. No sooner had I replaced the receiver than Kulmiye called me. He wanted to send a recommendation to Siad Barre who was then in Washington advising he agree to the signing of the contract. He asked me to draft a telex the way I saw things — but I knew that not even quotations from the Holy Quran would persuade Siad Barre to do anything other than reject the contract out of hand. Somalia's was the largest UNHCR program and Siad was determined that the control of what amounted to quite vast resources should remain at his own discretion. I reluctantly drafted a telex, but two other SRC members came by and joined us. I read out the draft. As I anticipated, they both instantly objected asking for Siad Barre's approval and asked Kulmiye why he was watering down a council decision. They advised him that he could only say his telex was for information. He agreed and I changed the text. Kulmiye signed it and a copy was given to Tarrah who then came in to conclude the contract. Thus was a successful outcome achieved to a long moral battle.

I never enquired whether Habib in Samatar's absence, had passed the message to Kulmiye: I doubted so because Kulmiye would surely then not have moved at all, no matter what pressure might have been exerted by the other SRC members. I did however learn from the Somali ambassador in Washington that Siad Barre was very bitter when he received news of the acceptance of the contract and had maintained that his constitutional preeminence had been violated. I was sure that I enjoyed the confidence of both the UNHCR officials and the representatives of the donor community but my personal motive was to fight corruption which was being encouraged, if not actually instigated, by President Siad Barre himself.

Some members of the donor community, like the Germans, though not necessarily heeding our advice — an embassy official quite frankly told us in May 1989 that, for moral reasons, aid already approved which was then in the pipeline could not be cut off—

nevertheless satisfied themselves as to the prevailing situation and thereafter phased out their bilateral aid. Others, like the Italians and the United States Department of State, did not follow the German example, despite the availability of the same kind of evidence. They would argue that the country would disintegrate if Siad Barre left the scene. Eventually, checking international aid definitely helped bring about his demise. But it fell to Congress to suspend aid from the United States and meantime much suffering continued. Some Americans may now be satisfied with what appears to them the fulfillment of their earlier predictions, because Somalia slipped into chaos and broke into pieces. If so, they would still be in the dark and far removed from ever appreciating the realities of the current Somali scenario. In truth the country had already disintegrated at the hand of Siad Barre. He had personally sown all the seeds of division by continuously arming certain groups of people against others, even during the time that his regime was strong.

In 1989, another UNHCR official — the representative, Abdulla Said of Sudan, was also declared *persona non grata*. Among other stands, he had questioned a refugee count and had objected to Siad Barre's policy of arming refugees. When later both the World Food Program and the UNHCR ceased food issues to armed refugees, I was surprised that the Italian government hurriedly donated emergency rations of rice specifically destined for the armed refugees in northern Somalia. The politics of interest groups on the Somali scene are very complex. In the meantime, the Secretary General of the United Nations himself intervened, perhaps at the urging of some important donor, and the United Nations Development Program (UNDP) took over all operations whereby food was distributed in the northern war zone. Thereafter, it could only be delivered through Siad Barre's army! As a Somali saying goes, "it was just like the rat leaving the baby with the cat for safe custody."

CHAPTER FOURTEEN

RESTLESS POLITICS IN THE AFTERMATH OF THE OGADEN WAR

T HE GAMBLE THAT THE Somali regime had made, not so much in assisting the oppressed population of the Ogaden or Western Somalia, as it was called by the Somali media, but in committing the nation's regular armed forces, has been mentioned. The failure of the regime to secure significant Western or Arab support is well known. So also is the massive intervention, on the side of the revolutionary and supposedly Marxist government in Addis Ababa, by the Soviet Union and its satellites — but of course it was Siad Barre who had invited Soviet intervention in the internal affairs of the horn of Africa in the first place and he was accorded little sympathy in the rest of Africa.

Yet the scale of the operation left all Somalis gasping. From late 1977, more than 250 heavy military transport planes — Tupolev 760, Antonov 22s etc. — conducted an airlift of men and advanced war materiel to Ethiopia. The supplies included ground to ground missiles, howitzer batteries, rocket launchers mounted on trucks (Stalin-organs) and other artillery. T55 and T62 tanks, machinery and planes — Sukhoi fighter bombers and MIG 21s and 23s were airlifted or shipped, together with massive quantities of fuel, rockets and ammunition. Cuban, Yemeni and Russian officers, pilots and ground crew vastly reinforced and revived the heretofore demoralized Ethiopian military. The result, when it came in early 1978, was a foregone conclusion. The only question was whether or not the juggernaut would stop at the

Somali frontier, which it did. The easy availability of light and heavy arms, too, was to prove a dangerous legacy.

It is rare in history for leaders suffering defeat on such a scale to survive and Siad was to be repeatedly challenged. Many, myself included, stayed our hands out of fear for the future of the nation, but life's difficulties increased accordingly. Not long after the debacle of the Ogaden war and a failed military coup attempt led by Mijertein officers, the Somali Salvation Democratic Front (the SSDF) was formed and armed resistance to Siad Barre's regime—aided by neighboring Ethiopia, began in earnest in the predominately Mijertein areas. Alarmed, Siad Barre foresaw another possible challenge to his authority from the powerful Isaaq clan in the north. At the same time, he kept an eye on the Hawiye, the largest clan, who predominated in and around the capital. He began a policy of harassment, first against the Mijertein and secondly against the Isaaqs. It soon became apparent that he harbored a special hatred for the Isaaq and soon his ultimate goal became clear—to reduce them to the level of impoverished nonentities.

Siad's hard feelings were based on at least three factors. First, Siad Barre considered himself to be an incarnation of the famous Somali resistance leader, Mohamed Abdille Hassan (the Mad Mullah) whom, although he was never captured, Siad believed had been defeated by the British only with the active support of Isaaq clansmen. Early in this century, the Mad Mullah's forces, the *Darawishta* (Dervishes), looted hundreds of thousands of head of livestock from the Isaaq people, depriving thousands of their means of livelihood. It was hardly surprising that the Isaaq should have joined forces with the British to defeat the looters and recover their property. Secondly, not unlike many other African dictators, such as Idi Amin and Mobuto Sese Seko, Siad Barre set great trust in soothsayers who told him that the Isaaq were bent on his downfall. Typically, soothsayers are intelligent people. They do not tell fortunes by magic but rather study the subject's psychology and collect information about worries, suspicions and aspirations until they are finally able to reveal something readily acceptable. Lastly, the Isaaq were northerners and Siad Barre was a southerner and felt he had little in common with them.

The Isaaq people enjoyed a numerically disproportionate and very visible representation in the civil service as well as in the armed forces, until 1975 and Siad Barre's consolidation of power. Thereafter, a concrete program was launched to eliminate members of the clan from government positions. Some were expelled, others prematurely retired, while still others were subjected to constant pressure forcing them into involuntary resignation. Isaaq resignations were readily accepted, unlike some others. There was a unique case in which twelve such applications from engineers were accepted while the thirteenth application, from a non-Isaaq, was rejected on the grounds that he was adjudged indispensable. Many who remained in the service suffered discrimination, frustrating experiences and poor placements. Over the years the majority of Isaaq clan members in high positions including ambassadors, directors, educators, bankers and other professionals left government service. Many emigrated to the Arabian Gulf or took exile elsewhere — for, as has been pointed out, Somalis are great travellers. In the forthcoming struggle, the flow of funds from such expatriate communities was to be of great significance.

Isaaqs overseas enjoyed relative freedom and were thus better organized. Those within the country, although much greater in number, took longer to organize. The activities of the overseas Isaaq only reinforced Siad Barre's suspicions which in turn reflected adversely on the Isaaq masses within the country who also were subjected to systematic harassment and deliberate miscarriages of justice. To that end, the so-called Isaaq politicians within Siad Barre's government institutions and the party, (of which I was one) recognized the danger of the people's unpreparedness to respond to Siad Barre's provocations. Despite his defeat in the Ogaden war, they were unprepared for a political showdown with him. Although shaken, Siad remained very powerful at home as he was cashing in on the political gains of his first nine years. The Isaaq people had urgently to be organized. That started in late 1978, with a sifting of ourselves (the so-called unelected politicians) to decide who should be involved, and who should be dropped, and who held, for the time being at least, at a safe distance from any knowledge of meetings and secrets. The process took several months but for the first time in almost a decade, people were beginning to be blacklisted among the Isaaq for being pro-Siad Barre.

The second goal on the conspirators' agenda was to strengthen and consolidate clan unity. Groups were formed within the various social groupings i.e. politicians, businessmen, intellectuals, teachers, adult students, civil servants, and in the armed forces. Every such group had its own committees, cells and sub-cells, without any written rules and regulations to avoid leakage; they depended upon unwritten rules of conduct for their guidelines. There would be weekly or bi-weekly meetings of individual politicians with other group and cell leaders. At first, most of the activities were centered in Mogadishu. There were briefings, debriefings, exchanges of views and secret instructions were imparted.

Siad Barre soon knew how the underground was functioning, for there were defectors and informers but they were almost invariably easily identifiable and could be neutralized and isolated. Siad Barre, meantime, unleashed his offensive. His entire security apparatus, terror organizations and other officials, were instructed to respond quickly to any manifestation of Isaaq dissent, real or imagined, with the utmost degree of brutality, by way of arrests, detention, torture, imprisonment and the confiscation of property. Such practices were systematically implemented throughout all areas of the Isaaq homeland, where, unlike Mogadishu, the mass of people were not so well organized.

Siad Barre liked personally to deal with the so-called politicians by interview, accusing them of subversion. It was effectively blackmail. One easy accusation would be involvement in tribalism, which he had supposedly rendered taboo, but with which he was himself quite obsessed. The pattern was simply to deny those accusations, for usually he lacked accurate details of day-to-day activities. Siad Barre would, however, use his own rationale and continue with his pressuring interviews aimed at harassing and weakening individual politicians. Secret contacts continued and the victims sought ways of responding to that pressure. Ahmed Mohamoud 'Silanyo'—later a Chairman of the Somali National Movement (S.N.M.) a predominantly, though not entirely Isaaq movement—suggested that we should no longer deny our clan involvement because that was the language which Siad Barre understood best.

This tactic was communicated to all concerned and was agreed upon as a future strategy, at least as far as the politicians were concerned. It worked very well. Thereafter, anyone so accused by Siad Barre would counter by accusing him of similar involvement. I would always update myself with information on his latest tribalist or nepotic activities. But Siad Barre would never accept responsibility for his failures and had always to find scapegoats to blame. His work style was irregular and set a bad example for all his institutions. He was also impulsive and would often go back on his commitments. This made it difficult for him to deal with many Somalis, particularly from the north. However, Siad Barre displayed one positive element in his public relations. One could argue with him at any length, so long as it was *tête-à-tête*, with no third person within hearing distance. This facet of his complex make-up was used to advantage for years, until later on he lost patience as clear evidence of his family's corruption mounted, and he could not bear to have it openly discussed.

Siad invariably made one last attempt before he would write Isaaq politicians off. He would ask some prominent Isaaq businessman to mediate between those so-called Isaaq politicians and himself. He briefed elders with his own side of the story, that we were 'not co-operating with him' or even that we were 'troublemakers.' One such would-be mediator was the late Farah Harbi who contacted, among others, Ahmed Hassan Musa, Ahmed Silanyo and myself and informed us that the President wanted to talk to us. Farah said to me that Siad Barre had specifically asked him to see Ahmed Silanyo and myself.

Silanyo and I met one day and considered the pros and cons of accepting or rejecting such overtures. We were already quite conversant with Siad Barre's tricks and propaganda ploys and were sure that he was not doing this for our own good or even in the national interest. If that were the case, he would have called us himself as he had always done, instead of approaching us through third parties. We assessed, in retrospect I believe quite rightly, that at the very least he wanted to embarrass us by making the accusation among his rubber stamp institutions that we had approached him to make a (forbidden) tribal representation. Hence, we decided to suggest to Farah that we were ready to talk to the president if he so wished, and he should call us either individually or collectively, whichever suited him, but without any mediation. I then checked with Ahmed Hassan who supported this line.

Farah Harbi met me again one evening at a mosque after prayers. He had seen the president and as a result claimed to be worried about our safety. Siad Barre clearly was blackmailing us through the unsuspecting Farah. He said to him, after Farah had conveyed our message, "Don't leave us alone," which means "Don't blame me later." It is actually clearer in Somali: *Nimankaas ha noo kala tegin, haddii kale hadhow hay eedayn.* Farah, who was about to go abroad, reported Siad's exact words and also briefed Silanyo. We met and resolved to ignore the threat.

After that, Siad Barre negotiated with us no further and tried the stick. Henceforth we were turned over to his security men for their special attention; open surveillances, telephone tapping and continuous reporting on our movements. I frequently played golf on the American golf course, the only one in Mogadishu, and one day I received a message from one of Siad Barre's party activists, a non-Isaaq northerner, to the effect that a security agent who was his clansman had informed him that he had been following me for a year and was so bored that he had applied for a change of duty and a substitute had been detailed.

The party activist offered to find out who the replacement was and let me know. I thanked him and asked him not to bother. I mainly drove around Mogadishu and was sure that I was never followed by any other car since I always checked and would have detected any such trailing. I reasoned my follower must therefore have been one of the caddies at the golf course, as I had long suspected. I lived inside the police headquarters compound and permanent watch on my house was an accepted fact of life. Furthermore, I knew that my telephone was frequently tapped. Sometimes I would get a warning beforehand. One day I visited a ministerial colleague in his office who was considered to have been in the good books of Said Barre, but because I had visited him, it was ordered that same evening that both his house telephone and mine should be tapped. It mattered little for we were always careful and most of the National Security Service (NSS) personnel, particularly those who had previously served under me, treated me with friendship and respect—even well after I disassociated myself completely from Siad Barre's government.

Corruption developed apace. One area was the self-help programs which were set up in the early stages of the Siad Barre regime. Both the need and the initial achievements of those programs were generally appreciated both in Somalia and abroad. Useful structures were built for various social services such as schools and nurseries. Other important activities involved largely unaccountable expenditures and sometimes substantial income. These were soon either mismanaged or diverted by Siad Barre's mediocre appointees drawn from among his party demagogues.

In the north, where the overall economy was largely in the hands of private entrepreneurs, ordinary businesses flourished as a direct reflection of the economic boom in the neighboring oil rich Gulf countries. Where little control or accountability existed, the conduct of mediocre officials also left much to be desired. Complaints from the public were unheeded by higher officialdom. Financial abuses and demands for bribes amounting to a system of debilitating extortion, were applied with utmost tenacity over a prolonged period. Accepted practice was actually indirect taxation, with no tangible results by way of development or services. Such levies were never credited to the general revenues of the state. They were solely used, with Siad Barre's full knowledge and blessing, as additional income for inept officials who would not neglect to send tributes to their patrons in Mogadishu, either Siad Barre's family members, including Siad Barre's senior wife, Khadija, or figures from the middle echelons of the party hierarchy. Such tributes even included cars imported through Berbera port and paid for from the self-help contributions, on which no customs duty would be paid. Khadija even received similar tributes or bribes, either in cash or in kind like watches, etc., from some ministers and other senior officials who owed their appointments to her.

Hargeisa only had one hospital which had been built by the British Administration in the early 1950s. Since then, the city had grown fourfold. It was in total disrepair; medicines and dressings were in short supply; patients were neglected without hospital rations and had to lie on the floor for lack of beds. All this, despite generous cash contributions given by the public monthly for the overall self-help schemes. A group of young graduates who had returned from abroad to re-establish their livelihood in their own country were greatly dismayed by those conditions and decided to take action. They held discussions over local issues with government officials, including visiting ministers, and disclosed the public abuses. Furthermore, they held orientations for the people and formed social committees of local elders to manage the resources raised for self-help schemes. These early communal steps resulted in the total rehabilitation and furnishing of the general hospital and the cash provision of twenty-five Somali shillings for each patient's daily ration.

The impact of their enthusiasm and honesty was truly spectacular, but the vested interests of Siad Barre's officials, not only those in the region, but also many in Mogadishu, were seriously threatened. The regime moved rapidly to concoct very serious charges of sedition and subversive activities aimed at the overthrow of the government, against about twenty of those young graduates who were arrested. (See Appendix I.) Their subsequent trial was marked by widespread demonstrations and violent uprisings took place for the first time since the military takeover thirteen years earlier. The trial had to be postponed on several occasions. Eventually harsh sentences ranging from life to various terms of imprisonment were handed out, and the young patriots were held in isolation and solitary confinement. (See Appendix II.) They came to be known as the 'Hargeisa Group' and were adopted by a number of human rights organizations including Human Rights Watch and Amnesty International. The US Academy of Sciences continuously addressed their case until their release in early 1988. On the other hand, Siad Barre used the incident as an excuse to intensify repression in the north as well as to accuse the Isaaq politicians in Mogadishu of having masterminded an uprising.

From January 1982 onwards, the political and security situation in the north worsened. The towns and cities were the scene of many riots and arbitrary arrests, confiscation of property and all sorts of legalized atrocities. In January 1983, the SNM raided the Mandera central prison, between Hargeisa and Berbera about four miles to the east off the main road, and released all the political prisoners incarcerated there. Siad Barre's forces retaliated by bombarding the nomadic settlements within a thirty miles radius, including the *Ga'an Libah* forest mountain, continuously for almost one month. Siad Barre himself visited the north at the end of February/early March, 1983 and on his return reported to a select group of his top aides.

President Hassan Gouled of the Republic of Djibouti had paid an official visit to Mogadishu in 1981 and had returned by way of Hargeisa where he stopped over for a night. Siad developed his own interpretation of the intentions of the Isaaq people. *Inter alia*, he claimed that they wanted to secede and unite with the Issa Somali of neighboring Djibouti. He blamed President Hassan Gouled for having sown the seeds of dissent during that stop over two years earlier. The Djibouti President is believed to have warned Siad of simmering dissatisfaction in the north. Siad told his entourage that the Isaaq had to be ruled with an iron hand and if that failed they could eventually leave and go wherever they wanted, but only after they had lost everything. The situation ten years later surely reflected the outcome of that plan. Siad's cruel mentality largely explains the subsequent destruction of the main towns in the north. Rule with an iron hand certainly continued and Siad Barre's relatives, officials and forces engaged in all sorts of activities — travesties of government — committing atrocities, and acting with such unlimited excess that they must have had the blessing if not the instigation of Siad himself. They clearly believed there was no accountability whatsoever.

On one occasion, an army patrol in the vicinity of Hargeisa encountered two young virgin girls tending their sheep and goats. They raped them both by cutting the stitches of their circumcision with bayonets and left them tied together by their hair. Both bled to death. On another occasion, after an SNM attack on a military garrison, all the women of a nearby town were collected together and ordered at gunpoint to take off their clothes and to parade in the main street. They were marched naked to the military barracks where they were forced to satisfy the soldiers, before being released to find their way home still unclothed. Such was the shame in our society, although guiltless, some committed suicide.

Whenever elders and others complained to Siad Barre about the excesses and abuses of his officials, he would always demand, as a precondition for redress, the dismantling of the SNM. He failed to understand that the SNM was born out of his misrule and drew strength from those very atrocities meted out to the people.

Siad's government maintained a rationale of disinformation that the unrest in the north was all engineered from Mogadishu. This resulted, on 9 June 1982, in the arrest and imprisonment of seven high ranking officials. They were Ismail Ali Aboker, third vice president; Omer Arteh, deputy speaker of the national assembly and former foreign minister, both Isaaq, and five southerners — General Omer Haji Mohamed, minister of health and former minister of defence, Osman Mohamed Jelle, head of the research and higher education bureau of the Somali Revolutionary Socialist Party and a former SRC member, Dr. Mohamed Adan Sheikh, former minister of health, Mohamed Yusuf Weyrah, former minister of finance and Warsame Ali Farah. All seven were long time comrades-in-arms of Siad Barre dating from his assumption of power. Ismail Ali Aboker, Siad Barre knew, was the real co-architect of the coup which had brought him to power. He saw Ismail not only as a legitimate claimant to power sharing, but also as an immediate threat to his one man rule.

Omer Arteh was Siad's second target: he had a number of reasons to move against him, apart from the fact he, like Ismail, was Isaaq. First, he maintained a comparatively lavish lifestyle which invited jealous reactions from Siad Barre. Secondly, he had gained some popularity in Afro-Arab diplomatic circles while serving as Foreign Minister and that was always a source of irritation to Siad Barre. Thirdly, both Omer Arteh and Osman Mohamed Jelle had been Siad Barre's special envoys to Arab leaders and he had long sought to distance them both from the determination of crucial policies and curtail their contacts with Arab governments. That had not always been possible. Soon after Omer Arteh had been replaced as foreign minister in 1977, Siad Barre had met Sheikh Zayed Bin Sultan Al-Nahuan, the ruler of the United Arab Emirates, in Cairo during the joint Afro-Arab Summit

Conference and had asked him for substantial assistance, using an unseasoned interpreter, as Siad Barre did not know Arabic. Sheikh Zayed was embarrassed by the crude way in which the request was presented and by the absence of the diplomatic flavor which had characterized such previous meetings when Omer Arteh had acted as interpreter. The latter was also in Cairo as part of the Somali delegation, but Siad Barre had wanted to dispense with his participation.

Sheikh Zayed did not give any immediate response. Siad Barre returned home as soon as the conference was over, but Sheikh Zayed proceeded to pay visits to the (then) two Yemens. Upon his arrival in Sana'a, Sheikh Zayed's protocol director contacted the Somali ambassador there and asked him to inform Siad Barre that Sheikh Zayed wanted Omer Arteh to come and meet him in Sana'a. The ambassador sent a message at once, but Abdurahman Jama Barre, Siad's cousin whom he had made foreign minister and who envied Omer Arteh bitterly, shelved it. The message was not shown to Siad Barre and there was no response despite repeated reminders by the ambassador during Sheikh Zayed's stay in Sana'a. His Highnesses' protocol director again suggested to the ambassador that Omer should then come to Aden instead. The ambassador, bewildered at the lack of response to his messages, just took a Somali Airlines scheduled flight to Mogadishu that same day and Abdurahman Jama Barre was unable to delay Sheikh Zayed's message any longer, because every visiting Somali ambassador would see the president. Siad Barre at once provided Omer Arteh with a special plane to meet Sheikh Zayed in Aden. It transpired that Sheikh Zayed had not exactly understood what Siad Barre really wanted. Omer did not know either, because he had been excluded in the first place and he had to come back to Siad Barre for a briefing and then return to Sheikh Zayed in Abu Dhabi. Whatever Sheikh Zayed gave through Omer Arteh could not, in the circumstances, satisfy Siad.

When Prince Nawaf Bin Abdul-Aziz of Saudi Arabia visited Somalia during February–March 1982, Siad Barre and his close aides again saw to it that both Omer Arteh and Osman Mohamed Jelle were excluded from all official functions in honor of the prince. However, the Saudi embassy gave a dinner party on the last evening of the visit over which the Somali authorities had neither influence nor control. Both men were among the official invitees and met the prince, much to the annoyance of Siad Barre's representatives. Soon afterwards, Siad Barre decided on the detention of the two men.

Siad, by all accounts, had already established a plausible rationale of his own against Omer Arteh as being among the Isaaq officials who were stirring up unrest in the North and he had to concoct a similar accusation against Osman Jelle. Siad later told some of his close collaborators that Osman Jelle had telephoned the Saudi Embassy, in order to meet with the prince, who had turned him down on the grounds that he was a guest of the president and therefore he would prefer not to meet anyone without the president's approval. Although it appeared to be an absurd story, I was interested at the time because if at all true, the information must have been obtained through telephone tapping. I asked Osman Jelle about this, after his release from detention six years later, and he assured me that he had never telephoned the Saudi Embassy during Prince Nawaf's presence in Mogadishu. I believe him rather than Siad Barre.

During the 1980 October celebrations of the anniversary of his coming to power, Siad Barre, always obsessed by the occasion and the supposed need to make some sensational announcement, re-established the Supreme Revolutionary Council (SRC) which had been dissolved more than four years earlier. The pretext was to correct the mistakes and failures of his regime. Dr. Mohamed Adan Sheikh mustered a pressure group of intellectuals to advise the President that he should appoint a prime minister if he really meant to make positive changes. By so doing they were only trying to act in the best interest of the regime and the nation. After exhaustively presenting their viewpoints through many meetings and discussions over nearly a year, Siad Barre unleashed a campaign against the group, accusing them of anti-militarism. At the time they managed to disperse unscathed, some of them, like Mohamed Said Samatar whose wife was French, choosing voluntary exile. Siad Barre neither forgot nor forgave Mohamed Adan, but bided his time for an opportune moment. A year later, the political situation in the North was deteriorating. It was a time of arbitrary arrests, torture, detentions without trial and complaints of other abuses. Mohamed Adan lobbied for a political solution, which ran counter to Siad Barre's already determined military option. By his honest actions, despite a closeness to Siad—he is a Marahan—Mohamed Adan thus almost offered himself as a candidate for inclusion in the arrest list.

Mohamed Yusuf Weyrah had been out for only a few months from an earlier one-year detention which had seriously undermined his health. He had continuously demanded proper medical treatment, which was only available outside the country, but at a time when many of Siad Barre's senior officials were defecting. Weyrah had twice before been minister of finance and he knew too much. For example, Sheikh Zayed paid twenty-four million US$, during his first visit to Somalia in 1971/72, for the construction of a T.B. hospital for the people of Mogadishu. It was never built and Siad Barre used the money for other purposes. Only Weyrah knew what and how. His defection would have been very damaging and renewed detention was the best guarantee against any embarrassing revelations.

Warsame Ali Farah, who died in detention, was a communist and Siad Barre had suspected him of encouraging the defection of leftist group members after relations with the USSR had been adjusted.

The last case was General Omer Haji Mohamed. In the past, Omer Haji had been groomed to become head of the Army, as the only 'suitable' Marehan officer. Over the years he had overtaken, one by one, everyone in the higher military hierarchy finally taking over from Lieut.-General Samatar in 1981. The President's senior wife, Khadija, had long been the hidden authority over army personnel matters. Most promotions, appointments and transfers of officers were decided upon her recommendations. However, upon assuming the command of the army, Omer Haji asked Siad Barre to approve reorganization plans for the proper safeguarding of the regime, to which Omer Haji was seriously committed. His plans ignored or upset many of Khadija's placements. In short, he defied her hegemony over military matters, underestimating her influence over her husband. A serious conflict ensued, whereupon the ever impulsive Siad Barre bristled and removed Omer Haji within ten months, appointing him, at very short notice, as minister of health. It was after this removal that Omer Haji was accused of planning to overthrow Siad Barre, but it seemed more likely that the latter just did not want to take chances. He must have decided that the disgruntled general's detention was his best insurance.

One evening, Omer Arteh was supposed to come by and together we would go to meet a group of intellectuals in a house near the prison. He came much earlier to tell me that he had been called to a meeting at General Samatar's office at army headquarters. I said that sounded suspicious. He replied he would be going there and asked me to greet the group on his behalf; among them I met Suleiman Mohamoud Aden and Omer Mohamed Handulle. That evening, my wife and I were taking two of her relations from Berbera out to dinner at a restaurant which I had selected for its telephone facility. I kept dialling Omer Arteh's house to see if he had returned but the telephone went on ringing unanswered. I made several calls to no avail so paid the bill, sadly without giving our guests enough time to relax and talk.

I drove near to Omer's house, pulled the car to the curb and walked to the gate. One of Siad Barre's security men was at the gate. We recognized each other. I asked him what was going on and he said that there was some sort of an operation and nobody was allowed to enter. I had not in fact asked to do so, for I quickly realized that Omer had been arrested. Neither my wife nor our guests noticed anything before I dropped them, and proceeded to see Omer Mohamed Handulle. He informed me that Ismail Ali Aboker had also been arrested. I learned of the arrest of the other five the following morning.

Although the individual circumstances of those arrested had little similarity — the only common denominator being the supposed need to silence them — they were jointly accused of plotting to overthrow Siad Barre and his government. All were members of Siad Barre's rubber stamp parliament. Ahmed Silanyo, who had already voluntarily exiled himself or he too would have been arrested, took their case to the attention of the Inter-Parliamentary Union and the International Commission of Jurists. The former called for their release and the secretary-general of the Inter-Parliamentary Union visited Somalia but failed to persuade Siad to release them. Somalia was condemned for abuse of international laws regarding the rights and privileges of parliamentarians. Siad Barre normally sought to accommodate international opinion, but it conflicted with his own dictatorship policies and he accepted wide condemnation rather than compromise those policies. Professor Greenfield, the British political adviser in the foreign ministry, also wrote to the government citing Ismail Aboker and Omer Arteh's case and advocating their release.

Instead, Siad Barre intensified his campaign of terror, mainly to frighten those of us who had not yet been arrested and to solicit new defections or informers. He implemented his campaign through his rubber stamp institutions: the party, the parliament, the council of ministers, and through the social (mass) organizations. I belonged to the first three and abstained from any meetings for almost a month. I did that because many of his published accusations seemed to refer to people like me and I was not prepared to submit to humiliation.

About two years later, when the council of ministers was debating a program of the International Monetary Fund presented by the minister of finance, I noticed that one minister first spoke in favor of the proposals, but later voted against—having discerned that the president wished to undermine his minister of finance. Another minister who also spoke in favor of the proposals pretended to be asleep during the vote. We were one of the worst examples of repressive government in Africa and perhaps it was justified to be afraid, but I could not have acted like that.

We were unsettled and it was a time of great strain. I recall that on the evening following the arrests, a ministerial colleague came to my house and invited me for a drive in his car. After about 150 yards he turned and entered the compound of the house of the Foreign Minister, Abdurahman Jama Barre, Siad Barre's cousin. I got annoyed and demanded to know why he had brought me there. Realizing my disapproval, he said he was only checking whether his wife was visiting. He got out of the car and popped into the house and out again in a matter of seconds, perhaps just to prove his statement. We drove for about twenty minutes without either of us uttering a word. Eventually, as I was getting out of the car, he said he would contact me the next morning. I supposed he had been aware of some danger from which he wanted to save me.

He kept his word and called me the next morning and we met.

Referring to the arrests, he said that what had happened had happened, and "of course there will be someone appointed to represent the Isaaq in the highest organs of the state." He was again referring to a possible replacement for Ismail Ali Aboker, who before being detained was a vice-president and a politburo member. He said that he would like me to be such an appointee, adding that the president had a high opinion of me. I replied that if I were to try to be close to Siad Barre for twenty years, I could never do for him what Ismail Ali Aboker and Omer Arteh had done and they were both behind bars. He took my resolve seriously. We remained friends and continued to meet occasionally. About two years later he was appointed as an ambassador. I met him at a reception, but it was too crowded for us to talk. At the end of the reception, he wished my wife good-bye and twice said that he was leaving in two day's time. This is how we had to behave: he was giving me to understand that he wanted us to meet before he left, so I visited him the following morning. He went over the circumstances that had surrounded the arrest of the seven politicians and only then informed me that I had been included in the list of those to be arrested, but by sheer luck Siad Barre had at the last minute deleted my name, adding that even while doing so, the president remained convinced that I was one of the big troublemakers. I wondered if that was why my friend thought that Siad Barre was well disposed towards me but said that I could only thank God.

It had in fact already leaked out that both Ahmed Hassan Musa and Mohamoud Jama Jugeh, the latter a fellow Marehan clansman of Siad's, were also included in that list. Siad Barre had deleted my name and that of Ahmed Hassan at the last minute. An arrest order had in fact been given for Mohamoud Jama but about midnight the arrest party had reported that they could not find him. He may well have been tipped off and had retired into hiding. Only then had Siad Barre said, "Leave him." Had Mohamoud Jama been arrested, there would have been three Marehan out of the eight, more than a third!

Amongst his favored groups and individuals, Siad Barre appeared always to support whoever was closest to him—among the Marehan, the closest of kin; it was mere arithmetic, and the essence of tribalism. He must have known, when appointing his inept cousin, Abdurahman

Jama Barre as foreign minister, that there were more capable Marehans in his institutions such as Dr. Mohamed Adan Sheikh and Mohamed Said Samatar who were more suited to the job, let alone members of other clans. Amongst those disloyal to him, however, he would hit the Marehan hardest. Mohamed Adan and Lawaha's are cases in point. There was a Marehan officer Captain Hassan Halane 'Afdhuub' also nicknamed *Haruuza* who was tortured to death: to his credit he failed to yield any information implicating General Omer Haji Mohamed in any conspiracy. Major Hussein Dirie Shire known as Hussein *Aabi* also died under interrogation. The eleven sheikhs executed in January 1975 not only included a Marehan but one who was a very close relative of Siad Barre.

Even so, the majority of the Marehan people were nomads, with the normal Somali commitment to traditional clan loyalty and they continued to blindly support Siad Barre's policies, without under-standing the real consequences. That nomadic quality was not lost on Siad Barre and as mentioned above he would overnight create from scratch, scores if not hundreds, of illiterate entrepreneurs from among his fellow sub-clansmen. The example of Abdi Hosh, at first a driver, who was allowed to become the business partner of Siad's senior wife, Khadija has been mentioned. When later the interests of that partnership conflicted, Siad Barre decided to create his family's own entrepreneur by discarding Abdi Hosh altogether and installing a young graduate, Abdurahman Jama Barre's nephew, in a highly prestigious office with all the business infrastructure in place.

Not that there were not conflicts within the family. When Siad Barre was badly wounded in a road accident in May 1986, Abdurahman Jama Barre coveted the presidency to the utter annoyance of Khadija who had groomed her own son, Maslah. Upon his recovery, Siad Barre sided with his wife and son, appointing the latter army chief of staff and thus supposedly undisputed heir apparent. It was with that internal power struggle, that the Barre family enterprise concept collapsed, Khadija promptly re-established her business connections with a much chastened Abdi Hosh.

Siad Barre, would make sudden inspections inside Mogadishu for the sake of publicity. The official Press had always to prominently report his activities. He once visited the ministry of public works where Ahmed Hassan Musa was the incumbent minister. But Siad Barre had an ulterior motive; he wanted to talk to Ahmed Hassan about politics. Ahmed Hassan, unlike myself, continued attending the council of ministers meetings, but avoided seeing the president privately. That however was basic to Siad Barre's style of work: it was how he conducted his real business. He told Ahmed to tell his friends (us) that we should either work with him properly (meaning that we should participate in his political maneuvering) or else resign, adding that Ahmed should report that those were the words of the president. When Ahmed asked to whom he was referring, Siad Barre retorted that he knew well enough.

Ahmed bravely said he could only convey the message to colleagues specifically named by the president. Siad then named the minister of transport and civil aviation (me), the vice-minister of higher education, Suleiman Mohamoud Aden, the vice-minister of education, Dahir Warsame, and, "others" unspecified. The significant name he missed was Omer Handulle 'Bobe' so we assumed that the "others" referred to him. Ahmed Hassan delivered the message to each of us but I proposed that we should all meet together so that he could repeat it. We agreed to meet the following Friday morning at Suleiman's house. There we resolved that Siad Barre had no need of our resignations as he could dismiss anyone at his discretion. Indeed, he hated people resigning from his institutions, always preferring to dispense with them. No one would resign without first clearing it verbally with Siad, who would reject the resignation on the grounds of indispensability to the nation. However, he would soon afterwards drop the applicant as a punishment. The only known case of successful resignation, after the necessary clearance, was that of a former finance minister, Abdurahman Nur Hersi, who resigned to take up an appointment with the Islamic Bank.

In our case, Siad Barre was clearly provoking us to seek audience so that he could talk to us, and assess how much our resolve had weakened after the arrests and how far he could use us for his own ends. I proposed that we leak the whole story to many senior government officials. Each would contact one senior official and inform him of our having received such a message; while showing our readiness to resign, we would ask merely the favor that he seek confirmation from the president. As anticipated, Siad Barre totally denied everything, saying that Ahmed Hassan must have misunderstood him. He further denied having mentioned our names. He was to drop all four of us (including Omer Mohamed Handulle) in his next reshuffle.

About a month after the arrests, I did go to see Siad Barre on official business. As always, it had to be in the evenings or at night. Only his security men and those asked for by him could see him during the day-time. Some disagreement had arisen between the Somali Airlines and Lufthansa. The German ambassador had called on me, since I was minister of transport, to present the Lufthansa case and I undertook to see him again after I had heard from Somali Airlines. My appointment with the ambassador was due the next day and since no minister could take a decision, no matter how trivial it might be, without Siad Barre having okayed it, I had to see him that evening. There were occasions on which I endeavored to circumvent the president in the national interest, but this was not one of them.

I joined the usual queue and at last found myself face to face with Siad Barre for the first time for more than a month. After completing my business with him, he asked if I had anything else to say. I said, "No," and stood up, thinking that it was his wish to call the next person. He asked me to sit down again and reminding me that I had not attended many council meetings (I did not think that he would remember as it had been as long as a month) and asked whether that was not a provocation. I said that I did not think so but admitted I had a duty to attend meetings and offered my apology. He then said that he wanted me to work with him. I asked him how exactly. He replied he wanted me to go to the North and talk to the people, "Who had been misled." I had to state frankly to him that he and I differed: I believed that the people were not misled but were being mismanaged and oppressed by his own appointees who were not fit for their jobs. I told him I would go and endeavor to fulfil any task entrusted to me but on one important condition, namely that I had authority to solve problems on the spot, and redress and correct any acts of mismanagement. He declined, saying I should report any such problems to him. I insisted that if he wanted the people to believe me and accept what he wanted me to tell them, then they should also be convinced that I had the authority to solve their problems.

Siad Barre had known of my reluctance to undertake any such missions to the north on his behalf since 1979 when, as minister of interior, on the last evening of my visit to Hargeisa I witnessed the rounding up by his regional officials of fifty-seven schoolboys accused of Islamic fundamentalist activities. In reality, the arrests were over their refusal to attend marxist orientation classes: instead they had gone to the mosques to receive Islamic religious teachings. Even after readjusting his relations with the Soviets and expelling their numerous advisers in 1977, Siad Barre was still preaching scientific socialist rhetoric for the dual purpose of seeking adoption by China and retaining his rigid totalitarian grip on the Somali people. The members of his new society had every reason to preserve the status quo upon which their prosperity and even means of survival, very much depended.

The boys had been taken to a specially arranged court which detained them for three months. They were transferred to the Mandera Prison 113 Kms away the same night. Siad Barre's officials had not felt it necessary to inform me, even of their side of the story. They had endeavored to keep their actions totally secret from me so that I should not interfere until they were *fait accompli*. Once detained by a court order, the youths could only be released by a decree signed by Siad Barre. I had been informed of the arrests the following morning at the airport by the parents and relatives of the boys, as I was about to fly to Mogadishu. I had seen Siad Barre immediately upon my return to the capital and demanded that the officials involved be subjected to disciplinary action for not keeping me informed of such serious developments despite the merits or otherwise of the case concerned.

At the time, the president had said that he would consider this after receiving the official report on the issue. I had no doubts in my mind that he had already approved the arrests, for the regional authorities could rarely resort to such actions of their own accord. Thereafter, Siad Barre did not allow any Isaaq senior officials to visit the north unless they were his own trusted agents willing to execute his special policies of divide and rule. But these were no longer effective. He had lost the trust of the people. Yet he wanted me to go there! We continued talking until day-break without achieving any agreement. At one point he accused me of wanting to create a government of my own within a government. I retaliated by accusing him of not delegating necessary authority. At long last he said that we should just agree to work together for the good of Somalia. I agreed and we did not discuss politics again for the next 23 months until his next government reshuffle on June 1, 1984. Then my colleagues and I were dropped, which I never regretted.

While in Siad Barre's institutions one would be immune from search, arbitrary arrest, etc., unless security men were unleashed or instigated by himself. One felt less secure having left those, otherwise unholy, institutions. I remained deeply involved in politics being very much opposed to Siad Barre's domestic policies, but I was increasingly vulnerable. I considered I needed some sort of hobby to legitimize my movements. Farming was one such possibility. I had owned a plot of agricultural land, since 1964, at Afgoye, just 24 miles south-west of Mogadishu along the Shebelli river. I cultivated it and made a viable farm which I enjoyed very much, besides establishing quite a plausible reason for my movements. Any time I might be wanted by other than close friends, I would be 'on the farm.' But it remained necessary to take care and pretend to be uninterested in politics. I never participated in any meetings held by Siad Barre or his officials with the Isaaq elders. I realized that none of my sons had either the aptitude or the desire to work on the farm, so I would have eventually to dispose of it. That, however, could await the fall of Siad Barre. As it happened, because of the turn of events in Somalia in general, and Mogadishu and its periphery in particular, I was unable to sell up. The farm lies derelict, along with so much of Somalia's development and infrastructure.

Meantime, in the north, major SNM attacks on the towns of Burao and Hargeisa in May/June 1988 were seized upon by Siad Barre as opportunity to destroy them with artillery fire and aerial bombardment. He sought to realize a long held dream of settling other clans in the Isaaq homeland. The destruction of those towns, parts of which were dynamited, forced the flight or evacuation of the local Isaaq population whom he supplanted with former refugees from across the border with Ethiopia. They were installed in Isaaq owned houses. His officials repeatedly tried to present those squatters to visiting representatives of the international community as Isaaq 'returnees,' but no one was deceived.

Despite Siad Barre's corruption, maladministration and blatant human rights violations, the US administrations, initially of President Reagan and later of President Bush, long committed themselves to unqualified support of his regime. When the SNM attacked the main towns in the north in 1988, the US airlifted large quantities of M-16 assault rifles with which Ethiopian refugees were armed to fight in a civil war on the side of Siad Barre. Embassy officials in Somalia even coerced the UN agencies and other international organizations as well as Arab diplomats to support the dying regime and some assistance was forthcoming thereafter from certain Arab oil producing countries. When U.S. Ambassador Crigler was appointed to his post, it was widely believed that he had refused to meet with Somali exiles in Washington who had asked to see him. We were justifiably angered and wryly quipped that perhaps only in Siad Barre's Somalia could Libya and the US Administration find an area of indirect co-operation!

Curiously, in those days when the world scene was dominated by hostility between the two superpowers, Siad often secretly hankered to return to the Soviet fold. Whenever he did not get the support he sought from the United States, he would publicly emphasize the danger Mengistu's Ethiopia posed to world peace. Privately, however, he felt that he could not co-exist with non-totalitarian western systems of government. He longed very much for readoption by his erstwhile Soviet patrons. Upon his return home from the United States in 1982, he had summoned his ambassador to Belgium, who had studied in the former East Germany and had some orientation in socialism. Over the head of the foreign minister, his own cousin, he instructed the ambassador to open dialogue with his Soviet counterpart to seek rapprochement and accommodation with the former Soviet Union, once his closest ally. Among other things, Siad Barre secretly offered cancellation of the newly signed military co-operation agreement with the United States and requested the USSR to reconcile him with Mengistu.

When Moscow received the report of their ambassador in Brussels, they summoned the Somali ambassador accredited to the Soviet Union and gave him their verbal response to the two points specifically relayed from Siad Barre. When they discovered that the ambassador had no prior knowledge of the matter, they briefed him and even quipped that when they had to communicate anything to Somalia it would be channelled through their ambassador there. The response to the two points was that the cancellation of the military co-operation with the US would be a positive step, once Siad Barre had realized his mistakes, and with regard to the reconciliation, Siad Barre had to first renounce his territorial claims against Ethiopia. It was a snub. The Somali ambassador then submitted his report through the proper channels, to the foreign minister. The latter immediately recalled the ambassador to Belgium and subjected him to disciplinary proceedings and harassment for failing to keep his minister informed of such important matters. Siad Barre did not defend the ambassador since the latter's special mission had borne no fruit and he had to resign. Later, Siad Barre had the Somali ambassador to Moscow recalled, and would seldom allow him to leave Mogadishu because he knew too much—he was lucky not to have been detained or physically eliminated, and he eventually managed to defect. It was not only at home that Siad Barre had run out of viable options and credibility.

CHAPTER FIFTEEN

THE SOMALI NATIONAL MOVEMENT AND THE UNITED SOMALI CONGRESS

THUS IT WAS, WITH attacks on the northern capital of Hargeisa, and on Burao, that Siad Barre's long simmering confrontation with the Isaaq people came out into the open. To trace how events had reached the point of no return it is necessary to examine the origin and development of the Somali National Movement (SNM). It was not the first liberation movement—that distinction belongs to the Somali Salvation Democratic Front (SSDF), a largely Mijertein organization, but it was the SNM that may justly be said to have broken the back of the Siad Barre regime, and prepared the ground for the eventual *coup de grace* administered by the United Somali Congress (USC) in central Somalia and Mogadishu.

A full study of the SNM has yet to be written and the writer will not attempt that here but some detail is vital to understand the depths which the dictatorship was prepared to plumb in its frantic struggle for self-preservation, and the crimes against humanity suffered in the process by so significant a segment of the Somali nation as the Isaaq. If drawbacks and failures appear stressed unduly, it is only that a young nation might learn from them.

The SNM was formed in April 1981 by a group of largely, but not entirely, Isaaq exiles in London. A few years later, military operations were begun from bases at first in eastern Ethiopia close to the common border, and then in the heart of the North, in the Isaaq homeland itself, following the intensification of Siad Barre's oppression against the civilian population. In retrospect, it is worth noting that had Siad Barre succeeded in absorbing the Ogaden into his realm during the 1977–78 war over that territory, the Isaaq people would have enjoyed no neighboring base or sanctuary from which to launch their liberation struggle.

The movement scored initial and spectacular successes by breaking into maximum security and other strongly guarded lock-ups and freeing detainees, including many condemned prisoners awaiting execution for political offenses. The cost was however heavy. Several of its best military commanders were killed in combat: among them Mohamed Hashi *Lixle,* Adan Suleiman, Mohamed Ali and Ahmed *Gaab* to name but a few. Adan Mohamed Sheikh Abdi *Shina* was also killed under dubious circumstances, perhaps by Siad Barre's agents, as was Abdulqudir Kossar. Ibrahim Yusuf Mohamed *Kotbur,* Mahdi and others died of 'natural' causes, due to lack of adequate medical facilities. Many other fighters and many civilians died for lack of medical care in those early days.

Meantime, to be Isaaq in Mogadishu began to have its hazards. Siad Barre and his regime fought tooth and nail to divide the Isaaq people. First they tried to bring about the disintegration of the movement, and later to form an Isaaq puppet counter-organization. All was in vain. Even after the destruction of the main towns and the consequent revenge killings, which Siad Barre thought he could use to discredit the SNM, the unity of the Isaaq in Mogadishu though threatened, could not be broken.

Harassment had the positive effect of deterring defection from the SNM. The very few who defected, though not important, found it hard to live among the lsaaq population nor could their names be publicized for fear for their safety. Defectors from the SSDF, on the other hand, had always seemed to be welcomed by their clans-folk in Mogadishu. Siad Barre would publicize defections through the official media and would appoint some SSDF defectors to prominent managerial and other senior posts. In this way, the SSDF was rendered almost defunct, until after the fall of Siad Barre, when it at once revived.

Not all Isaaq were patriots, nor was the SNM itself without problems — far from it. Since its inception, the SNM leadership was always the center of controversy from within, due to continuous power struggles which often almost paralyzed the organization's management, and prolonged the struggle, perpetuating the suffering of the people and unduly delaying the overthrow of the dictatorship. Siad Barre continuously monitored such activities and particularly the weaknesses of the movement, through infiltration and destabilization by his own agents. That was quite apparent from the accurate information he was getting.

Since the movement's inception, no leader remained in office for more than a year, with the exception of Ahmed Mohamed Mohamoud *Silanyo* who steered it through stormy weather and rough waters for a good six years. Siad Barre contributed dearly towards Ahmed Silanyo's overthrow, which he wanted more than his head. Although an attempt was made on Silanyo's life when he was undefeated after a second re-election. He was eventually succeeded by Abdurahman Mohamed Ali *Tur*, but in a constitutional electoral process. Despite the many criticisms levelled against him, it was through Ahmed Silanyo's skill and patience that the movement remained intact and survived long trying years of self-defeating debacles.

The achievements of the SNM fighters were considerable, especially if one realizes that the efforts of the people — the young fighters, elders, financial contributors, and the Isaaq communities at large, wherever they might be — were constantly betrayed and undermined. According to information we received over a long period in Mogadishu, which was later overwhelmingly confirmed by testimony eventually collected after the overthrow of Siad Barre, the blame rests squarely upon the shoulders of several former senior officers who had defected from Siad Barre's army — the so-called *Qaaxo* Group. There were also a few individuals who acted purely out of ambition and other parochial motives. Many a time, an armed operation against Siad Barre's forces was deliberately foiled by the cutting off of supplies from SNM fighting units or by orders to disengage some of the units without warning, thus imperilling others still fighting. There is ample evidence available today from SNM fighters to prove crimes committed against the people. Also, certain SNM fighters who expressed dissenting views were physically liquidated.

Hargeisa totally fell to the SNM fighters in December 1989. That they held it for a few days, was clearly ascertained from messages relayed from the commander of Siad Barre's beleaguered and overrun forces, to which we gained access. The SNM fighters, however, had to withdraw for lack of supplies. They had been intentionally cut off by certain military commanders, and government forces were thus able to retake Hargeisa and hold it for a further thirteen months. The city was not permanently liberated until the fall of Siad Barre in Mogadishu. The rules of the game played by the opportunists were that the SNM should never succeed in overthrowing Siad Barre or in forcing his troops out of the North unless and until certain officers could seize the leadership of the movement. It appears they only wanted to substitute another military dictatorship for that of Siad Barre. The otherwise courageous organization was thus sometimes paralyzed and long continued to suffer from lack of a mechanism to require accountability for the betrayal of the many martyrs who gave their lives for the common cause. Many still believe it to be the duty of their surviving comrades to render them this minimum justice posthumously, not least for consolation of their families, but others fear it would be too divisive.

In Mogadishu, we met in secret cells and rejoiced at the victories but were all too frequently dismayed to receive negative reports concerning betrayals. Such reports first filtered through Siad Barre's sources, for he relied on destabilizing activities; they were later confirmed by Isaaq travellers and undoubtedly contributed to Siad Barre remaining in power for so long. One of our Mogadishu cells consisted of Ahmed Hassan Musa, Omer Mohamed Handulle *Bobe* and myself; another of Mohamed Hawadleh, Mohamed Haji Hassan *Salah* and again myself. We discussed what contributions we could make, being determined to avert collapse of the movement. These meetings dated from the movement's first operations from Ethiopia in 1982.

An important contributor to the cause of the struggle, although not by attendance at any secret meetings, was Osman Jama Ali among whose gifts were good public relations. He had contacts with people, both friends and foes, and especially with members of Siad Barre's politburo. He would always know something, often very useful to us. I would see him only once or twice a month in order not to jeopardize his activities. He finally defected to the SNM in late 1989, after Siad Barre had criticized him for undermining his regime in which he was then a minister.

Hundreds of Isaaq people made positive contributions but there were many other Isaaq who, though they contributed to the struggle in the early years, became intimidated after 1984 when the Siad Barre regime started reckless killing, often over trivial matters and based on flimsy or false and uncorroborated reports. Forty-four men, including the local police commander, were summarily executed in Burao in November of that year, after a mock trial lasting only a few minutes. None were granted legal aid or opportunity to appeal. Twenty-six other men were similarly executed the same month in Hargeisa as were fifteen persons, including a woman, in Sheikh. The woman was accused of having ululated — chanted in celebration — when some SNM fighters ambushed an army convoy on the Sheikh pass. How such shameful activities developed into 'clan-cleansing' and policies tantamount to genocide, will be revealed below. Suffice it here to note that the Isaaq people in Mogadishu and elsewhere remained united and stood solidly behind the SNM, despite unceasing attempts by Siad Barre and his few Isaaq stooges, to divide them. In reality the SNM became like the 'PLO' in Palestine, as far as the Isaaq people were concerned, but it is an open question as to whether all the movement's leadership lived up to such high expectations.

Unfortunately, information very often obtained at great risk, was not invariably put to good use by SNM officials. An exception was Siad's son-in-law's infamous "letter of death," which was leaked to *New African*'s contributing editor, Richard Greenfield. In it, General Morgan made detailed and quite horrendous proposals for the elimination of the Isaaq peoples. The world press took it up. What was passed on to the SNM was more typically deductions from personal conversations held with Siad Barre himself, other key players of his regime and various party and state officials. Siad was not only talkative, but a great waffler and one could always extract useful information, unwittingly imparted. Ahmed Hassan Musa was one source who contributed a great deal of information. I reached a point where almost every significant Isaaq living in Mogadishu would either make reports to me or come for information about the latest SNM activities against the hated regime. I often wondered how much of this Siad Barre might have known. I had to take every possible precaution.

I devised a system of managing my secret operations, including the storage of important documents. I was a member of the American Golf Club, located within the premises of the embassy compound. Most golfers, myself included, would hire a steel cabinet for storing clubs, golf balls, etc. I always stored my confidential papers there, including copies of the reports I sent to the SNM and any documents of value whether stolen from the regime or otherwise. As far as I know, the United States authorities had no knowledge of this. It was the best solution available, but I felt vulnerable. If Siad Barre's agents came to know of this, they could easily have burgled the club, disguising themselves as common criminals. They could even have been given American permission to search my cabinet in order to still further improve relations with Siad Barre. At times some senior members of the US Embassy were in favor of doing just that but were overruled by Washington. I had to get a reliably dependable lock for my cabinet. A nephew of mine and another golfer, Ibrahim Gulaid, found me a combination lock of the right size and I used it for more than six years.

My confidential file got enlarged over the years and once in a while I had to take it home in the evenings in order to dig out references. After working on it, I would lock it over-night in the back of my car which would be parked in a garage away from my residence. Private homes were searched at random, usually midnight onwards, during the Siad era.

In September 1988, the respected Hawiye human rights activist, the late Dr. Ismail Jumale Ossoble, who was about to depart on a visit to Europe, spoke with an Isaaq elder about the possibility of contacting the SNM leadership. The elder said he would think it over and sent for me. I was thrilled by the idea, hoping to break the political isolation in which the SNM found itself as far as other Somali groups were concerned, despite continuous military successes. I knew Dr. Jumale well and went straight to him and said that I was responding to his conversation with that elder. In those days Siad Barre's security felt justified in executing anyone implicated as an SNM sympathizer, let alone someone in contact with them. In order to win my trust, Dr. Jumale put all his cards on the table and informed me of Hawiye decisions to plan the overthrow of Siad Barre's tyrannical government. He wanted to meet with the SNM leadership to establish a working relationship and co-ordination to consolidate opposition to the regime. Despite a recent Ethio-Somali peace accord, the SNM still seemed to be receiving Ethiopian support so he would like to explore the possibility of similar co-operation and inquired whether the SNM could be a bridge.

I asked Dr. Jumale whom he would like to see? "Silanyo," he said, meaning of course Ahmed Mohamed Mohamoud, the long time Chairman of the SNM. He gave me a code name, 'IGO,' based on an acronym of the three initial letters of his full name. It was a Monday and he was leaving by the Somali Airlines flight late Wednesday that same week. We agreed to meet Wednesday morning and I immediately wrote to Silanyo's wife, Amina Sheikh Mohamed in London. I always addressed letters to Ahmed 'Silanyo' through her, so that even friends who would usually post my letters abroad would not easily know about my contacts.

My letters were normally carried by foreigners who were friends and were not politically suspect. I also used Somalis on occasions and always accompanied my couriers to the airport because even some foreigners were searched for undeclared foreign currency. Most of the security people there were my former staff when I was the head of the special branch and they always respected me and never searched people I was escorting. At one time my couriers had been Somali Airlines crew, as they were regulars, but on one occasion, some of the crew were found to possess narcotics when they got to Cairo and thereafter they were subjected to regular searches before leaving Mogadishu and I had to stop using them.

In my letter to Amina, I alerted her to Dr. Jumale's purposes and asked her to expect a call from Rome on the following Saturday evening. He would use his code name and she would have to respond by calling him Ismail. As agreed, Dr. Jumale and I met the following Wednesday morning and gave him among others, Amina's telephone number. All went well for Dr. Jumale. Amina managed to connect him with Silanyo that same Saturday evening, who was staying in Diredawa from where he was directing his movement. At the same time, he was in close contact with the Ethiopian authorities upon whom the SNM depended. Dr. Jumale returned with a high opinion of the SNM as a properly organized opposition and immediately briefed the underground Hawiye Committee of which he was Chairman. It is safe to assume that his trip and the encouragement he received from the SNM served as a stimulus to the already simmering resolve of the Hawiye to commit themselves to the armed struggle against the dictatorial regime. All considered, and in hindsight, this was to prove a crucial breakthrough.

From October 1988 onwards, a secret committee of elders met in Mogadishu, composed of Engineer Ali Sheikh Mohamed, Jirdeh Hussein, Ismail Dualeh Warsame, Abdurahman Haji Deria, Dr. Iman Mohamed, Abdulkarim Ahmed Gulaid, Mohamed Abdi Skerse, Dahir Haji Mohamed and myself. Other Isaaq people who were still government officials, knew about our meetings and sent contributions in the way of information and advice, though they did not themselves attend meetings. We would discuss problems facing the SNM from within and would often send emissaries or messages to places abroad in order to reach those who tried to set themselves up in opposition to the leadership. We were invariably unanimous in our view that once the SNM leadership was popularly elected, it had to be supported, come what may, until the end of its mandate. We would remind those opposing it, that the alternative could only be dissolution of the movement and a free rein for Siad Barre.

Our aim, however, was also to broaden the struggle. At that time, still prior to the formal establishment of the largely Hawiye United Somali Congress, we resolved to request the caucus of the Hawiye leadership, to use their influence over Hawiye army personnel stationed in the North — who were in fact the majority of Siad Barre's forces — to persuade them to disengage themselves. The Hawiye elders promised to address this issue with the utmost urgency. They sent several missions to the North and invited some ranking officers to find an excuse to come to Mogadishu to confer with them. The elders spent a lot of money on those missions and finally reached an agreement with the officers to bring about the mutiny of some army units, who would thereafter join the SNM. It was assumed the North would then fall to the freedom fighters by not later than the end of that year. The Hawiye elders also provided enough money in cash for one week's expenses for the army units who would mutiny. More than that could not be transferred to Hargeisa but thereafter the Hawiye elders pledged to maintain those units with no cost to the SNM or the Isaaq population. For that purpose they opened a proxy bank account in neighboring Djibouti from whence they could secretly pay for necessary supplies. The SNM were accordingly so informed through their London office.

To our astonishment, reports came back from the Hawiye army officers in Hargeisa that the SNM commanders had rejected their offer. We could not believe it and even suspected the Hawiye officers of deceiving their elders and just collecting their money. The Hawiye elders sent for some senior officers to come to Mogadishu at the first available opportunity. It was arranged for me to individually interview two of the officers in the home of Dr. Ismail Jumale. The rejection on the part of the SNM was thus verified and it was urgent to discover the reasons behind it. The officers I interviewed differed in their individual deductions, but neither of them voiced the SNM officers' real motives as we now know them. They simply did not want the job finished until they were successful in assuming leadership of the movement. Some of Siad Barre's Hawiye army officers did in fact mutiny with five tanks, and joined the SNM attack on Hargeisa in December 1989, after their original mutiny plan became known through the delay in its execution.

I wrote about these developments to Abdurahman Tur, then the SNM representative in London — our first line of communication — but never received any reply. I later interviewed Ahmed Silanyo who, as I have emphasized, has been the longest key player in the movement. He gave me a good deal of his time, defending the overall struggle of the SNM in general as being the best humanly possible under the conditions which the people had to endure, without much assistance from any quarter, despite the resources which were all the time available to their formidable enemy. He considered the movement's occasional setbacks as being the minimum to be expected in similar situations. He was right. Despite my disapproval of many aspects of the SNM's performance, it nevertheless goes without saying that Siad Barre could neither have been ultimately defeated, nor could the USC forces have dislodged him from his stronghold in Mogadishu, had his war machine and manpower not been irreparably incapacitated by the long, debilitating armed struggle waged against his brutal regime by the SNM and its supporters.

Ahmed Silanyo charitably defended the role of the senior ex-army officers, most of whom had been opposing him throughout his tenure of leadership, and while he did not deny their militaristic ambitions, he said that he gave them the benefit of any doubt, since they led combat operations and exposed themselves to great personal risks, during which many of their comrades were killed. He also minimized the seriousness of the attempt on his life, but could hardly deny its motive as being the militarist ambition of others.

I am less sanguine about those particular military officers, for they seem to have only been fighting the Siad Barre regime to keep the rebellion alive. They would have lost all the remittances of money and other assets that were so generously contributed over the years by the Isaaq supporters of the armed struggle worldwide. The Isaaq business community and intellectuals in Mogadishu paid dearly to assist the defection of all the Isaaq military and security personnel remaining in Siad Barre's forces. When these people tried to join the SNM, after enduring great risks and hardships, they were not infrequently kept at a distance and their services were not taken advantage of despite the need. A few did force their way into the movement, when their sub-clans brought pressure to bear on the SNM military commanders, a pattern which was eventually to have a negative effect after the fall of the dictatorship. It strengthened loyalty to the parochial sub-clans at the expense of central authority. I asked Ahmed Silanyo about the rejection by the SNM military commanders of the offer for some of Siad Barre's Hawiye forces to mutiny. He replied that he had never been informed of it, but added that SNM policy was that any such offer would only be acceptable if it were made without any preconditions. To the best of my knowledge the Hawiye leadership laid down no preconditions.

Compared with the Mijertein and the Isaaq, the Hawiye, for a long time lived in relative peace and accommodation with Siad Barre and without any direct opposition to his regime until the formation of the United Somali Congress (USC) in March 1989. Although they provided the backbone of the Mogadishu business community, and were the largest clan, they were not spared the regime's notorious system of public harassment, nor had there been belief on the part either of the Hawiye or Siad Barre, in any everlasting truce.

The interest of segments of the Hawiye business community in a change of government—especially as the economy spiralled towards total collapse—has been mentioned. As Siad Barre' regime degenerated, early in 1988 a caucus of Hawiye elders had been established secretly in Mogadishu, as any such organization had to be those days. Under the chairmanship of the late Dr. Ismail Jumale, it started to organize and orientate, both in and outside the country, in order to prepare the Hawiye sub-clans for an uprising and subsequent power bid. Counting on the personality and popularity of Dr. Ismail Jumale, who had long stood up for the value of human life, they agreed in principle that their next leader should be from his Abgal sub-clan. They anticipated confrontation with the regime, as Siad Barre would tolerate no competition for power, even if he were dying, and it was recognized that he would eventually move against the Hawiye.

They decided to organize their own force for armed struggle in the face of possible challenge. With the consent of the other elders, Dr. Ismail Jumale contacted Brig. General Mohamed Farah Aidid who was then Somali Ambassador to India, Sri Lanka and Singapore and invited him to leave his post and organize armed opposition among the Hawiye people in Ethiopia against Siad Barre's regime. Aidid agreed. Though not of the same sub-clan—Aidid is Habar Gedir—mutual trust and understanding had always existed between Dr. Jumale and Aidid. The majority of the Hawiye intellectuals placed their hope for a better future on these two men.

The birth of the USC was hastily, even prematurely, announced by the Hawiye people abroad, who established their own leadership structure and organization with a head office in Rome. Ali Wardhigley was elected as its chairman. While the Hawiye elders in Mogadishu held the real power, they gave their blessing to the Rome-based USC group, with an eye on better publicity and mobilization. Mogadishu still made the decisions on all important issues. It was this dual-pronged organizational arrangement that, on Dr. Ismail Jumale's death in July 1990, engulfed the USC and the whole Hawiye clan in internal conflict and subsequent bloodshed. The death of the Rome based USC chairman, Ali Wardhigley, which in fact preceded that of Dr. Jumale, had the effect of adding to an apparent leadership vacuum. A serious and chronic power struggle ensued.

Aidid considered himself to be Dr. Ismail's heir apparent, and was regarded as such by a majority of the Hawiye people as would be confirmed by his subsequent popular election as USC Chairman in July 1991. Meantime, Ali Wardhigley's former deputy in Rome, Hussein Ali Shido, claimed constitutional heirship to an 'interim chairmanship' until the next Congress. Aidid, who had never recognized the Rome based group whom his USC wing had always regarded as mere demagogues, proceeded to Ethiopia and was elected as 'interim USC chairman' by the fighting forces that he commanded. Back in Mogadishu, not wishing to be sidelined, the Hawiye caucus styled itself as 'Executive Committee of the USC' with a new Chairman, Hussein Mohamed Bot. Bot was an Abgal, but was otherwise unqualified as a replacement for Dr. Ismail Jumale. The Rome based USC and the Hawiye caucus co-operated and opposed General Aidid but the latter was supported by both the Somali National Movement (SNM) and the Somali Patriotic Movement (SPM) that is to say the three movements actively engaged in armed struggle against the Siad Barre dictatorial regime. They later issued a joint communique on their military co-ordination, providing also for post-Siad-Barre transitional arrangements. Both the USC Rome and the Mogadishu executive committee not only denounced the tripartite agreement but went so far as to deny Aidid's authority to represent the United Somali Congress in any way, thus making future civil conflict amongst the Hawiye sub-clans a virtual certainty, once Siad had fallen.

Our Isaak committee meantime developed ordination with the Hawiye opposition caucus, both at committee level, with the two sides always meeting at short notice, as well as on individual to individual basis for the following two years. We all recognized that although the Isaak and the Hawiye, united, could overthrow Siad Barre, they could not alone form a basis for a new united, democratic and peaceful Somali Republic. Through arrangements initially organized by Dr. Jumale, opposition co-ordination was therefore further widened and included prominent representatives from the Darod clan mainstream like General Mohamed Abshir Musa, Mohamed Ahmed Abdille *Sakhraan* and Prof. Ibrahim Mohamoud Abyan, former Dean of the Somali Institute of Development Administration and Management (SIDAM).

The last Siad Barre government dismissed Siad's son, Brig. Gen Maslah, as chief-of-staff of the armed forces, after he had ignored the ministers and refused to attend their meetings. It had been common knowledge for a good two months prior to his dismissal that Maslah was seldom available for his demanding job; he would often be unreachable during emergencies even when he was wanted by the president. Siad Barre came to ignore his son's existence and became his own chief-of-staff until Maslah's dismissal. He must have already written off his son or he would never otherwise have tolerated it. Maslah was replaced by Siad's son-in-law, Brig. General Morgan. According to information that later filtered through one of Maslah's mistresses, father and son had differed and parted ways after the former had rejected Maslah's advice that they should avoid confrontation with the Hawiye clan. His private business was managed by a Hawiye man who was in partnership him and perhaps it was under the latter's influence that he proffered advice to his father. If all this is true, despite being dull, Maslah was right, for it was the Hawiye rising in Mogadishu that finally put paid to Said Barre's dictatorship.

The development of a more broadbased opposition suffered a severe setback when sections of the business community prepared and presented the first of a number of manifestos against the regime, in May 1990. Their main objective was to substitute peaceful opposition for the armed struggle in which the SNM had been fully involved for almost a decade. Moreover the SNM had already been joined in the armed struggle by two other movements: the Somali Patriotic Movement (SPM), drawn largely from Ogadeen clansmen, and the United Somali Congress USC). Naturally, the Isaaq committee was totally opposed to this development — which we suspected was at least in part foreign inspired — on the grounds of practicality. But many influential personalities of the Hawiye caucus from which the USC drew its support, were among the signatories of the manifesto, including Jumale who gave me a copy of the manifesto while still in draft form. I called a meeting of the underground Isaaq committee in which it was discussed and rejected outright. We considered that it was only a dream to assume that a peaceful opposition could be effective and that a change of tactics would serve only to destroy the armed struggle. We were soon proved right when the regime rounded up all those who signed the manifesto for peaceful opposition. The Isaaq people had not only been involved in a full-fledged civil war, they had virtually lost all their assets and the notion of peaceful opposition, could not possibly be sold to them. I returned the draft to Dr. Jumale and explained our stand to him. We disagreed and he said that the sponsors would go ahead.

In the interests of unity, at first I even suggested a few amendments, but when other manifestos were produced by a number of interest groups, it became clearer by the hour that the whole idea of proposing last minute peaceful opposition was the brainchild of some western circles, especially the Italians. It came far too late. These western powers meantime continued to aid the Siad Barre regime without seriously addressing his human rights abuses. I too had contact with the Italian embassy and when both Dr. Jumale and General Abshir many times tried to convince me that peaceful opposition would only be complementary to the efforts of the SNM and not otherwise, I remained unconvinced.

CHAPTER SIXTEEN

THE SIAD BARRE
REGIME COLLAPSES

For many cruel years, Siad Barre and his close associates got away with horrendous atrocities, particularly in the north; at home through intimidation and abroad through the efforts of his diplomats to sustain a news blackout. Another factor was that international correspondents preferred the climate and comforts of Nairobi in the highlands of Kenya, to Mogadishu, let alone Hargeisa, Burao and Berbera.

So unprincipled was Siad Barre's regime that, despite its membership of the Organization of African Unity and the United Nations, the presidency and the regime's last foreign minister were quite prepared to deal behind the scenes with Apartheid South Africa, in a search for weapons with which to contain mounting insurrection. Deals were negotiated through avaricious foreigners and even Somali contact men. Hassan Jahi Ahmed Wehelie, a businessman and nephew of the late General Hussein Kulmiye Afreh, a former vice-president, is a case in point. His company, Winterfreight Ltd, was in contact through its Johannesburg office with the Department of Foreign Affairs, South African Airways, the Defence Force and Armcorp (the government manufacturer of military hardware). Top officials from Mogadishu, prepared to break U.N. sanctions if necessary, visited South African arms factories. South African ministers and officials, arriving in small planes with falsified flight plans, visited Mogadishu and Kismayo and were welcomed by ministers and even Siad Barre himself.

We smuggled evidence of the deceit to the BBC and others. After an article by Richard Greenfield set it all out in *African Events*, we were delighted to learn that the black caucus in the United States House of Representatives had taken the matter up. Even so, it is a matter of record that the Siad Barre regime's secret contacts with the former racist regime in Pretoria, continued from as early as 1983 right up until November 1990, only weeks before the dictator fled from Mogadishu. And all this time the regime perfidiously called for the restoration of human rights and the release of Nelson Mandela and other political prisoners—provided they were abroad.

The outside world knew of the existence of dissent at home and even of political unrest in the Somali northern regions, and elsewhere, but precise details of the extent and the root causes of the problems were often lacking. It was one of the main failures of the SNM not to have publicized the situation more. We kept sending their London office regular situation reports, obtained with considerable risk and under stress, but it seemed to us the SNM seldom made full use of them. Only in the last few months of the struggle when Suleiman Mohamoud Aden became secretary for international relations, did we receive some acknowledgement and feedback. Generally press coverage remained sparse.

Notable exceptions were some of the African magazines, particularly *New African* in London and *Africa Report* in New York. Some articles also appeared in *Africa Events* and others, but considerable pressure was at once exerted by Siad's diplomats against editors and correspondents of these papers. Later the *Washington Post*, the *Christian Science Monitor*, and in England, Richard Dowden of the *Independent* took an interest. The traditional academic and other societies interested in Somalia proved very reluctant to come to terms with what was really happening and seized on every propaganda ploy by the regime and its supporters as evidence of a change of heart.

After failing to get the SNM itself to publish adequately, we managed to establish contacts such as with Dr. Hussein A. Bulhan, of the *Somali Relief and Rehabilitation* organization in Boston, Massachusetts, USA, and sent him copies of whatever we sent to the SNM. During 1989–90, Bulhan and a few colleagues promptly and continuously issued a monthly newsletter entitled *Crisis*. The limitations under which Somalis abroad worked are clear from the *Crisis* editorial which persistently pointed out:

> CRISIS appears monthly. It has no budget, no paying audience, and no supporting organization. The bulletin emerged out of a sense of urgency and duty. Its voice is presented by the least expensive and most efficient means. Readers who find a copy can xerox it, make as many copies as they can afford, and send it to anyone they wish.

We could hardly keep up with this publication and when we did not meet deadlines, it would still be published, sometimes reproducing Hadrawi's poems which were always descriptive of the situation. *Crisis* was not, of course, the only Somali news pamphlet in the outside world, but we would duplicate the copy we received each month and distribute it to the foreign community in Mogadishu. Xerox copies of other articles and video tapes of news features also circulated clandestinely in the capital and beyond.

A small but significant segment of America's opinion-formers were alerted and in due course the US Congress, supported by many other American institutions, acted to deprive the US Administration of its former freedom of action and end its policy of unqualified support for the Siad Barre regime. For example, the US Congress on 8 February 1989, released an accurate and damning report submitted to it by the Department of State on human rights practices in Somalia in compliance with the Foreign Assistance Act of 1961, which requires human rights reports on all countries that are members of the United Nations.

The contribution of reports issued by various Human Rights organizations such as *Human Rights Watch* and *Amnesty International*, also helped curtail non-bilateral assistance. Examples of such important reports might include the testimony of Holly Burkhalter of *Human Rights Watch* before the House Foreign Affairs Subcommittee on Africa, on 9 March 1989 and before the Subcommittee on International Development Institutions and Finance, on 20 June 1989. Comment by the Lawyers Committee for Human Rights and reports by concerned committees of the US National Academy of Science and the Institute of Medicine were also valuable. Another important factor was the Somali Language Service of the BBC. Its normal broadcasting routine ran counter to the seriously guarded policy of news blackout. Siad Barre frequently complained of its "interfering in Somali internal affairs" and his regime sought to influence and even discredit and change the personnel the BBC employed.

Probably the hours of quiet but effective lobbying put in by friends and the Somali communities abroad can never be evaluated, but it is certain that Siad Barre was not only defeated in the armed struggle but even more by the withdrawal, albeit belated, of international aid. This sapped the morale of his regime and eventually determined its collapse. The German government was among the first donors to totally withdraw assistance. With the general curtailing of international economic aid, Siad Barre found it difficult to maintain his large army including several thousand armed irregulars spread over all parts of the country, not to mention the thousands of Ethiopian refugees in the North whom he armed to fight side by side with his forces against the civilian population.

Unfavorable publicity worldwide, soon had a tremendous effect upon most members of the international donor community, with the exception of Italy and some Arab OPEC members. Eventually even Italian support began to wane as Siad Barre continued to lose credibility. Both the Italian parliament and the press were critical of Siad Barre's corruption and human rights violations but they were powerless to emulate the US Congress, and successfully cut off Italian aid. There were friendships and dubious business connections between members of Siad's family and the families of leading Italian politicians, among others. Italy was also a major supplier of arms and munitions—possibly, over the years, as important if not more so, than the Soviet Union and the United States. Even when Congress cut off all aid, armaments said to have been in the pentagon pipeline continued to arrive to reinforce Siad Barre's forces almost to the last minute. Likewise support from several Arab OPEC members was received right until the very end of Siad Barre's rule.

Inside the country, commerce was severely inhibited by shortages of cash. This was caused by failure on the part both of bank management and government authorities to apply proper banking practices. That excessive credits were granted has been discussed above, and government deficit financing soon spiralled out of control. Substantial withdrawal of deposits by ordinary clients ensued. Currency was instead hoarded in private safes or hiding places. Difficulty in cashing personal checks was only overcome by the use of circular checks in normal transactions, bringing about a money exchange mechanism substantially outside the banking system. Whenever a considerable number of such checks were to be cashed, as often as not the banks would not have the liquidity to meet the demand. Moreover, general insecurity, particularly the conflict in the North, resulted in the destruction of a substantial proportion of national business operations. To further complicate matters, cash used by the government as bribe money in a vain attempt to keep certain sections of the society on the government side, again especially in the North, was drawn on deficit from the banks to the extent of well over 10 billion Somali shillings. Much of this cash became bottled up in remote regions and did not circulate freely. Moreover large stashes of cash were kept in certain government garrisons, particularly the headquarters of 77 Command, for political contingency. The pumping of more 'money' into the banks resulted only in greater withdrawals; massive isolation, but no deposits. From the mid '80's, public trust in the country's banking system had been apparently irretrievably lost.

As international pressure mounted and economic aid dwindled, Siad Barre suddenly presented a human face by announcing the introduction of a multiparty democratic system and promising to release all political detainees. He also decided to allow representatives from the US Academy of Science's Committee of Human Rights and from Amnesty International to visit the country. No Somali saw this as other than a ploy, but some foreigners were taken in. I had lunch with the US Ambassador on February 17, 1989 and when I said that I did not believe in the least in Siad Barre's declaration, he dismissed my skepticism as mere cynicism. Neither delegation was, in the event, allowed to see or interview any of the detainees, but Amnesty International's visit in June 1989 coincided with the release of scores of politically held or politically convicted prisoners. Several hundred more prisoners still remained in detention centers in the North of the country and a few others nearby in the notorious Labaatan Jirow prison, despite government claims that all political detainees had been released.

I had previously had contacts with Amnesty International before they ever came to Somalia. Soon after their arrival, I was telephoned early one morning by the human rights activist, Dr. Ismail Jumale. He just said, "They are here." He could not have been clearer in his expression than that, as his telephone was liable to tapping. I immediately went to his office and met the two delegation members, one of whom, Martin Hill, I had met before during a Conference on African Refugees held in Arusha, Tanzania in May 1979. Dr. Jumale then left us and we set up subsequent meetings and venues.

The delegation members had only a short stay, and were living at the Croce del Sud hotel, very near to Dr. Jumale's law office which, although they would be shadowed, was always very crowded and offered good cover for we could meet privately in the study. The office was inside the large Lloyd Triestino compound with its wide area for parking. I would always drive in through the back gate and park my car there, while the delegates would enter by the front gate facing their hotel.

Our second meeting place was the American Golf Club. We met several times in one or the other venue, hopefully having shaken off Siad Barre's surveillance. I would then deliver any messages. Martin and I had a rendezvous early one morning at the Golf Club and had breakfast there together. Among other things, Martin expressed a desire to meet former foreign minister Omer Arteh who had been released only a few months earlier after six years detention. I knew Omer Arteh would be willing and advised they should go to the Haraf bush restaurant at exactly 5 p.m. that same day. They were to release their taxi on arrival and I would pick them up at about 6 p.m. I arranged with the restaurant manager that he should delay the taxi until ten minutes before 6 P.M., since any taxi driver from the hotel could only be a security agent or else he would have been shut out of business. The Haraf restaurant was 8 miles outside the town and the driver would naturally report his passengers' whereabouts to the president's surveillance team. The team could otherwise ride back in the same taxi to the restaurant to see who was meeting, or even worse, break up that important meeting. The restaurant manager paid the taxi driver for waiting. I arrived there at 5:55 P.M.; the taxi had just left and Omer Arteh and the delegation had just stood up and wished each other good-bye.

I then hurriedly drove off my important passengers, by a different route towards the town, to the house of the Michael Mariano family where they met more than a dozen former detainees who had been waiting there and they were uninterrupted for six hours. About midnight I dropped the delegates one block behind their hotel.

The authorities somehow figured out the Omer Arteh meeting, I think only by deduction, rather than on evidence, perhaps based upon information the taxi driver might have given. Omer Arteh was a frequent visitor to that restaurant where he often entertained guests. A spokesman for the regime, Mohamoud Gaileh, said later that the delegation were allowed to see anybody they wanted to and included Omer Arteh in his list.

The Amnesty International delegation, although not satisfied with the overall situation, had nevertheless to acknowledge, by the time they published their report, that there was some improvement in the human right's record of Siad Barre's regime. Had events not developed as they did, Siad's plan was probably to provide sufficient time for the US Administration to try to convince Congress to release some aid, at least that already approved but frozen.

I had warned the delegation that they should be careful because the release of some detainees, though a relief to the individuals concerned and certainly helpful to their families, by itself meant little in the overall Somali political scenario. The regime would have no difficulty replacing those released with new detainees. As it happened, hardly two weeks passed before Siad Barre was involved in the most appalling bloodshed. But even during the visit of the delegation, the activities of the newly established United Somali Congress (USC) were already having a visible impact on the Somali capital of Mogadishu. Leaflets were being scattered in the streets. Wall posters portrayed Siad Barre in caricature as a wanted criminal and appealed that anyone finding him should arrest and deliver him to the nearest police station.

Siad's 'socialist' regime had always had an uneasy relationship with the nations religious leaders. Serious confrontation had occurred for example over defining women's inheritance 'rights'. In times of national, as well as personal difficulties, most folk tend to turn to religion and Somalia was no exception. But that is not to say that the more extreme organized religious fundamentalist groups existed in Somalia as they do in certain other Muslim countries. Nevertheless, several Imams of the Mogadishu mosques took the opportunity of Friday prayers to deliver speeches critical of the government for not curbing what they saw as anti-Islamic religious activities. Then one day, one of those Imams also accused the Roman Catholic Church of being involved in proselytizing. Siad Barre immediately seized this opportunity to endeavor to silence Islamic religious criticism. On the following Wednesday evening the Catholic Bishop, Salvatore Colombo, was fatally shot in the chest at very close range, in his own cathedral. He was dead within two hours. The killer ran away un-detected and unidentified.

According to an Italian nurse who worked at the police hospital where the bishop was taken and where he died during an emergency operation, Siad Barre arrived there before the hospital staff had received any request for emergency surgical treatment. Nor had the nurses even heard about the shooting. Other observers reported that the French ambassador arrived at the hospital some thirty minutes after the shooting of the bishop and he too was surprised to learn that the president had already offered his condolences and left.

The first police officer on the scene, Colonel Sulieman Kujog, deputy head of CID, instituted an enquiry and traced the flight of the assassin to the presidential Villa Somalia. He similarly traced a vehicle that had been used in the getaway. However, he was ordered to hand over all enquiries to the ministry of interior, then headed by one of Siad's sons-in-law. Shortly afterwards, the colonel, who had previous-ly clashed with Siad's relatives over his enquiries into the smuggling of narcotics and ivory — in August 1986, he had stumbled upon arrange-ments for a sale of some eighteen thousand elephant tusks, actually on police premises — went into exile where he set down the facts as he knew them in a sworn affidavit. There was little doubt in the minds of the majority of the Somali people that the murder of the bishop had been engineered by Siad Barre and carried out by his agents. This suspicion was shared by many Italians, but the Italian embassy played it down.

The bishop had been in Somalia for more than forty years and his murder came as a great shock to many people. He had come first as a young priest, and over the years had established good relations with many Somalis, including pious and devout muslims, because of his commitment to social welfare. Since his appointment as bishop, the Roman Catholic Relief Organization, Caritas, had built many schools and hospitals in various localities in the South and upon completion the keys were always delivered to the community leaders. Nurses had been willingly provided for the hospitals but only where requested.

I was prompted by that murder to seek a more personal knowledge about the Roman Catholic Church, but not all that I was told by other muslims, proved accurate. I later sought additional information from one of the very few catholic Somalis but still could not fathom any apparent motive for the killing. I was well aware however, that had the killer been an Islamic extremist he would never have run away, but on the contrary, would have shouted, "Allahu Akbr" (God is Great), and would have given himself up to his martyrdom. My mind thus turned to examine the popular suspicions.

I pondered, had Siad considered that his opponents had been too much encouraged by his earlier announcement of political relaxations and had they come to pose too great a danger to his one man rule? Had he not, perhaps, foreseen that he must silence them before it was too late? On the other hand, surely Siad Barre also knew only too well the effect such a crackdown would have in eroding and discrediting his declared new policies. Did he believe it possible, therefore, to orchestrate a situation suggesting the emergence of 'Islamic fundamentalist terrorism', solely for the western Christian world's consumption? Being already at bitter odds with the Islamic revival elsewhere in the world, would the Americans not then accept him and his repressive regime as a lesser evil; an acceptable alternative to a future Islamic fundamentalist state in Somalia? There are elements in the west who so misunderstand Islam that this seemed just possible.

Anyway two days later, Siad Barre laid a siege around most of the mosques in Mogadishu, just before the Friday prayers — we suspected in order to provoke riots as a pretext for detaining the most outspoken religious leaders. The worshippers in several mosques played into Siad Barre's hands when their sheikhs were prevented from delivering the usual speeches. Serious riots erupted and Siad's chosen soldiers were not short of targets. They left several hundred dead and many others wounded. The Imams of several mosques were arrested and a dusk to dawn curfew imposed. Then similar arrests were made of political figures including the human rights activist lawyer, Dr. Ismail Jumale.

Siad Barre appeared mistakenly to believe, after the Mosque riots, that only the Isaaq, who had been hardened by the long war in the North, could have dared to confront his forces in such open fighting. In fact, the Isaaqs in Mogadishu, apart from meetings and other secret activities, were amongst the most law abiding of citizens: they did not feel it was their responsibility to act; after all, it was Southerners who were being forcibly conscripted and sent to the Northern front where many were killed. If they were willing to put up with that continuously, so be it. An exception was one single act of sabotage, planned by some Isaaq young men, to involve the blowing up of a Somali Airlines 707 plane which Siad Barre was using to airlift men and weapons to the North. The plane was technically grounded before the contemplated plan could be effected.

Having failed to present the 'Ethiopian' refugees in the North as Isaaq returnees, Siad Barre desperately tried to get Isaaq evacuees back to the sites of their destroyed homes, in order to ward off some international criticism and create a cover for the presence of resettled 'foreign' refugees. As all other means failed in achieving that objective, he pronounced — but only as a ploy for international consumption — his readiness for reconciliation and dialogue with the opposition. At the time, the only effective opposition was the SNM, but both the SPM and the USC were in the process of establishing themselves.

The Italian and Egyptian governments, with the blessing of many other countries of the western donor community, took the initiative to bring about a dialogue. All those countries wanted to achieve, was to commit Siad Barre to democratic reforms. That could never suffice, for the people of the North would never have accepted Siad Barre remaining as their president, even for one more day. Clearly any such talks were doomed to failure. Nevertheless, after discussion, we urged the SNM leadership to seize the opportunity of accepting the invitation, even if talks were to break off immediately, like those between Eritreans and Mengistu's dictatorial Ethiopian regime held in Nairobi. We knew that Siad Barre himself did not in fact want talks to take place as he had nothing new to offer. He could only repeat his outdated slogan of an 'amnesty'. We felt the SNM should not play into his hands by refusing talks. They could lose ground by antagonizing the international community, the majority of whom were simplistically committed to peace through dialogue as some kind of worldwide panacea. Agreeing to meet did not necessarily mean accepting the proposals of the other side. The SNM, however, rejected talks, stating they would not sit face to face with the Siad Barre regime. The immediate reason could well have been that because of their internal power struggles and the weakness of their leadership, they were not in a position to reach any consensus. However, in retrospect, it is clear that any opportunity for fruitful talks had long since passed, for the bloodletting continued unabated.

On the night of 16–17 July, 1989, army units under the command of Siad's son, Brigadier-General Maslah, collected as many mainly young Isaaq men as they could lay their hands on, during a swoop on houses in the city. The forty-seven men apprehended, however, included two professors in the National University's College of Education, one of them the only Somali who taught chemistry at that level. Their offence was merely being Isaaq. They were herded together and shot, before dawn. A mass burial site was chosen near the Jezira beach about 13 miles south-west of Mogadishu. One survivor of these mass murders, albeit buried alive, was able to dig himself out of the desert sand after the killers had left the scene. He reached Mogadishu about noon the following day but being in a state of severe shock, if only wounded slightly in one arm, he hid himself in a house because he knew too much. (See Appendix II which also mentions this dreadful incident.)

Information was communicated to an army general who, after interviewing the victim and inspecting the mass grave, reported direct to Minister of the Interior Ahmed Suleiman, as stated, a son-in-law of Siad Barre. The two went to the president who instructed the minister to take charge. But no sooner had the minister left, than Siad Barre warned the killers of the discovery of their crime. Meanwhile Ahmed Suleiman, known as *Dafle* (the blade), arranged that the survivor be questioned by a panel of officials, in his presence. By the time his staff had made necessary arrangements for the exhumation of the bodies, Siad Barre's men had returned to the scene of their crime and sealed off the whole area. The minister's men, the police investigators and their escorts, were all chased away by the threat of firearms. They reported back to the minister, who indirectly acknowledged his father-in-law's complicity but took no further action.

I was invited by a prominent businessman to his office so that we could report the massacre to people outside the country. He had several telephones, but one line was free, protected by his hired security agents from any tapping, and after we had transmitted our messages, my host warned our distant interlocutors that whenever they called they should use only that line. The awful news made the international press and of course shook the whole nation including hitherto passive members of Siad Barre's institutions. The extent of murmuring from all corners prompted Siad Barre to attempt to placate public anger by appointing a bogus committee of inquiry. Even before the committee started its work, he pre-empted its finding by talking about the incident in public and dismissing it as false and malicious propaganda against his regime. The committee did report an apparent commission of a crime but Siad Barre neither published the report nor passed it on as a basis for a proper investigation.

The regime's days were clearly numbered, but still the Italians and the Egyptians struggled to forestall the inevitable. Apart from the genuine opposition movements, certain other opportunistic groups emerged to register their voices, often through the BBC Somali service. Most were not in the least engaged in armed struggle. Some were even financed by Siad Barre himself to counter true opposition. However, because of prior refusal, on the part of the SNM, invitations to reconciliation talks were extended to several such 'opposition' groups. Had it not been for a dramatic increase in the pressure exerted on Siad Barre in the South, those talks would have taken place in Cairo on 13 December 1990. The SNM was perhaps fortunate thus to escape a measure of unhelpful international pressure and possibly condemnation. Meantime, however, the sharp decline in international assistance, long since diverted for military use, took its toll. Siad began to lose control not only of his army, but also of most other pillars of his dictatorial rule, including his terror organizations. The latter were beginning to distance themselves from Siad Barre and found it necessary to 'buy' favors for themselves. On one occasion the palace guard nearly mutinied, complaining about the effects of mounting inflation. When the officer in charge reported the incident, Siad Barre ordered that the men be filed before him. He just snatched a rifle from one and said, "He who has this can never get hungry," and with that he left. This was an appalling and irresponsible remark with far-reaching consequences.

That same evening, his guards raided the hawker's market at El-Gab and looted sacks of money. The whole crowd at the busy market rose up against them and they fired at the crowd, killing some and wounding many others. They fled with the public in hot pursuit and entered the palace, the Villa Somalia, but a precedent for looting had been set. A few days later, three elderly businessmen, Abdulqadir Mohamed Aden *Zoppo*, Jirdeh Hussein and Osman Ahmed Robley, went to see Siad Barre to talk to him about opening a private bank in response to his earlier pronouncement that economic restrictions would be removed. After their discussion, Osman Ahmed Roble brought up the El-Gab incident and reminded the president that the looters had taken refuge in the presidential palace. He replied, "Let them be looted because they would not put their money in the banks." He later issued a warning to the general public which was repeatedly publicized in his official media, exonerating his government of any responsibility for money looted which was not deposited. Siad Barre mistakenly calculated that he could still overcome the people's resolve by forcing them to deposit their money in his banks, where his regime could use it at its discretion, or alternatively by encouraging his army to commit acts of legalized looting.

All this Machiavellian maneuvering was fast becoming irrelevant. The country was rising and closing in on the regime. Siad's adversaries were soon to dub him 'Mayor of Mogadishu.' His power nationwide was rapidly slipping away. Even in his last times, it did not seem to matter to Siad that he was setting a most dangerous example. Many lawless groups, not under his control, could and did follow suit. During the eighteen months prior to Siad Barre's final fall, Mogadishu was to all intents and purposes in the hands of scores of armed gangs. One or two may have belonged to Siad Barre's forces but they all robbed and even killed foreigners and Somalis alike, and almost daily looted motor vehicles, mainly from the international community.

People able to do so made their own private security arrangements. Every senior official, politician and businessman of Siad Barre's Marehan sub-clan, enlisted ten or so kinsfolk from Siad Barre's already beleaguered army for their own personal security. Many other soldiers deserted. Siad Barre was no longer capable of disbanding the terror gangs even after he discovered that his forces had no monopoly of the spoils of banditry. The distraught president resorted to the inflationary printing of currency notes to lessen his guards' need for theft, and he is said even to have had foreign currency, including that of neighboring countries, forged abroad and imported.

United Somali Congress forces began closing in, having twice overrun the military garrison at Bulo-Burti, 220 Kms north of the capital, killing the commander there. Yet even while USC commando groups were actually infiltrating the city and forces led by Brigadier-General Aidid were sweeping through the center of the country, the Italians never let up in their efforts to stave off collapse. Meetings were held, manifestos were circulated, new appointments were canvassed and broadcast but the chaos deepened steadily. It might be news even to Siad Barre himself that on Saturday 29 December 1990, it was actually his own soldier bandits who provoked the final escalation of fighting in Mogadishu.

Some gangs, including Siad Barre's men, had become highly organized, collecting information and choosing their targets for looting forays. On that particular day, a group of army bandits acting upon correct intelligence of the availability of a large amount of cash in a Hawiye owned store, took two military vehicles with artillery guns and raided the store. They killed the owner and seized sacks of cash. It was about noon and the noise of their firing sent warning signals throughout the nearby surroundings. Anyone with a gun rushed to the scene. Some of the bandits were killed there and then. One of the two vehicles was immobilized. The money was recovered, but the remaining bandits escaped in the other vehicle and fetched reinforcements including a tank from the hitherto vaunted 77 Army Group.

This clash developed into the final phase of civil war in the Somali capital which did not cease until Siad Barre fled on January 26, 1991. All able-bodied men in both the Army and the Police crossed over on the night following the flare up and joined the USC forces. Siad Barre became short of infantry manpower to halt the USC advances. He resorted to the indiscriminate bombardment of large civilian populated sections of the city. Meantime his officials, led by his son-in-law, Ahmed Suleiman, struggled to organize a Darod-based armed civilian militia. He met with some success amongst Dolbahante, Mijertein and related clansmen, although the Ogadeen and other Darod refused to fight on the side of the dying regime against the USC. Regrettably, this nevertheless triggered off another phase in the civil war and led to eventual Darod-Hawiye ethnic retribution of serious dimensions and far reaching consequences, long after the aged dictator, Siad Barre, had been bundled into an armored car and hastily evacuated to the temporary safety of his clan homelands.

CHAPTER SEVENTEEN

CONFUSION AND THE DECLARATION OF THE "REPUBLIC OF SOMALILAND"

U PON SIAD BARRE'S DEFEAT and flight from his besieged
official residence in the Somali capital, the USC Mogadishu faction
complicated a difficult situation by hastily and unilaterally installing
a rich, but comparatively unknown hotelier, Ali Mahdi, as interim
president claiming full control over the whole country, while in fact
this faction was not even in proper control of Mogadishu itself. Ali
Mahdi is an Abgal by sub-clan, and it seems clear that the original
Hawiye choice of Dr. Ismail Jumale's leadership was still being
interpreted by the elders as assuring an Abgal right of succession to the
presidency. Brigadier-General Aidid very strongly opposed the
nomination and disassociated himself from any subsequent
developments. The other two fighting movements also denounced the
installation of Ali Mahdi as an usurpation of power and rejected the
claim of total control over the country. Ali Mahdi countered by
dispatching a delegation to Rome and confirming a northerner, Omer
Arteh Ghalib to head the government as interim prime minister. (He
had already been so appointed in the dying days of the dictatorship.)

In the wake of the rejection by the SNM, the SPM and General
Aidid of the new interim president, Mohamed Haji Hassan *Salah* and
I grew alarmed and we met Omer Arteh and asked him to postpone,
at least for four days, the formation of a new government until we
could try and see the SNM leadership, in order to seek common

ground for developing a consensus. He agreed. When I met Omer Arteh the following morning, however, he said that he would announce the names of his new ministers that same day or the day after. I asked him why he had changed his mind, but he gave no reason. I learned only that he had seen Ali Mahdi the night before. Doubtless the latter had objected to any consultation with the SNM whom he knew would support Aidid. Omer Arteh was an experienced and able diplomat, and he secured recognition from the Organization of African Unity, the League of Arab States, the non-Aligned Conference and many — but by no means all — individual governments. But the non participation of the SNM, of which he was not a member, greatly eroded his government's standing at home. Conflict with Aidid's forces, not to mention an opportunistic but brief recovery by Siad Barre and his supporters, contributed further to the imminent collapse of the Somali state as we had known it.

The hasty and unilateral decision on the part of the Mogadishu based USC faction — the so-called 'executive committee' — not only to install their own president, but also to form a 'government', greatly angered the people of the North, as did the new 'president's' apparently total disregard of their ten long years of arduous struggle and sacrifice. He seemed only to acknowledge a campaign of no more than seven months duration in the South against the former dictatorial regime. This step contributed to the eventual separation of the North, and political developments there must be examined.

Certain weaknesses and chronic rivalries within the SNM have been mentioned. They can best be explained by an appraisal of their nature and the realities of their background. Although continuously engaged in armed struggle since the beginning of 1982, the movement was not cohesive. It had not even styled itself as a revolutionary organization, as it probably should have because of the situation in which the masses, from whom the SNM drew its main support, found themselves.

A dearth of revolutionary spirit resulted in a leadership dominated by coalitions of groups with diverse vested interests and ambitions, over which no leader could exercise much effective control or proper discipline. The situation was further compounded by the willful cover-up of the prevailing lawlessness which had developed, encouraged by group factionalism. The community elders seem to have felt that addressing such serious issues on their merits might bring about division among clan members whose unity was their only viable defensive weapon against Siad Barre's unceasing tactics of divide and rule.

The SNM was ever a frail structure. Its contradictions had led Abdurahman 'Tur' to threaten to resign the chair and had obliged its leadership to practice the minimum possible level of damage control, just to hold the organization together. That was the exact situation in which his predecessor, Ahmed Silanyo, had found himself for a good six years. Apart from the usual power struggles mentioned earlier, a good part of the criticism and the malicious propaganda directed against him was financed by Siad Barre and cleverly implemented by his own agents within the movement. They were supported by others who had joined the movement, not for its cause, but being misfits even in the Siad Barre regime, in order to seek some alternative standing and accommodation in society. Miraculous achievements from an organization so beset with internal obstacles and bickering were not to be anticipated. Another factor was the absence of any radical institutional framework for the expulsion of undesirables. The attempted destabilization of the SNM by certain officers has also been discussed above. Their main motive, formerly, was sheer ambition; this became complicated by fear of accountability for past crimes. Factional interests could not, after the defeat of the Siad Barre regime, be sustained in their original form and the interested groups therefore orchestrated an agenda for wider clan conflict. Had this not been rejected by the overwhelming majority of the general public, major confrontations with destructive consequences would undoubtedly have resulted in the North as they began to in Mogadishu and Kismayo in the South.

Apart from long standing rivalries and power struggles, corruption also played a big part in the instability which followed the defeat of Siad Barre. The SNM inherited abundant stocks of fuel supplies, besides other assets, from the defeated Siad Barre forces. If properly managed, there should have been sufficient to meet local needs for more than six months. But they were disposed of within a much shorter time without the least accountability, to the utter disgust and resentment of the war-crippled and other former guerillas who were denied any compensation. For a time, some resorted to indiscriminate looting. It was sad that genuine SNM fighters felt driven to turn to terrorism because of malpractices on the part of some of their leaders.

The leadership did not move fast enough to ensure a workable system of accountability, nor did it at once re-establish law enforcement mechanisms such as a police force. The honest and sensible ones were overwhelmingly outnumbered and frustrated. On the other hand the movement had one real strength — the will of the Northern masses. They had stood tightly together, not necessarily so much because of a commitment to Isaaq clan unity (which neither existed before the Siad Barre era nor has been adhered to with any great seriousness since the defeat of the regime) but rather because of collective reaction to atrocities directed against the Isaaq people as a common target. Siad's hatred made no distinction as to where the ordinary individual's loyalty might lie — religion, nationalism, tribalism or ideology. It became simply a matter of genocide on the one hand and survival on the other.

The vicious behavior of Siad Barre's officials in the north before and during that long era of armed struggle, whatever their titles or designations: governors, the likes of *Afar-Jeeble*, the 'man with four pockets', a sobriquet inferring bribe taking, and the *buulles*, judges, senior army and police officers or the other so-called administrators, was so devoid of human decency and compassion, that it was seen by all who witnessed it as un-Islamic and un-Somali. Corruption, rape, looting, arbitrary arrests, detentions without trials, torture and killing, although religiously and ethically condemned, were continuously meted out to the civilian population. This bred hatred and desperation. The overwhelming majority of all repressive government personnel, whether civilian or in the armed forces, were southerners whom the people came no longer to see as co-nationals, but rather as an alien occupying force. Over the years, there developed a rejection of anything and everything southern.

However, despite all the bad feeling among the people of the

North, prior to the overthrow of Siad Barre, it had never gelled into a general consensus for a unilateral declaration of independence (UDI) before the decision of the United Somali Congress, Mogadishu faction, to usurp power. Before that time, neither the majority of the senior members of the central committee of the SNM, nor their constitution, had contemplated any such separation. They had not even considered it among suggested solutions to the problems of the people of the North. Article 6 of the SNM's (Mujahid's) Constitution adopted at the 5th Congress, 1987, specifically stated "The Somali National Movement is committed to the total liberation of the Somali Republic and shall oppose any division of the country into regions or mini-states that are prejudicial to the unity of the country."

It has been argued by some that there was a parallel between Somaliland and the case of Eritrea, but that is not so. Eritrea had a totally different historical background. International involvement was necessitated by the defeat, in the Second World War, of Italy, the former colonial power. At that time the people of Eritrea were divided over their future. Some wanted independence, others wanted federation or a union with Ethiopia, while still others wanted a union of at least a part of the country with the Sudan. The UN General Assembly finally passed a resolution federating Eritrea with Ethiopia, whereby Eritrea was to enjoy a full internally autonomous system of government with its own legislature, finances and a separate police force. Ten years thereafter, Emperor Haile Sellassie of Ethiopia illegally violated the UN resolution on the federal status of Eritrea and reduced it to a mere province of Ethiopia. He abolished the Eritrean internal constitution and all the relevant institutions attached thereto and appointed his own governor-general for direct rule from Addis Ababa. This was the basis for the subsequent long years of liberation struggle. After the defeat of dictatorship in Ethiopia, the new rulers of both Eritrea and Ethiopia wisely agreed on the holding of a plebiscite in 1993, with observers from the United Nations etc: the Eritrean people overwhelmingly opted for independence and they have thus received both international acclaim and understanding and Eritrea as an independent nation has been admitted both to membership of the United Nations and the Organization of African Unity.

In the case of Somaliland, on and before achieving independence in 1960, the people were never divided on the issue of Union with the South and had overwhelmingly opted for that Union, without UN involvement or outside participation. Any reversal of that option would seemingly require two conditions to be fulfilled prior to an acceptable declaration of independence: first, a dialogue with the other contracting partner to the union, namely the South, to negotiate such withdrawal (since there was no united South a notice to that effect would probably have served the legal purpose of showing goodwill and would serve to satisfy international public opinion) and second, the holding of a plebiscite for the people of the North with or without international supervision.

Representatives from five regions—Awdal, Northwest, Togdheer, Sool and Sanag—met in the port of Berbera 15 to 27 February 1991. They decided to reconsider the Act of Union which the government of the former British Protectorate had passed on 27 April 1960. A congress which included 99 members of the SNM central committee met in Burao in 27 April 1991.

At this crucial moment, the SNM leadership lost control and failed to advise the people and present considered options and their probable consequences. On the spur of the moment and with (understandably) embittered emotions paramount, the representatives of the Northern people reached the snap decision on 18 May 1991, to unilaterally and at once withdraw from the Union of the Somali Republic and to rename their region "The Republic of Somaliland." The merits or demerits of that decision apart, and notwithstanding its being precipitated by a unilateral action on the part of the USC, Mogadishu faction, and a sudden burst of emotion, there is no doubt whatever that it reflected the wishes of the overwhelming majority of the people of the North at the time and since. The procedure followed, or the lack of it, in arriving at that decision was, however, inappropriate, to say the least, and the newly declared republic suffered in consequence a total lack of international recognition. International isolation jeopardized rehabilitation of the almost totally destroyed cities and main towns and the infrastructure, such as it was. Moreover, no country accepted any Somali passport with a 'Somaliland' stamp on it and Somaliland citizens were obliged periodically to approach Somali Republic embassies, where they remained open, including those still held by supporters of the ousted president, for the issue of new passports. Where available, these proved expensive.

In fairness to the SNM, a positive development to its credit since the fall of the dictator, has been the partial reconciliation of the northern communities among whom Siad Barre had engendered internecine strife. That said, however, the non-Isaaq communities within Somaliland, who had a combined total of thirty-three percent of the parliamentary representation at the time of independence, should not be expected to automatically continue support and loyalty to a system offering perpetual Isaaq leadership but not necessarily a stable system of government which could guarantee undisturbed minority rights.

The Isaaq too, who constitute the majority of the population of the former British Protectorate, may never have been so united as they were during their struggle against the dictatorial regime of Siad Barre. More than anything else, they need to preserve a measure of unity, which once lost, may never be regained. They may only maintain it if they can compete with other Somali groups of similar standing, like the Darod or the Hawiye; it will be difficult to sustain if they compete only amongst themselves. That has been proved in history and may partly account for serious intra-clan strife and instability in 1991-2, which not only disrupted humanitarian relief efforts but even threatened disintegration of the fragile newly declared 'republic.'

By separating without any negotiations with the South, the newly declared 'Republic of Somaliland' many have forfeited outright any claim to the former assets of the Somali Republic and what might be recoverable from the improperly accumulated private coffers of Siad Barre, members of his family and from his close associates. Moreover Siad Barre and his regime will not easily be brought to justice for crimes committed. Siad Barre left behind a huge foreign debt which hangs round the neck of all the Somali people. Somaliland, under laws governing the succession of states, may well not avoid a proportion of that debt obligation.

Last, but not least, there is the economic factor. Somali people on both sides of the former colonial frontier with Somalia — which again becomes the common border between Somalia proper and the newly declared Republic of Somaliland — have since independence in 1960, considerably developed mutual co-operation, trade and extended markets. Reversing that situation must cause a great deal of economic loss and disruption. Some apologists for UDI narrowly argue that Somalia-Somaliland economic links are easily replaceable by new trade connections with Ethiopia. While their assumption might have some validity, it will only be for people who live west of a line drawn from the Gulf of Aden at Berbera, through Burao up to the 8th parallel at Bohotleh. It will be quite the opposite for those who live east of that line, the majority of whom are already greatly dependent on the port of Bosaso and its hinterland. Trade with Ethiopia is a positive new development which can be quite viable because of geographical proximity and it should be encouraged and extended at all levels. It is, however, clearly preposterous to argue that while some people in Somaliland after more than thirty years of social and economic intercourse with other Somalis, can complain of differences in ways of life to the extent that they can no longer co-exist yet at the same time claim they can do just that with the people of Ethiopia, most of whom have different languages, religions and customs. Indeed, it seems to me that nothing can be achieved by total separation that could not have been achieved while maintaining some sort of loose association with the Somali Republic. Much more can and sadly probably will be lost.

Whether the Somali nation will endeavor to come together again, only time will tell, but the will of the Northern people has been vindicated to some degree. They have thanked and retired the SNM and the military leadership and steps have been democratically initiated by the elders in council to return the new Republic to civilian rule — but the transition has been none too smooth and is, in any case, another story, which I hope to analyze and discuss in due course. My present purpose has been to illustrate and catalog the tragic costs and consequences of my country's sad slide into dictatorship.

UNFINISHED BUSINESS

S INCE I BEGAN THIS BOOK, the sad legacy of dictatorship has bequeathed yet more civil strife, irresponsibility, lawlessness, banditry, suffering and starvation. Many a patriot, such for example as Professor Ibrahim Mohamoud Abyen, after twenty years of dedicated opposition to dictatorial rule, has been savagely murdered by mindless clan militia drunk on Darod-Hawiye animosity. In Ibrahim's case only one day after Siad Barre fled. Although absent, the responsibility was clearly his. My sad country has once again witnessed the generosity of western donors but we have also seen well-intentioned foreign and international interest and actions degenerate into high-handed violence. Nor were we at all guiltless. Since the whole Somali scenario remains fluid and surrounded by uncertainties, it is neither easy nor indeed feasible to recommend specific common courses of action. But such are our responsibility: that at least is established. We have to rebuild trust in one another.

I have long recommended that serious consideration be given to the establishment of a National Council, or Councils, of Elders, whatever other institutions are revived and retained, with powers to appoint and dismiss the head of government and to approve the formation of governments, perhaps only during a transitional period possibly not exceeding two or three years within which elections should be held. Such a Council should be based on proportional communal representation in order to usher in a sense of trust and belonging by all concerned and to create a climate conducive to fostering re-commitment to a common identity and destiny. We live in a changing world and such a Council need not necessarily be limited to the traditional leadership, but neither should it exclude it.

It now seems impractical — even impossible — for the people of the newly declared 'Republic of Somaliland' to abruptly reverse their verdict *vis-a-vis* the South. Nor does the disintegration of the South offer any encouragement for the exploration of any attempt at such a reversal. The continuation of the *status quo* therefore seems inevitable. I remain convinced of the necessity for the cessation of all hostilities, planned reconciliation and some kind of inter-Somali association and relationship, whatever system of government or governments prove acceptable to all sides. In the South some form of a confederation or something similar may emerge. Meantime the opportunity has presented itself, for the first time, for the Somalis in Ethiopia to protect their ethnic interests and play their proper role in the modern state with their rights and obligations recognized by all parties. Political realities have vastly changed and there is no more talk of 'Greater Somalia'; but every Somali group in Ethiopia remains genealogically linked with one or other clan in Somalia-proper or Somaliland.

But, allow me to return to my main theme, the cost of dictatorship, for there remains some unfinished business. Unless we emphasize the dangers and learn the lessons, we and others could be dragged again down that slippery path. A constructive peace in our country or countries must be restored, that is clear, but lest we forget, I invited Dr Adam Yussuf Aboker, the former medical director of the Hargeisa hospital to contribute a small personal note by way of an appendix on how repression began in Hargeisa. I am grateful to him and to Mohamed Barood Ali who has agreed to relive painful experiences by recollecting his frightening prison years...it could have been any one of us, so arbitrary were the arrests.

For my part, as a former police officer and student of law, let me in conclusion turn to the unfinished business. Despite some moves by the appropriate authorities first in Canada and then in the United States, many of Siad Barre's evil henchmen, not to mention the dictator himself — along with Mengistu of Ethiopia and others — are still allowed to enjoy their ill-gotten gains in comfortable exile and I wonder why. Villas in California and luxury apartments in Virginia come to mind, but so do residences in Abuja, Nairobi and elsewhere.

The crimes committed by the Siad Barre regime were legion but many formed part of a planned policy of extermination aimed at one particular clan, the Isaaq people. It is not denied that others suffered; far from it; it is merely suggested that these are sufficient to constitute the international crime of genocide. According to the definition of the UN Convention on the Prevention and Punishment of the Crime of Genocide (1948), Article 11, which defines Genocide. "Genocide means any of the following acts committed with intent to destroy in whole or in part:"

(a) killing members of (the) group
(b) causing serious bodily or mental harm to members of the group;
(c) deliberately inflicting on the group conditions of life calculated to bring about its physical destruction in whole or in part."

Many innocent people were brutally killed en masse, solely because of their clan membership or upon mere suspicion of anti-regime activities. In November 1984, forty-four men including the local police commander were publicly executed in the provincial capital of Burao, the second largest northern town, without the minimum legal formalities: neither recourse to any legal aid nor to an appeal. They were instantly buried in a mass grave. Another twenty-six men were executed in the northern capital of Hargeisa and a further fifteen people — including a woman — were similarly executed in the town of Sheikh, during that month. They all belonged to the Isaaq clan from which the then leading opposition group to Siad Barre's rule, the Somali National Movement (SNM), drew its main support. The only charge against the lone woman victim was believed to be that she had ululated for an SNM ambush against a convoy of Siad Barre's army. During the SNM's main offensive against the main northern towns in May-June 1988, not only was the predominantly civilian populated city of Hargeisa indiscriminately destroyed by aerial bombardment and ground artillery fire, but even the human columns of refugees fleeing on foot, women, children and the aged, alike were continuously strafed from the air every day of their flight until the survivors reached the Ethiopian border. Apart from the many who died in the carnage resulting from the destruction of the cities, hundreds of civilians as well as members of the Armed forces were deliberately massacred by the regime.

Several hundred other Isaaq civilians were rounded up at night time during June 1988 in the port city of Berbera. Significantly, and unlike Burao and Hargeisa, no conflict ever took place between the SNM and the Siad Barre forces in Berbera at that time but people were nonetheless executed in the same manner and buried *en masse*. A certain European who worked in the construction of a cement factory in Berbera was believed to have retained some evidence of those mass murders. His particulars were supplied to Amnesty International at the time, but it is later believed that he was reluctant to make a statement perhaps then hoping to return to work in Berbera, he feared reprisals.

More than a score of people were murdered either individually or in groups in various parts of the Gabiley District west of Hargeisa, again where there had then been no direct confrontation between the forces of Siad Barre and those of the opposition. One hundred and seven civilians, mostly pastoral nomads, were massacred in various locations in the El-Afwein District, about 55 miles west of Erigavo. After a military vehicle was blown up by a land mine, killing all the occupants, the authorities ordered that all men found in the vicinity of the incident be rounded up. Forty-seven men were reported to have been machine gunned as they were being thrown off a tipper like quarry stones — murdered before they touched the ground. The overall death toll has been conservatively estimated at fifty thousand by witnesses later interviewed by the Human Rights Africa Watch (see their report: "A Government at War with its Own people").

Then there has been the intentional destruction of private properties. Many houses in Hargeisa, including privately owned gynecological clinics and other medical centers which had escaped the initial bombardments, were later dynamited by the Siad Barre regime. Their ruins are still in evidence. The whole of Hargeisa and its suburbs, as well as many other centers including Gabiley and Odweina and the countryside at large, were heavily mined. Loss of human lives and the maiming of both people and their animals continue to this very day.

Even those engaged to lift the mines have suffered injury and amputations.

During popular riots against the Siad Barre regime, on 14 July 1989, in the capital city of Mogadishu several hundred civilians were presumed killed by the regime. Forty-six Isaaq men and one non-Isaaq who lived with an Isaaq family, were rounded up from their homes during the night of 15/16 July, on the basis of clan identification. They included two professors of the College of Education at Lafole near the town of Afgoye. They were all shot to death on the night of their arrest and hurriedly mass buried at the scene of the murder, a beach in the suburbs of Mogadishu. Many more people would surely have been liquidated in the same manner during ensuing nights had the secret killing not been made public by a lone survivor, who was left presumed dead. After mounting international pressure, Siad Barre appointed a commission of inquiry, consisting of members of the armed forces and chaired by a hand picked general. Before the Commission could have its first meeting, Siad Barre went public on two occasions at least and falsely denounced reports of the massacre as being baseless and malicious rumors intended to discredit his regime. The Commission nevertheless reported that there had been commission of a serious crime. Evidence could be available to that effect from some of the commission members.

Other acts of individual or group murder as well as other atrocities meted out to the Isaaq people, and others, continued unabated. These include mass arrests, detentions without trial, some for a whole decade and in solitary confinement, tortures, rape, extortion, arbitrary confiscation of property without compensation and economic strangulation. There was a policy of Isaaq depopulation by settling other Somalis and non-Somalis in the main centers of the Isaaq homeland. Curfews were imposed from 12:00 noon until 6 a.m. the following morning and there is ample evidence of large numbers of cases of trauma. Foreigners have also been involved, apparently without risk, in the destructive exploitation of the nations national resources and fauna.

A Canadian television team who visited Somaliland during June–July 1992 witnessed and filmed the exhumation of human remains from mass graves. The film was released to the public on 6 October 1992. The television team's interest arose, following a complaint from the Somali refugee community in Canada against the granting of refugee status to some of Siad Barre's former officials. Likewise accusations against supposed jailers previously employed by the regime of Colonel Mengistu Haile Mariam, the deposed Ethiopian dictator, have been heard in United States courts.

But why are only minor officials prosecuted? That at least is one cost of dictatorship that it would surely be politically healthy, in this modern world, to endeavor to refund.

Why We Were Arrested

by Dr. Adan Yussuf Abokor

The Group Hospital in Hargeisa was built in 1954 during the colonial days by the British but since then it has hardly been maintained, let alone refurnished or re-equipped. When I was posted there in 1980 as the Hospital Director, the laboratory was hardly functioning due to lack of chemicals and equipment. The blood bank, the emergency and out-patient departments were closed. The x-ray machine had been out of action for the previous two years partly due to lack of films and partly due to the malfunction of some of its parts. The drainage system was completely blocked and at night patients usually relieved themselves outside.

To be admitted, patients had to bring their own mattresses, bed-sheets and pillows. One had to buy ones own drugs (including parental fluids) as well as meals. The only 'service' the hospital offered was frustrated and demoralized doctors and paramedics. Whenever possible, people used to avoid the hospital and instead utilized the pharmacies which lacked doctors and qualified pharmacists. The amount of drugs sold to these pharmacies by the government agency was so meager that the owners were compelled to go to certain regions in the South to buy more drugs. In fact, the drugs officially allocated by the government to the North-West region (one of the most populated in the republic) were about equal to those provided to the smallest region, population wise, in the country. This was not due to bad adminis-tration but was done intentionally. The issue used to be raised with the authorities whenever possible but always in vain. Also, the few available medicaments lacked both quality and variety. As a result, people used to order drugs from Djibouti and Saudi Arabia for their sick relatives.

Vital drugs such as insulin, coagulants, anti-coagulants, parental fluids etc. were neither available in the hospital nor in the pharmacies in the city.

Many patients died due to lack of these essentials. Moreover, the hospital did not have a generator of its own. It was supplied by the city's power station which was a very poor and unreliable supply. Many times power failed with the doctors in the middle of surgical operations. On other occasions, operations had to be delayed because of lack of electricity. The maternity ward had only 20 beds for a region with a population of more than 500,000 (not including the five big refugee camps that were located near Hargeisa).

The maternity ward did not have a single delivery bed or any other facilities except old beds without mattresses that were left behind by the British in 1960. The pediatric ward had only 10 beds. One of the most painful experiences for the staff is to have to send home a mother with a seriously sick child, because of lack of beds or even space on the floor.

We used to complain to every visiting official, whether from the ministry of health or from other government institutions, about these hideous conditions. Always the response was "Please write me a report and I will see what I can do." Not even once were requests fulfilled. In the end we refrained from complaining to the authorities but never lost interest in exploring other ways of improving the health care offered by the hospital.

We were working under those conditions when a team of volunteers from Germany, The German Emergency Doctors who were already working in the refugee camps, offered assistance to improve services in the hospital. The Germans had noticed that although the region was badly neglected, the population was willing to help itself.

During the 1980's there was an influx of young professionals and intellectuals into the region. Most were born in the North and every one of them realized that they were badly needed here to help. Some returned from USA, some from Europe while many others took transfers from other regions of the country. They were doctors, teachers, engineers, economists and businessmen. Initially we used to get together as we were all acquainted with each other from childhood and had attended schools in the region. After a period of time, it was agreed that we hold more regular meetings to discuss various community matters concerning the city of Hargeisa. It was during those meetings that we decided on some self-help programs to improve the conditions in the hospital and schools. We agreed that some of us would voluntarily teach in schools and that the teachers among us would exert more effort to improve and raise the quality of education. As for the hospital, we decided to repair the buildings, clean the compound, and raise public awareness of health matters by using Hargeisa Radio and other means.

The German doctors brought new beds, mattresses, bedsheets, pillows, mosquito-nets and many essentials for the hospital. They repaired both the buildings and drainage system. They repaired and fully equipped the emergency room and the out-patient department and then supplied the drugs that were desperately needed in both departments. Furthermore, they provided the hospital with a generator and re-installed the electric system. German doctors and nurses worked fulltime in the hospital for varying periods.

Simultaneously, we contacted some established businessmen to participate in the self-help program. They formed a committee of six men who were supposed to study our needs and then collect necessary funds. The idea was a blessing. The German doctors increased their effort when they realized that the people were enthusiastically participating in the self-help schemes. The committee of businessmen built a laboratory for the out-patients beyond the hospital compound; laid the foundation for a new maternity ward and allocated funds for the construction of a second pediatric ward.

The German doctors, the committee of businessmen, the young professionals and the hospital administration met more often to discuss the needs and the contributions each group could provide. It was decided to give the hospital staff bonuses in the form of rations and to supplement their devastatingly low salaries so as to motivate them to work harder. We also contacted the bus-owners union which agreed to exempt hospital staff from paying bus fares. In short, everyone in Hargeisa was coming forward to help because they saw the tangible improvements that were taking place. The work was not limited to the group hospital but extended to mother and child health (MCH), the nursing school and the ambulance service in the city. We were even able to donate some drugs to a number of districts and villages to improve local health.

We continued to improve the conditions of the city whenever possible. Some of us taught at the nursing school and others in the clerical training center (CTC) as volunteers. Throughout this time, the authorities both in Hargeisa and Mogadishu were watching our activities very closely. At first they tried to convince the head of the German team that the project was more needed in Mogadishu than in Hargeisa. Then they brought some officials from Mogadishu to interrupt our activities for they considered them a danger to President Siad Barre's system of government. They insisted that the committee of businessmen should operate under the administration of the governor's office and 'cooperate' with the local authorities. Everyone avoided confrontation with the regime and whenever we finished a project we used to invite the governor or his representative to give his blessings on behalf of the president. Whenever an official arrived from Mogadishu we used to seize the opportunity of showing him or her the success of our efforts. Unfortunately, this served only to increase the regime's contempt for and hatred of our activities.

By the end of 1981 although the condition of the hospital was vastly improved, our German colleagues still had 2 million marks to spend on medical facilities in the city. It was during those days that we heard a rumor that the authorities were going to arrest some of the professionals. On 2 November 1981, the first of our group of volunteers was arrested: the second on the 4th after midnight: on 19 November two national security service (NSS) officers and several paramilitary police came to my house and woke me at 1:00 A.M. I went with them under the impression that this was a case of mistaken identity. I was wrong. The madness that has brought about the catastrophes affecting our country to this day had begun. The suffering and the destruction we, the Somali people, have since experienced at the hand of the dictator, Siad Barre, is beyond the range of human imagination . . .

Inside Labaatan Jirow Secret Maximum Security Prison

an abridged report by Mohamed Barood Ali

The knocks came just after 2:00 A.M. Although I had expected them to come any day, I was terrified when it happened in reality. My heart started beating faster and harder. I put on a pair of jeans, a shirt and shoes. They knocked harder and harder. A friend of mine had been arrested on November 2nd, 1981 two days before and we had heard there was a list of people to be detained.

I was a classical example of the belief that horrible things happened only to other people. In spite of many stories that I heard of innocent people being arrested in the middle of the night and the systematic torture of prisoners who were perceived to be against the regime or simply not actively for the regime, somewhere in my mind there was a nagging feeling that the victims must have done something wrong. When my turn came I could not think about it objectively. The first few hours went by in a blur and even today it is difficult to recall exactly how it had happened. The most haunting image I remember is the terror I saw in my wife's eyes. We had only been married for 4 months. Her eyes were pools of love overwhelmed by fright and helplessness. I could not bear looking at her. She suggested repeatedly that she open the door by herself but in the end we went together. There were four men in civilian clothes with AK47 assault rifles and a vehicle at the ready. A fifth man, obviously their leader, carried a pistol in his hand. He instructed me to go with them to the National Security Service headquarters. I asked them who they were and whispered to my wife to go and wake up our neighbor who was an army officer. They tried to stop her but were too late and the neighbor arrived. This upset the leader. The last thing they wanted was to be seen arresting people in the middle of the night. My neighbor confirmed that they were N.S.S. officers and I asked him to come with us and make sure I was taken to N.S.S. headquarters. They reassured my wife, with disarming civility, that I was going to be back within the hour, but I was to spend seven years and six months in prison, mostly in solitary confinement.

On that first night I was not taken to the N.S.S. headquarters but to a police station on the other side of town. I was put in a tiny crowded cell with no windows and light. The fetid suffocating smell of human excrement overwhelmed me. I had to feel my way through a huddled mass of people of different ages, different professions, different outlooks: different in every thing, but united in a kind of inexplicable brotherhood. Everyone realized we were all thrown down to the lowest level a human being could experience — that of struggle for survival. Most of my fellow prisoners were petty thieves, drunkards etc., but we got acquainted with each other quickly. All reservations were thrown to the wind. During the following four months I was transferred from one N.S.S. center to maximum security safe houses and to military police centers — all equipped for the torture of political prisoners. Sometimes our tormentors concentrated on routinely sensitive parts of the body: on other occasions there were brutal and indiscriminate beatings of the whole body; dipping in water; etc. The torturers were military police officers, specially trained for the purpose, supervised by the N.S.S. officers leading the investigations. The N.S.S. officers often took part in our torture and seemed to enjoy it.

It all began when, after being held for about a week in the main N.S.S. center without charge or contact with my family or friends, I was suddenly called to the N.S.S. chief's office. There were five officers with him. I learned immediately that they were especially sent from Mogadishu, for the 'investigation' of the cases of 29 people arrested in November and early December 1981. They were an elite band of interrogators and torturers led by the chief investigating officer of the N.S.S., an organization modeled on the KGB which had trained many of its officers in the Soviet Union. They possessed unlimited powers of search, detention without trial, torture and confiscation. That first meeting was short. The leader of the group bragged about his exploits in extracting confessions from detainees. He described in graphic detail how he succeeded, where others had failed, in extracting a confession from Col. Cirro, the leader of a failed coup attempt in 1978. Walking to and fro in the interrogation rooms with a heels-first step and always stopping behind me and putting his hands on my shoulders, he finally made a proposition that he would make me a witness and if I cooperated I would be released. I told him I did not know anything about his allegations which were not even specific. Eventually, he said my friends and I were members of an illegal organization with intent to overthrow the government. I denied this. He immediately asked the military police guards waiting outside to take me back to my cell. I was handcuffed behind my back. They took away my mattress and blankets. I had no food or water. The following day I was not allowed out of the room even to go to the toilet.

Next evening at 7:00 P.M. the lights were extinguished throughout the building. I heard footsteps approaching my cell door. Two military police officers and one of the interrogation team entered; they told me to stand up and searched me for the tenth time that week. Then they blindfolded me and put me in the back of a Land Rover. Forty-five minutes later I was made to get out still blindfolded and handcuffed from behind. They tied my feet together and I was forced to kneel down. A heavy weight was placed on my back while four soldiers held me. The weight was held on either side of me by two other soldiers who let it descend gradually while the leader kept asking me if I was ready to confess. I kept silent for a while but eventually cried out with excruciating pain. But there was no let up and finally I fainted. When I regained consciousness, I was wet. Apparently they had thrown a bucket of water over me. As soon as I opened my eyes the leader asked me to sign a prepared statement. I declined. He ordered that I should be given the water treatment. They forced my mouth open and poured in large amounts of water till I almost suffocated. I vomited. They repeated this several times. By now I was so weakened that they decided to take me back.

At the office, my blindfold was removed and a new officer asked me in a sweet voice what had happened. I explained everything to him and he started cursing the others telling them that it was no way to treat a human being. They lowered their heads as if in repentance. He told me it would never happen again. He ordered a sandwich, a cup of tea and a cigarette but before they arrived, he asked me the same questions which were raised by the others. I told him what I had already told to the others. It was a technique, for suddenly he was transformed into an animal. He started screaming at me and threatening that he would shoot me on the spot if I did not sign the prepared statement. When the sandwich and tea arrived, he threw them out of the window and assured me that I would soon follow them if I did not cooperate. He then ordered me back to my cell.

I lay on the floor for the rest of that night without having eaten or drunk water for more than 30 hours, but I did not feel hungry or thirsty. I could not sleep either. I kept worrying about my situation, knowing I was innocent of all crimes, but helpless against these people who did not listen to reason and were motivated by the single notion of breaking a prisoner and making him 'confess' to imaginary crimes. They were engaged in a cruel game in which they made the rules and were allowed to use all kinds of weapons and techniques. By contrast, the prisoners were stripped of everything and could not even use their reason.

At exactly 7:00 P.M. the second night they came with their blindfold. They took me away and went through the same routine with the addition of kicks on my shins, and cigarette burns on the inner sides of my legs and on my ankles. There were short periods of rest during which they again exhorted me to sign prepared statements. This continued for about a week when suddenly they stopped coming. I learned later on from one of the military police guards that was because there were so many other prisoners to be interrogated. Having been through physical torture, I was less worried by the pain, hunger and thirst than the psychological effects of detention and solitary confinement. I was overwhelmed by the sense of loneliness and being abandoned and forgotten by my family and relatives. Yet I knew this was unreasonable for they themselves were helpless. It almost became a relief when the interrogators came to beat and torture me. Physical pain became easier to cope with than doubts and fears during the day and night.

After two weeks, I was called to the interrogation room. The chief told me that they had uncovered new incriminating evidence against me. Some of my friends were prepared to testify against me and he did not need my cooperation anymore. He mentioned the names of some familiar people and asked whether I knew them. I admitted that but no more. The most incredible accusation came when he asked me why we called ourselves *Barood* (gunpowder), *Olad* (struggle), *Abby* (defense), *Dagal* (war) if we were not involved in a conspiracy. These names were the traditional names of the fathers and grandfathers of my fellow detainees. I countered that some of my other fellow detainees were called *Warsame* (good news), *Dualeh* (blessing), *Madar* (rain) to which he made no comment. During the eventual trial I found out that some of my fellow detainees had undergone similar tortures. Some had suffered even harsher methods including one whose testicles had later to be removed.

Four months passed and there was no release or even trial insight. But on 19 February 1981 we were all served with indictment papers. We were officially charged with high treason. I was charged under two articles. Article No. 54 section 1 for allegedly belonging to an illegal organization, and article 17 section 1 for publishing seditious material. I was not familiar with these laws. I managed to send a note through one of the guards to my wife to find out what these articles meant. Her brother contacted a secretary in the security court. He sent back a note explaining that each article carried a mandatory death sentence by hanging. When I read the note I was floored. I could not think, sleep or eat. It was definitely the worst week of my life, for I was forced to look at the ugly face of death. When I thought of the track record of Siad Barre — the way we had executed all his opponents or those perceived to be opponents; the security court's history as his puppet; the inordinate haste with which accused had been executed in the past — all boded ill for me. Even worse than my fear of death was obsession with the manner of death — hanging or *Daldalaad* in Somali. Somehow my distress, the confinement of the cell, the loneliness and the absence of any consolatory points in the grim picture, all contributed to my being unable to think clearly. I just concentrated on the horrors of dying by hanging. I spent all my time thinking about stories I had heard or books I had read on this most terrible manner of execution. I was so sure that I was going to be hanged that I even imagined that I could smell death. I had read Hemingway's *For Whom the Bell Tolls* only a few months before my arrest. I was reminded of one of the central characters talking about the smell of death. I never understood this before, but now I felt sure I smelt death or maybe fear of death. That I was unable to talk to anyone about this exacerbated my fears.

One morning, 20 Feb. 1982, I heard sustained gunfire not far away. There was even sporadic artillery fire. The shooting seemed to be coming closer and continued until 4:00 in the afternoon. The same happened the following two days but there was no one to ask what was happening. There were no interrogation sessions from the first day of the shooting but on the third day the interrogation team arrived with two others whom they said were judges in the security court. They charged me formally but when I requested to see a lawyer, that was denied. Two days later I was taken out of my cell with 28 others, most of whom I knew. We we reordered into two buses, half of whose seats were taken up by *Dhabar jebin* soldiers known as the 'back breakers' or 'fifth column'. For the first time we saw burnt buildings. Armed soldiers, armored vehicles and tanks, stood along the route to the court which was completely empty of civilian cars and people. There was a dragnet of commandos around the court and beyond. Inside most of the seats were taken up by uniformed commandos. The last two rows were reserved for relatives of detainees — one relative for each of us. Only after the trial, when we were taken to the main prison, did we learn of the extent of the riots and the resulting death toll.

Our 'trial' took only 10 hours, from 9:00 A.M. to 19:00 P.M. including a break of one hour for lunch. None of us was allowed to say a word other than to briefly answer preliminary questions such as "How do you plead to the offense described?" All 29 defendants pleaded "not guilty." Our defense lawyers, who arrived from Mogadishu two days earlier, only met us the night before the trial in the presence of the interrogation team. They had only 10 minute individual interviews to learn our names, ages, professions, etc. Being veterans of many previous political trials, they knew that it was immaterial whether or not they presented a case, because, the final judgment lay not with the court, but with the government and more specifically with Siad Barre, the president.

The case against us, as presented by the prosecution, was that we belonged to an illegal organization with intent to overthrow the government and that we had published a pamphlet in which we spread pernicious propaganda against the regime. The evidence presented to the court was a list of names. Not all those accused were named while others in the list were not present at the trial. The list had been compiled by an NSS informer called *Laangadhe* who, earlier on, escaped to Ethiopia after he received a check for 40,000 Somali Shillings, then about US $2,000, for his services. The security police knew about his escape but they did not want him at the trial to be questioned by the defense lawyers. The main prosecution witness, the chief interrogator and torturer, claimed that *Laangadhe* told him that we used to meet and criticize the regime and plot in his presence. Vainly the defense lawyers objected to the list and its having been compiled by an unprincipled man whose mercenary allegations could not be considered as evidence since the accused were unable to question him. The judge, a police captain with no legal training, immediately overruled them.

The other piece of evidence presented by the prosecution alleged that by cleaning up health facilities at Hargeisa Group Hospital and improving educational, cultural and general social services in the region, the accused were trying to show up the government as inept, thereby gaining popular support for themselves. They also cited the riots that preceded the trial which in fact occurred because the people were unhappy with the detention and torture of prisoners throughout the region. We were being accused of instigating riots which took place four months after our arrest and solitary confinement!

All the prosecution did was repeatedly recite that each prisoner was accused of such and such a crime. They did not make any effort to convince the court with hard evidence. Nor was there time for 29 people to be accused of high crimes against the state, punishable by death, let alone for defense lawyers to rebut this. No one expected any fairness from such a court. It seemed that everyone, including the judges, the prosecution, the defense lawyers, the audience and, in a sense, even us the accused, were in collusion to let the charade take its course. We all knew that once accused of a crime against the state, the only issue was whether or not the death penalty would be imposed.

There was a sigh of relief from everybody when, as a result of a furious diplomatic shuttle between Mogadishu and Hargeisa by two government ministers — one a politburo member and a son-in-law of Siad Barre the president — none of the accused were sentenced to death, even though two of us were sentenced to life imprisonment. This was why the defense lawyers, as if admitting to our guilt, concentrated on asking for leniency from the court since all other requests, including one to examine the wounds and scars left by torture during the four months of interrogation, had been denied. Looking back at the trial proceedings, there is no doubt in my mind that the presence of lawyers did not make the slightest impression on the court or affect the final sentences. The only thing it did, was lend a stamp of 'legitimacy' to the farce and that was the actual intention of the regime. This, of course, is not to question the ability or integrity of the lawyers. On the contrary, I have only respect for them and we all appreciated the effort they made in an impossible situation to help innocent victims of a cruel system. Nor were we saved from arbitrary execution through the magnanimity of Siad Barre, the President, as the judge read out in his summary, but rather because the regime was terrified of the possible consequences of such a course. Hargeisa, Burao and other major towns in the North experienced heavy riots in which 47 people, mostly students, were killed by the security forces. Hargeisa was still in turmoil. Only the slightest excuse was needed to spark off further riots. Testimony to this is the way the final sentences were wrapped up and packaged. The two ministers involved promised the families of the accused that we were going to be released soon after the trial had run its course, but that was not to be.

The court rulings for the 29 detainees were as follows:
— 9 — released for 'lack of evidence.'
— 2 — sentenced to life imprisonment
Ahmed Mohamed Yusuf *Jabane,* Physics Teacher
Mohamed Barood Ali, Industrial Chemist (the writer of this appendix)
— 22 — 30 years imprisonment and a fine of 10,000 S.Sh.
Mohamed Haji Mohamoud Omer Hashi, Economist and Entrepreneur

Abdirahman Abdillahi H. Aden, Civil servant
— 1 — 25 years imprisonment
Mohamed Ali Ibrahim, Head of self-help at Hargeisa
— 9 — 20 years imprisonment
Adan Yussuf Abokor, Medical doctor
Hussein Mohamoud Dualeh *Berberawi,* Biology/Chemistry teacher
Aden Warsame Saeed, Economist and Businessman
Yussuf Abdillahi Kahin, Surveyor, Farmer and businessman
Bashe Abdi Yussuf, Accountant and Businessman
Mohamoud Sheikh Hassan Tani, Medical doctor
Abdillahi Ali Yussuf, Veterinary doctor
Osman Abdi Maigag, Medical doctor
Ahmed Hussein Abby, Banker
— 3 — 8 years imprisonment
Mohamed Ma'alin Osman, Biology teacher
Mohamed Abdi Jiir, Biology teacher
Ahmed Muhamed Madar, Biology teacher
— 3 — 3 years imprisonment
Ali Eghe Farah, Civil Engineer
Omer Isse Awale, Civil servant
Mohamed Ali Sulub, Medical doctor

All those sentenced remained in Hargeisa prison for the following eight months. At one time there were 400 school students, aged between 11 and 16 years, with us before they were transferred to the largest prison in the north at Mandera. They had participated in demonstrations for our release. One night the girls among them were taken to Berbera prison which shocked us, for it is reserved for women alcoholics, prostitutes and hardened criminals.

A female custodial guard, a woman who traveled with the school girls to Berbera, told us when she returned that at one time on the way to Berbera, the soldiers ordered the girls to get off the lorry. She had objected but was struck by a soldier from the military police with the butt of his gun. She believed that the girls were saved from rape and perhaps worse when soldiers saw the light of an approaching car. The students were released six months later, after fresh riots threatened to break out in Hargeisa and Burao.

After the sentence, my father and a relative of one of the other prisoners accompanied the two ministers on a military plane to Mogadishu. Siad Barre himself had earlier on asked for a meeting with a delegation of the relatives before he would grant our release. As usual, however, he broke the appointment and left for a 45 days tour of Europe and North America. His plane actually took off from Mogadishu Airport a few minutes before the delegation were due to arrive. This was typical of the man's deceit and wickedness. He knew that our relatives and elders were coming to see him in Mogadishu and fresh riots were unlikely to take place in Hargeisa while the elders remained hostage in Mogadishu. When he returned from his tour abroad, the president embarrassed the elders and sent them back with yet another empty promise to release us on the then forthcoming October anniversary celebrations of the 1969 'Revolution.'

There were heavy rains, and the track between Baidoa and Labaatan Jirow Maximum Security Prison was all but impassable. We were blindfolded as we left Baidoa to prevent us from knowing where the top security prison was. (We were also blindfolded from the prison to Baidoa when we were being released six and a half years later.) Inside the prison each one of us was taken to a cell where the blindfolds but not the handcuffs were removed. They were taken off a week later. The cell was completely empty, 7 x 7 feet with a hole in the right hand corner. This was the toilet since no one would be allowed to go out at all. The walls were unplastered and made of reinforced concrete. There were two successive doors for each cell. The inner door remained locked at all times and consisted of heavy steel bars. The outer door, which was opened from 7:00 A.M. to 4:00 P.M. each day, was one heavy sheet of iron without even a small hole on it. This door was normally closed during punishment periods which were quite frequent because the slightest sound constituted 'misbehavior' in the eyes of the guards.

There were 20 guards inside the prison, and about 150 soldiers outside equipped with heavy artillery and anti-aircraft guns. All the guards, both inside and outside the prison, were members of the military police. The guards outside were to protect the prison from attack. There were no custodial corps guards in Labaatan Jirow. Administratively, this special prison was run direct from the president's office in Mogadishu. The overall membership of the military police in the country was predominantly Marehan. They had wide powers of search, arrest, interrogation and their own detention centers. They also manned all control posts throughout the country, using their powers to extort property from the population. Every single member of the guards from the prison warden Colonel Deria Hirsi to male nurse Dheel Deria Yussuf, was a Marehan—the clan of Siad Barre, the president. The regime denied the very existence of a prison called Labaatan Jirow. In fact the only people who have ever seen it apart from Siad Barre himself, were either builders, prisoners or the prison administrators. (See a prisoner's sketch from memory, page 254.)

There were a total of 175 cells in the prison but only 35 were occupied during our stay. That was not because there were not enough political prisoners in the country to fill them, but because all the other cells did not have toilet facilities and the guards did not want to take the trouble of taking the prisoners outside, whenever the need arose. We learnt of others who had been detained there at one time or another between 1981 and 1989. They included

Ismail Ali Aboker, ex-vice president
Omer Arteh Ghalib, ex-minister of foreign affairs
Osman Mohamed Jelle, ex-minister of livestock and rangelands
Dr. Mohamed Adan Sheikh, ex-minister of information
Mohamed Yussuf Weyrah, ex-minister of finance
Abdillahi Mohamed Nour, army major
Warsama Ali Farah, ex-mayor of Modadishu who died in prison in 1983
Ali Easa Islam, police inspector
Mohamed Ali Jama, army capt, released in 1984
Mohamoud Islam (uncle of the above), army captain
Ahmed Hashi, army captain
Gaboobeh, army captain
Ahmed Dhore Farah, businessman, still in prison when we left in 1989
Mohamoud Malin, civil servant
Sheikh Mukhtar, lawyer
Yussuf Osman Samatar, in prison since 1968
Hussien Ahmed, an Ethiopian airforce colonel 1976 — still in prison
    when we left in 1989
Jama Ali Jama, imprisoned since 1978

On the second day after our arrival, I was given a blanket, an aluminum cup, a plastic plate and a small plastic bucket for water. Every day each prisoner was given a bucket of water for all purposes such as drinking and ablution before prayers, washing up the utensils and cleaning the toilet. We were not provided with clothes, and ours were taken away. I was left with a T-shirt, a *Ma-awis* (the traditional Somali cloth wrapped round the lower body) and a pair of sandals cut from an old tire, *Kabo shaag* in Somali.

We were given millet gruel for breakfast and boiled rice with a glass of powdered milk for lunch. This was the usual prison fare for the next six and a half years. Only occasionally, perhaps once every three to six months, a goat would be killed, boiled and each prisoner given a tiny piece with his rice. These were 'feast' days for us and they would be signalled the day before by the bleat of a goat. The 'feast' day itself would be confirmed by unusual movement and numbers of crows in the prison compound. A bleat one day and increased crow activity definitely indicated goat meat. A bleat therefore became a beautiful song to our ears. Every time one of us heard it, whether in the morning, afternoon or in the middle of the night we would immediately transmit the good news to neighbors who would pass it on until everybody heard and discussed with their neighbor the delicious part of the goat they would like to get and, in due course, the part actually received.

One comic incident comes into mind. Dr. Osman dreamt one night during a particularly meatless period, that he heard the bleat of a goat. He woke up and transmitted the news to his neighbors. Everybody stayed up the rest of the night discussing the good omen. The next morning, a group of crows chased one of their number holding a piece of red meat in its beak. We all saw this. It was more than enough to lift our spirits. We watched the lucky crows with hungry eyes as they flew back and forth playfully. Suddenly the lucky crow released the meat. We all waited for it to fall to the ground. But no; the 'meat' stayed up in the air, floating! The crows kept it playfully in the air; it was a piece of a pink cellophane bag.

Food in all such facilities is the main conversation topic. Even when alone, one daydreams about food. We made many a joke about our yearnings for food. Dr. Osman was asked once by his neighbor through the wall to name his best wish at that particular moment. Without hesitation he said "meat." Only after we asked him about freedom did he laugh and said of course. One became obsessed with food, which was brought in a big barrel pushed on a wheelbarrow. As soon as we heard the noise of the wheelbarrow we literally started to salivate, like Pavlov's dog, even for millet gruel.

The greatest problem was during the holy month of Ramadan, when Muslims fast from dawn to sunset. We were given food only during the night, to break our fast at six in the evening and 3 o'clock the next morning. The early evening was no problem but at 3 in the morning the soldiers violently opened the doors. If you were not ready at the door with your plate, they just locked up the door and that was that. Your next meal would then be fifteen hours later, at six in the evening. We usually solved this problem by assigning one person to stay awake each night. As soon as he heard the noise of the wheelbarrow he would wake up everybody. Even if we got the meal, darkness was a problem in the cell. The soldiers brought hurricane lamps with them, but as soon as they locked up, it was pitch black. With the smell of food came attacks from all quarters — cockroaches, mice and ants. We tried to cover the plate with one hand and eat with the other. The cockroaches were particularly vicious. They would fly from the walls above the toilet and land on your face and plate and refuse to take no for an answer. If you were squeamish you went hungry.

Confronted with poor food, shortage of water, lack of sanitation facilities, immobility, lack of reading material and isolation not only from the rest of the world, but from any fellow prisoners, the first few days in Labaatan Jirow were the most difficult. All contributed to a sense of incomprehension and depression. I tried to get in touch with my friends on either side of me. But as soon as one uttered a word, even *sotto voce,* a guard would be at the doorstep closing the main iron door. There were no warnings given in that prison. Very soon we learned that shouting to each other behind the doors would only bring more punishment. We had to content ourselves with knocking on the wall between the cells when the guards were not looking: it served to know that two friends on either side were at least alive. We were even warned not to write anything on the walls. It is literally impossible to desist from scratching something on prison walls in solitary confinement because that is about the only way left to express oneself. But we had to be careful. Every day during 'lock up' time, three soldiers would enter the cell ordering the occupant to stand against a wall. They would meticulously check for scratches on the walls, floor and even the ceiling. As soon as I arrived at my cell I checked for graffiti but there was none. Obviously my predecessors took their warnings seriously and did not dare to write on the walls. Only much later, while I was sitting on the floor and looking at the walls in front of me, I saw something. At first I could not believe what I saw, but soon I was laughing so loudly that my friend next door started knocking on the wall to warn me. At the bottom of the wall, where the soldiers could not possibly see was *EGAL* written in capital letters. This was the name of Somalia's last civilian prime minister much later to be 'president' of the Somaliland Republic. He spent 7 years here. The most powerful man in the country had been reduced to writing his name on that corner of the cell to express his protest. I felt for him at the time. It must have felt great seeing soldiers checking for signs on the walls and failing everyday. I imagined him chuckling under his breath.

I did see one grim example of protest graffiti in the large cell I shared with 20 friends in Hargeisa's main prison where we had stayed for 8 months before we were transferred to Labaatan Jirow. On a wall opposite where I slept, clearly written were the names of 7 male prisoners, every name apparently written by a different person. Every one added a comment after his name. Most of them wrote the name of somebody loved.

One had poignantly written "Siad Barre says we die tomorrow on the 28 April 1981 by firing squad—Siad Barre says but ALLAH did not say." But for those seven prisoners who signed their names on the wall of that grim prison, as for so many Somalis before and after them, there was no divine intervention. They were shot on the 28th. Now they rest in Allah's peace. They were all civilians belonging to the Mijertein clan, accused of belonging to the Somali Salvation Democratic Front (SSDF), the first opposition movement to fight the Siad Barre regime.

Looking back now at the many lost years, they seem a blur because almost every one of the 2375 days was exactly the same. I woke up at 6:00 A.M. The outer door was opened at 7:00, millet gruel was served at 7:30, lunch at 11:00 and the outer door was closed again at 4:00 P.M. Nothing else happened in between, except the guard going back and forth between the cells. Boredom, Boredom! Bone-crushing boredom! Some times it used to occur to me that I was in some kind of an Orwellian zoo in which the humans were inside cages with the beasts looking in from outside. The soldiers resembled beasts not only through my bitter view but also because they seldom uttered a word. They only made grunts when they disapproved of something or otherwise glared ominously.

One of the most cruel things was the treatment of detainees in illness. The guards would think that you were shamming if you told them you were ill. Even if they believed you, seeing that you were really in pain, they gave you insufficient doses or the wrong drugs. There was only one old male nurse for health care in the prison. We called him 'doctor No' because his first response was always negative. Later on when we learnt to communicate with each other through the walls between the cells, we were able to seek advice from the four real doctors amongst us. The doctors advised us to keep asking for drugs, particularly aspirins, sedatives, anti-pain drugs, antibiotics and chloroquinine against malaria and to hoard them even when we were well. This method helped us whenever one of us fell ill and 'doctor No' would not come to see him or refused to issue medicines.

We were able to pass medicines to each other because we had one exercise period of 10 minutes every three days, excluding Thursdays and Fridays. Exercise periods were taken one person at a time, but if that person had drugs to pass on he would inform the person next to him through the walls (more about the wall language below) who would pass on the information to his neighbor and so on until the person needing the drugs was reached. Medicines would be 'dropped' at a prearranged place for the ill person to pick up during his turn of exercise. The 'walk' took place between two doors 30 meters apart with one soldier at each end. We always dropped drugs near a small shrub half-way between the two doors. However, sometimes we were not given exercise periods for 3 or 4 consecutive months or even more. This usually coincided with periods of tension in the country as we found out later. For example we did not have exercise periods after May 1988 as a result of the war in the North. I have calculated that we came out of the cells during six and half years for only 72 hours.

Major health problems were mainly connected with immobility, tension, anxiety, fear, depression, insomnia and poor diet. Most of us suffered psychosomatic ailments and 'doctor No' always succeeded in aggravating these conditions. During our sojourn, two men died due to negligence. One of them, Warsame Ali Farah, who was in his seventies, was taken to Mogadishu but died there two days later. According to the official pathological report he died of kidney failure, but there is no doubt that he died of criminal negligence. He had been mayor of the capital city.

One of the detainees who fell very ill had been held since the 1978 coup attempt. Abdillahi Mohamed Nour had been asking for drugs for six months. On 1 May 1986 he started shouting at the top of his voice. The place was normally dead quiet and we all put our ears against the doors to hear what was happening. He started reciting his autobiography. The authorities closed the outer iron door on him. They came in the night, took him out and obviously beat him because we could hear him shouting "Allah. . . Allah." This continued on and off for about two hours. He never stopped his sporadic shouting until he was released in February 1989. The warders never attempted to treat him for his disturbance, as far as we know. When we were released, we found out that he had been badly maimed that night. Sadly, Abdillahi is still mentally disturbed.

We were informed, through the walls by a detainee, that 5 Ethiopian pilots were shot just before we arrived to make room for us. The pilots had entered Somalia voluntarily seeking political asylum. This was not an isolated incident. The same treatment was given to some 200 young Ethiopians, mostly students, who fled Ethiopia and were with us in jail in Hargeisa. They were transferred to Mogadishu prisons and shown to foreign journalists, as captured Ethiopian soldiers in 1982 when the Ethiopian army, together with some members of the SSDF occupied the Somali border settlements of Balanbale and Galdogob, in 1982–83. Afterwards we were told by a member of the custodial corps who accompanied them during the transfer to Mogadishu, that the poor students had all been executed.

Our knocking on the cell walls developed secretly into a fine art. We devised an alphabet from the two distinct sounds available to us — a loud note made with the knuckles of the middle fingers and a low drumming note produced by the side of the closed fist, 'O' and '.' on the diagram below. It took a few hours to memorize our alphabet but, since we had nothing else to occupy us, we were soon able to use it fluently, and within a week had become experts often understanding a word even before its transmission was completed. I cannot overestimate the value of our alphabet because, it was the only method of human contact left to us. The guards could not see us and never made the mental leap of deducing that we were able to understand each other by 'touching the walls.' Through the tapping on walls, we were able to know who had a cold, who was fine, etc. We were able to amuse each other and discuss almost anything. I was even eventually able to learn some German and Italian from my two neighbors. The most important use of the 'code,' however, was to seek the advice of one of our doctors. That helped us keep our sanity. In solitary confinement one always imagines the worst. The slightest cough, pain or weakness becomes a terminal illness. Reassurance was the more effective if it came from a trusted doctor.

THE WALL CODE OF HARGEISA GROUP
IN <u>LABAATAN JIRO</u> PRISON

A .	B 0	C ..	D .0	E 0.	F 00
G 0.0	H 0..	I ...	J ..0	K .00	L .0.
M 000	N 0..0	O 0.00	P 00.	Q ..00	R ...0
S	T .000	U ..0.	V .00.	W 00..	X 000.
Y 0000	Z .0.0				

Another, very important entertainment was bird-watching. There were many in the neighborhood, which was dry and the birds came to drink from a reserve tank. They usually sat in the trees planted in front of the cells to block the view. There is a whole world to learn and behold when you have time to observe these beautiful creatures. I had a favorite which I called Ruby for its red underbelly, this being a translation of *uur cas,* its Somali name. I liked its antics during play and its singing, not on one note only, but rather like a whole orchestra with wind, pipes, brass, strings, etc. During the afternoons after they had eaten the prisoners' leftovers, the birds performed a concert, I imagined, as a mark of gratitude for our generosity.

But even this small pleasure was not to last. The ignorance of the guards was such that, in 1987, they put poison into the leftovers. Most of our bird population was thus brutally exterminated: the few that survived emigrated to, perhaps, a more friendly environment. Apart from those tiny birds, we had ample time to watch other species which came to visit us at certain times of the day. The crow, that normally people seem not to like, was particularly interesting because it was very playful. For hours I observed its methods of fighting, mating, etc. Then there was the hawk, which despite its irregular visits was always a welcome sight. I remember one particular occasion when out of the blue a hawk suddenly dropped right in front of my cell door. I heard the whistling sound of a captive mouse crying for help. Suddenly the hawk released it and it scampered off a short distance and halted. The hawk looked everywhere but could not see the mouse whose color blended with that of the earth. The proverbial vision of the hawk briefly failed it, but the cowardly mouse could not remain still; as it endeavored to dart towards a small shrub, the movement alerted the hawk and it was on top of the mouse within no time. This time there was no escaping those cruel claws. The hawk flew away with its prey, chased by a gaggle of playful crows. Away, that is, from my restricted view. Away, away, soaring, powerful and unlike ourselves—free.

We played many games through the walls of the cells. But the funniest and at the same time the most serious, was the one we called W.H.O. after the World Health Organization's brief claim, in the late seventies, to have exterminated malaria in south-east Asia before realizing that new and stronger strains had developed. The prison area was a kind of oasis. Because the surrounding area had no water, nomads came to drink from the large tank near the prison. The prison area was thus rather swampy and became a breeding ground for mosquitoes. The buzz of mosquitoes in the evenings sounded more like the whine of jets than the sound of insects. Apart from the irritation of the sound and bites, there was the fear of being infected with malaria. We used to kill mosquitoes with our hands as we saw them. We had no illusions about our chances of exterminating them but we could not help trying and developed skills and techniques. The game W.H.O. consisted of knocking on one's neighbor's wall every time one killed a mosquito. Later in the evenings, the scores would be tallied from all the cells and a winner would be declared for every night, every week, every month and every year. He would be named 'the Blood Donor of the year': the greatest number of mosquitoes I killed in a single day and night was 175.

The ants, distinct colonies of which occupied certain corners of the cell, were considered a nuisance for the first few weeks and I even tried to get rid of them. But as time went by, and the confinement began to weigh on me, I realized that I was exacerbating its effects by ignoring all the tiny animals and insects living with me in the cell. I was alone in the cell as far as humans were concerned, but there were hundreds and maybe thousands of other 'beings' with me in the cell. To deny their existence seemed as foolish and as short-sighted as humanity denying the presence of the multiplicity of life-forms, and the integral part they play in this world. I studied them and for their part, they cleaned up my cell.

Often, for company I had a solitary house lizard improbably hanging upside down from the ceiling. But during the nights when the doors were closed, rats came out of the 'toilets'. Of course I hated these filthy animals who crawled all over one in the darkness of the cell. When I tried to frighten them away by stomping my feet, they seemed to realize that I could not see them. They just moved to one side and returned as soon as I sat down.

The nights were when fears, real or imagined, were heightened. As soon as the outside door was closed at 4 P.M. the cell would be in total darkness. At the beginning of solitary confinement, every sound that I heard, I interpreted as a sign that we were going to be released. But as time went by, even this defense mechanism of hope wore out. The sounds became ominous. Every door that was opened or closed during the night would increase the rate of my heart beat. Even the usual antidote to this fear — getting in touch with next-door neighbors through the wall — did not seem to work. The only remedy was the flash of dawn. By that time I may have woken up several times sweating and with my heart beating so fast that it seemed to be in my mouth. The first time I woke up in that way was in the beginning of 1984. I had been having nightmares for a few months, dreaming of the death of a loved one, a close relative or a friend. On occasions I might dream I was offered an appetizing meal, instead of the prison fare. Or I would dream of being released and be denied this at the last moment when I would wake up panting as if I had run a marathon.

Fear, tension and anxiety eventually reached such a level that my subconscious mind was always on guard. It refused to let me sleep even when very tired and badly in need of sleep. As soon as I was about to fall asleep my heart beat, instead of falling as is normal, would increase. Sometimes I would fall asleep but wake up even more tired, dropping off in the morning when the outside door had been opened. Later, after discussing my condition with Dr. Aden Yussuf Aboker, my next door neighbor, I slept better.

Indeed, the nights were the worst time in the dark cells for another reason: apart from the rats, the cockroaches and mosquitoes, the Colonel who ran the prison had a cruel habit of sending his soldiers to fetch one of the prisoners. They would come late at night. Two would open the outside steel door noisily, focus a torch on one's face and tell one to stand up. Each holding one handcuffed arm, they would march one to the colonel's office. He sat there smiling triumphantly with a dozen soldiers standing to attention behind his chair. He would start by asking one's name, profession, and length of sentence. Then he would ask if clothes, medicines and food were needed. Naturally he could see one needed clothes, food and sometimes medicines very badly. Whatever one said: Yes or No did not matter. He would then abuse one verbally, shouting that one deserved an even worse fate. Eventually he got bored and told the soldiers to take one away. There were ex-ministers, national assembly members and generals in the prison, and the colonel enjoyed humiliating ex-vice president Ismail Ali Abokor or ex-minister Omer Arteh more than I or one of my friends.

Even so, these night visits left their mark on me, I can easily understand why captives become confused and brain-washed and cooperate with their captors despite feeling hatred towards them. I remember how I felt whenever the soldiers, with their high boots, and uniforms passed in front of my cell. Sometimes they seemed supermen. As time went by, the stature of every soldier increased in my mind. The uniforms, the regular hours, the lack of communication with us prisoners, and of course our feeling of being abandoned and helpless all added up to make petty tyrants seem like immortals. When I happened to see one of those soldiers in Mogadishu after we were released, I was incredulous. He looked so puny and average that I felt sure he must be someone else. In hindsight, I am sure this sighting helped exorcise the feeling of inferiority from my own mind although I did not feel any particular bitterness towards him.

Occasional nightmares remained part of life, long after our release. Many friends have wondered aloud how we were able to survive and keep our sanity in those horrendous conditions. The only answer I am able to give is that people are capable of adjusting to almost any environment, however difficult. Furthermore we are much stronger and more resourceful than we realize. Only in very trying circumstances are we forced to tap all our potential but hidden resources. I feel if we could find a way to utilize these resources in normal times we might well solve many seemingly irresolvable problems . . .

Our release, when, after many a long year, it eventually came, was as dramatic as the manner of our arrest. One morning in mid-March, two soldiers, followed by the male nurse, stopped in front of my cell; and for the first time in six and a half years called me by name. They wanted to know whether I was called Mohamed Barood Ali. It took me a while to comprehend the meaning of the query, before I stammered yes. A cardboard box containing some few clothes was half pushed, half thrown through the bars of the inner door. They left me open-mouthed without saying another word. I could hear them stopping in front of my neighbor's door and talking to him, although I could not hear what they were saying. Suddenly I was overwhelmed by a thousand thoughts all incoherent and fantastic.

In a place like Labaatan Jirow, where one never hears anything from the soldiers, or from anyone else, one becomes used to deducing what is happening in the outside world from the slightest change in the habits of the guards and even their slightest change in facial expression. In my world of half-tints what happened that day was comparable to a newsreel in technicolor. And yet I found it was not easy to think further than the gate of the prison. Maybe we were being released, but to believe that needed a great leap of faith, and I ended up coming back looking through those steel bars as if they were part of my pupils and not a separate entity. As soon as the guards reached a safe distance I started communicating with my next-door neighbor who informed me that he was also given clothes. We continued to 'talk' happily for the next 10 minutes, concluding that we were definitely going to be released. But as soon as we stopped tapping the wall, I was not sure anymore. Doubts crowded out my fleeting happy mood.

This mood of uncertainty was reinforced by two most powerful indicators. I could see when the outside door was opened that the national flag, raised on a pole each morning was flapping normally. The rationale was we believed that we were not going to be released while Siad Barre was ruling and his death would surely be signalled by the flag not being raised. Hence my daily check on the status of the flag. After our release many of my friends told me they also looked out for any sign of the flag being lowered. The second indicator was that every morning without fail the soldiers would sing a particular song in praise of Siad Barre and his accomplishments. If for any reason, they failed to sing, which was very rare, I would listen all day for any unusual sign to confirm that Siad Barre had been, somehow, gotten rid of. That morning they sang and with particular gusto, I thought.

Even so, about 2 o'clock in the afternoon guards, all of them dressed for parade, stopped in front of my door and one of them told me to collect my things. There was nothing I wanted to take from that cell and I started towards the door almost running and breathless. They opened the door and handcuffed and blindfolded me. Somehow this did not dampen my spirits. They told me to walk. When they took off the blindfold, I found myself in a room with a table in the center. Sitting there was the male nurse, who was at the time assistant commander of the prison. He told me to sit down on a wooden form. I beheld coming through the door my friends, one by one, everyone blindfolded and in handcuffs. They all seemed strangers: I had not seen them for six and a half years. At first we said hello to each other as if we had only met a few hours ago. But then someone started laughing hysterically and we all started hugging each other and laughing. We were separated into three groups, handcuffed in threes, blindfolded, and put in the back of Land Rovers. We were never sure where we were going but reached Mogadishu after five hours drive. The blindfolds and handcuffs were removed on the outskirts of Mogadishu.

We were immediately taken to the *Villa Somalia,* Siad Barre's state palace on a hill in the center of Mogadishu. We saw the fabled cheetah royally kept and looked after by a platoon of guards. While waiting to be received at the court of the dictator, we had the first opportunity to speak to each other, because on the way we had been warned that if anyone uttered a word, he was going to be shot.

I was greatly saddened when shown the scars left on the feet and arms of one of my friends, Yussuf Abdillahi Kahin. He had been kept in chains day and night for three months for trying to speak to a soldier. The chains were too short for him to reach the toilet and he had to sleep next to his own excrement. I saw that the big toe of my friend Abdirahman Abdillahi H. Aden, injured during torture sessions and neglected, had become so badly infected that it had had to be amputated by 'doctor No,' who cut it off with a saw without the aid of anaesthetic. Six soldiers had held Abdirahman down. I was generally shocked by the sight of my emaciated friends who were comparable to survivors of a concentration camp. All had aged a lot. The effects of anxiety and solitary confinement, were all too visible on all their faces. Some were unusually withdrawn; others laughed hysterically, and yet others exhibited signs of morbid fear and nervously watched the guards as if expecting to be attacked at any moment.

General Siad, who usually worked at night, kept us waiting for a long time but we were never bored for a moment. We had so much to say to each other and a rising excitement replaced our usual mood of listlessness and apathy. I had heard many times before that Siad Barre kept political opponents waiting to consult an old lady who served as court witch-cum-magician-cum-clairvoyant. It was common knowledge among Somalis that Siad Barre was superstitious, ignorant, deceitful and vindictive. He was not an educated man, and there are a lot of anecdotes testifying to his ignorance in the face of something he did not understand and his suspicious reactions.

Finally, when we were summoned into the presence of Siad Barre, we found him seated behind a huge mahogany desk. He was smoking, as always, with an attendant standing one step behind him, holding a packet of cigarettes and a lighter. He appeared much older than I expected, with vacant, tired-looking eyes. There were eight in our group, but Siad ordered Dr. Mohamoud Hassan Tani to remain outside because he was of a different clan than the rest of us. This was typical of the man, who was always exploiting the clan divisions in Somali society to remain in power—setting Somali against Somali to prevent us from uniting and getting rid of our common enemy.

Siad inquired of each of us whether or not we had been guilty of the offenses for which we had been sentenced in 1982, more than seven years previously. But he did not listen or await any response. He started railing away at us, saying that we were traitors, responsible for the destruction of the northern cities, the death of tens of thousands of people, the widowing of so many Somali women and the losses of property suffered by all northern Somalis. All this was in fact new to us. It was the first time we had any hint of the magnitude of the destruction which he and his evil colleagues had visited upon our people. (Dr. Mohamoud Tani later revealed to us that Siad had predictably, asked him why he had involved himself with such a group of anti-government subversives as ourselves.) After delivering this monologue, Siad announced that we were pardoned but that we must refrain from getting involved in anti-government activities in the future. He dismissed us by standing up and we were ushered out of his quarters by a group of bodyguards who left us in the middle of the street. We had no money and we did not know where to go. It was about 3 o'clock in the morning.

After roaming around the empty streets of the capital for about one hour, we found an old hotel. There we met other people (Isaaqs who had also been released from prison). Early the next morning, the first of our relatives found us. Apparently they were expecting us and they had been checking all the hotels. Within no time the hotel was flooded with relatives, friends, and well-wishers. We found we were heroes. This was surely testimony of how the country desperately needed heroes. We had been put on a pedestal and it was frightening to think about the daunting task awaiting us in fulfilling those expectations. We were welcomed so heartily by so many people we wondered what we had really done to deserve so much adulation.

Even this welcome, however, was threatening to Siad Barre's regime. Three men who invited us for the first three days were soon afterwards arrested by the security (NSS) and held for a week before they were released on the intervention of a group of elders who went to see Siad Barre. He told them he was not aware of the arrests and ordered their release. But he also told them not to continue celebrations over 'criminals.'

The first day of our reunion with our families and friends was both happy and traumatic. Seeing them, speaking and holding them after six and a half years of solitary confinement was exhilarating. But some of my friends learned that their marriages had been annulled by government decree while they were in prison. It was also traumatic for us all because, apart from the fact that we were passing from solitary confinement into large, ebullient crowds, with no transition, we learned the shocking details of what had happened in the north for the first time. It was difficult to visualize all the destruction, devastation and cruelty that had been made manifest between our arrest in 1981 and 1989 when we were released. It was a story that started with the repression of the northerners, particularly the Isaaq, and their demands for equality which had led to the brutal use of the military power of the state against them. Not only the military power but the whole might — economic and military — that the Somali state possessed. It culminated in the final phase of an official plan — known to everyone as the 'Morgan Plan' — which had been sanctioned by Siad Barre and which called for the virtual genocide of the Isaaqs: — the freezing of bank accounts, diluting their numbers in schools and the population at large by resettling residents of the refugee camps, the destruction of large villages, farmland and animals, the poisoning or mining of watering holes and the replacement of Isaaqs in the army, police, NSS, prison service, etc.

We were angered to learn the details of the initial period of low-key repression; the dismissal or transferring of all business permits from Isaaq businessmen and encouragement of non-Isaaq businessmen by giving them easy access to loans on very favorable terms; the creation of neighborhood cells to facilitate spying on each other, until it reached the level of Orwell's 1984 — the mother and kids spying on the activities of the husband and father. Finally, this blossomed into full-scale warfare when the regime insisted on identifying every single Isaaq as an SNM member and enemy of the state. The regime carried out extra-judicial killings of civilians — massacres on a massive scale. They used artillery and aerial bombardment on heavily-populated civilian areas, such as marketplaces. Cities and towns were destroyed wholesale and the military even bombed refugee columns on the run for their lives before and even after reaching Ethiopia. Survivors tell of the harrowing and incredible sight of seeing Somali Air Force planes take off from Hargeisa airport and bombing downtown Hargeisa. These planes had been donated by the Government of the United Arab Emirates.

Foreign governments and individuals helped the regime and the military perpetrate atrocities during this oppression of the Somali people — as they had in their economic exploitation and the plundering of the national treasure, fauna and natural resources. War planes, piloted by South African and Rhodesian mercenaries, caused so much trauma that children who survived involuntarily dived under the nearest protection every time they heard the sound of an aircraft for more than one year after the war ended. Learning of so much cruelty and inhumanity served at least to save us from dwelling overlong on our own prison experiences — a sad type of therapy.

However, it soon became clear to us that it would be foolish to stay on in Mogadishu and risk being arrested again. We knew no excuse, other than the fact that we had been in jail, was needed to arrest and imprison us again. There were two options open. Either we had to go through the usual channels, get passports and fly out of Mogadishu airport, risking detection, or to leave by land. Both methods had their risks. We weighed the pros and cons and in the end decided to try the air route. The risks were higher but we were encouraged by the corruption and confusion of the whole system. We did not go to the immigration authorities ourselves but applied for passports using our own names. Instead we gave US$ 30 to a go-between who would share the money with his contact in the immigration department. Within two weeks we all had new passports. The only scary moment came when the name of one of my friends was discovered among a group of people who were listed as undesirable and ineligible for passports, but it turned out to be a different person.

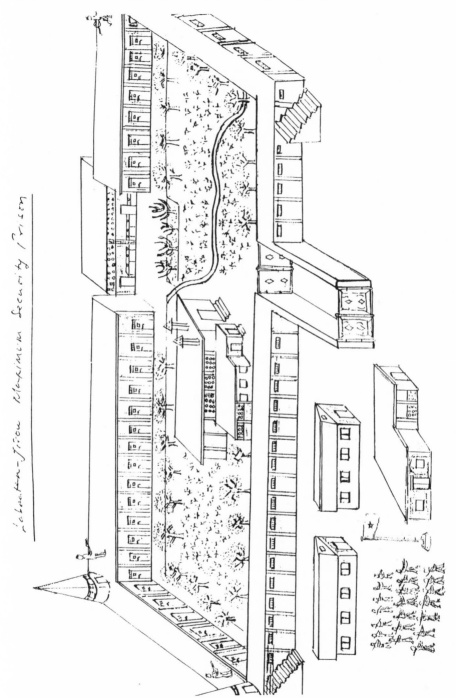

Sebastian-Straße Maximum Security Prison

After receiving our passports, we decided it best to endeavor to leave in small groups. Timing was of the essence. An Amnesty International delegation was visiting Somalia at this time and we knew the authorities would do anything to deceive and please this delegation and — more to the point — they might well crack down hard after the delegates had left. Most of us slipped away while they were still in the country.

I left with Hussein Mohamoud Dualeh on 27 June 1989. We had our luggage taken to the airport by friends who told us to come to the airport only at the last possible moment. The NSS were everywhere when we arrived. I reached the window where I had to have my passport stamped. An officer took it and handed it to another sitting at a desk who looked at it for a long time as if it were something he had never seen before. He looked first at me and then at a list of names in front of him. He gestured to the first officer and whispered to him for what seemed ages. Many thoughts passed through my mind. Should I run? But then he stamped the passport, called my name and gave it to me. I breathed again and went to sit in the waiting hall. I stayed as far as possible from my friend Hussein. We sat there not looking at each other and trying not to look frightened whenever someone came to look brazenly into the faces of the passengers. When finally our flight was announced and we went to the tarmac, there were more NSS officers standing next to the plane to have a last look at the passengers. In fact others even boarded the plane and checked our passports for the last time. Then the plane took off and as soon as we were able to unfasten our seat-belts we both stood up, left our places and hugged each other in the middle of the passenger aisle. The passengers and the crew thought we were crazy and it was not far from the truth. We were mad with happiness.

When the plane landed at Djibouti we had quickly to rein in our enthusiasm. The immigration authorities were notorious for the arbitrary nature of their decisions of whether or not to grant entry. Many people with bonafide documents have been denied admittance into Djibouti and returned to Somalia, even when it was clear that they might be in danger of their lives. It would be gratifying to end with this account with our 'escape' but in the interest of completeness one more fact must be chronicled.

Barely two weeks after the Amnesty delegation left, on 14 July 1989, there were demonstrations in Mogadishu, following the detention of a group of religious elders. The regime responded with its usual brutality, killing over a thousand people on the first day alone. According to eyewitness reports, most of the deaths were not caused by regular army units but by 'goon squads' belonging to Siad Barre's Marehan clan who were free to shoot demonstrators on sight.

A dawn to dusk curfew was declared during which on the night of 17 July, 'death squads,' led by Maslah Siad Barre (the son and heir-apparent) and *Anjeh* (his cousin) went to the predominantly Isaaq neighborhoods of Medina and Hodan. Knocking only at known Isaaq households, they picked up forty-seven young men and took them in two closed military trucks, beyond Jezira beach, some 13 miles south from the capital and shot them all. One solitary youth survived with minor injuries. He fell down with the rest thinking that he must have been killed. He got up only when the assassins departed after throwing some earth on top of the bodies. The Isaaq community in Mogadishu managed to spirit him out of Somalia and he lived to recount this harrowing experience.

A number of those killed at the beach had been regular visitors to our home while we were in Mogadishu, so it was particularly distressing to find out about their brutal death. At least four of my friends were still in Mogadishu and they had to change houses every night until they too managed to leave on 18 July. Unfortunately two of our friends who had been sentenced to death in 1988 with the group called the 'Parliamentarians' were stopped at the airport on the way to Mecca, to make their pilgrimage. They had their passports confiscated and while not imprisoned were unable to travel or work.

In conclusion, I would like to express a word of thanks to the numerous groups and individuals both inside and outside the then Somali Democratic Republic who selflessly fought to publicize our suffering and contributed immensely to the international pressure which eventually resulted in our release from prison. A special thank you is due too, to the school children who, unfailingly, used to demonstrate in Hargeisa, Burao and other Somali towns on 20 February every year, despite the certainty of harsh retaliation from the regime, to remind the authorities that we had been neither abandoned nor forgotten by our people.

Author's Note: Mohamed Barood Ali later recovered sufficiently from his ordeal to become Minister of Rehabilitation and Resettlement in the Somaliland Republic.

INDEX

This index is constructed in two sections: General and Individuals.

Somali spellings are difficult for westerners and are not followed. Since Somalis place great emphasis on nicknames (which at least initially are indicated by inverted commas or italics) some index entries may use them, especially in well-known instances. An attempt has also been made to avoid a multiplicity of individual listings under common names such as Mohamed, Ahmed, Ali etc. and entries should be checked for one or other alternate name if the first enquiry is not successful.

GENERAL

INDIVIDUALS